# CONTAINING THE SOVIET UNION

## Pergamon Titles of Related Interest

# CONTAINING THE SOVIET UNION
## A Critique of US Policy

Edited by

**TERRY L. DEIBEL**
and
**JOHN LEWIS GADDIS**

**PERGAMON-BRASSEY'S**
**INTERNATIONAL DEFENSE PUBLISHERS**
(a member of the Pergamon Group)

WASHINGTON · NEW YORK · LONDON · OXFORD
BEIJING · FRANKFURT · SÃO PAULO · SYDNEY · TOKYO · TORONTO

| U.S.A.<br>(Editorial) | Pergamon-Brassey's International Defense Publishers,<br>8000 Westpark Drive, Fourth Floor, McLean,<br>Virginia 22102, U.S.A. |
| (Orders) | Pergamon Press, Maxwell House, Fairview Park,<br>Elmsford, New York 10523, U.S.A. |
| U.K.<br>(Editorial) | Brassey's Defence Publishers,<br>24 Gray's Inn Road, London WC1X 8HR |
| (Orders) | Brassey's Defence Publishers,<br>Headington Hill Hall, Oxford OX3 0BW, England |
| PEOPLE'S REPUBLIC<br>OF CHINA | Pergamon Press, Room 4037, Qianmen Hotel, Beijing,<br>People's Republic of China |
| FEDERAL REPUBLIC<br>OF GERMANY | Pergamon Press, Hammerweg 6,<br>D-6242 Kronberg, Federal Republic of Germany |
| BRAZIL | Pergamon Editora, Rua Eça de Queiros, 346,<br>CEP 04011, Paraiso, São Paulo, Brazil |
| AUSTRALIA | Pergamon-Brassey's Defence Publishers, P.O. Box 544,<br>Potts Point, N.S.W. 2011, Australia |
| JAPAN | Pergamon Press, 8th Floor, Matsuoka Central Building,<br>1–7–1 Nishishinjuku, Shinjuku-ku, Tokyo 160, Japan |
| CANADA | Pergamon Press Canada, Suite No. 271,<br>253 College Street, Toronto, Ontario, Canada M5T 1R5 |

First printing 1987

**Library of Congress Cataloging in Publication Data**

Containing the Soviet Union.
Includes index.
1. Soviet Union—Foreign relations—1945–
2. World politics—1945– . 3. United States—
Foreign relations—Soviet Union. 4. Soviet Union—
Foreign relations—United States. I. Kennan,
George Frost, 1904— . II. Deibel, Terry L.
III. Gaddis, John Lewis.
DK282.C66 1987      327.73047      86–25295
ISBN 0–08–034947–1

*Printed in Great Britain by A. Wheaton & Co. Ltd., Exeter*

# CONTENTS

# PREFACE AND ACKNOWLEDGMENTS

Four decades have passed since the cold war began. It was in the years 1946 and 1947 that the United States reluctantly abandoned the vision of one world, peacefully managed by a concert of wartime allies, and turned its energies to resisting the expansionist pressure of the Soviet Union. Appropriately, the broad policy it adopted then was defined by a Foreign Service officer with long experience in Moscow. Writing anonymously in the prestigious journal *Foreign Affairs* from a post at the newly created U.S. National War College, George F. Kennan called for "a long-term, patient but firm and vigilant containment of Russian expansive tendencies." Although the United States has adopted many strategies towards the Soviet Union in the years since that famous "X" article appeared, the term "containment" has been used to characterize them all and now seems to be both a permanent and central feature of American foreign policy.

Yet, beneath this apparent continuity, enormous change has occurred in virtually every significant area bearing on the U.S.–Soviet relationship. Forty years ago, the Soviet Union was a country devastated and exhausted by war, while the economy of the United States produced over half of gross world production. Today the Soviet economy is rebuilt (if inefficient), while America, no longer a creditor country, creates only about 15% of the world's goods and services and struggles to maintain its overseas markets. In 1947, the United States held a nuclear monopoly, and the Soviets had no blue water navy; now Moscow's nuclear and conventional arsenals are at least a match for Washington's, and the Kremlin possesses considerable power-projection capability. At the beginning of the cold war, American decisionmakers worried about the subversive power of communist ideology, even in democratic Europe and particularly among radical independence movements in colonial areas. Today, communism has exhausted its ideological appeal nearly everywhere, and the Third World is well into its third decade of independence.

The essays in this volume seek to examine how these and many other profound changes in international life have and will continue to affect the time-honored policy of containment. They also, from their various perspectives, continue and expand the policy debate on what containment ought

vii

to look like in the years ahead and how the United States can more effectively deal with its Soviet rival. Those in Part 1 do so primarily through an analytical look at our experience with containment; those in Part 2 focus more on current and emerging policy issues. But all fuse history with policy analysis, the theoretical with the experiential. Also, all pay homage to the thought of George Kennan, beginning with John Gaddis' introduction. It outlines the intellectual contours of the containment debate, highlighting the critical issues that reappear in the pages to follow.

The focus in Part 1 on the history of containment begins with some contemporary reflections by Ambassador Kennan on the origins of containment and the differences between the worlds of 1947 and 1987. Professor Ole Holsti then surveys the changes in American public opinion over those four decades, and Angela Stent looks at the problematic effects of American efforts to use economic policy as an instrument of containment. George Quester's chapter addresses the important matter of how perceptions of the nuclear weapons balance have affected (and are likely to affect) containment policy, while Terry Deibel uses the background of Kennan's opinions on alliances to illuminate the impact of the three great postwar alliance systems created by the United States to execute the containment policy. Finally, Richard Ullman discusses how containment has affected and has been affected by major changes in the architecture of world politics, both between the superpowers and within and beyond their spheres of influence.

The first two chapters in Part 2 attempt to delve beneath the "surface" of the Soviet Union (the object of containment), to seek whatever lessons may be found there for American policy. Jerry Hough's chapter examines the political, ideological, and economic influences on the Kremlin's foreign policy, both in Kennan's time and in the Gorbachev era. James Billington probes the deeper cultural and generational factors in Soviet society, which he thinks demand a new and far more sophisticated American approach to containment.

Then, four distinguished commentators explore variations on the three logical alternatives to containment: settling the conflict, giving up the struggle, or somehow winning it. Alton Frye reviews the accomplishments in U.S.-Soviet relations as support for his proposal that containment be supplemented with a negotiated regime of policy coordination and mutual restraint among the superpowers, particularly in Southwest Asia, the Middle East, Central America, and on arms control. Earl Ravenal argues that the American crisis of solvency demands a global strategic disengagement, even in Western Europe, and a retrenchment to a policy of war avoidance and non-intervention. Dmitri Simes counters that the United States should not only defend its vital interests against Moscow's advances, but also pursue a dynamic containment of Soviet expansion throughout the Third World. Norman Podhoretz goes even further, offering a neoconservative's history of containment and calling for an aggressive policy designed to actively promote the breakup of the Soviet empire. Finally, Donald Zagoria urges a centrist position, declaring containment a success and warning equally against extremists who consider it either too dangerous or too passive — those who would either give up the struggle or give up trying to manage it.

The editors would like to thank the many individuals and institutions who were helpful in bringing this work to fruition. First mention properly belongs to the National Defense University (under which the National War College now resides), which honored George Kennan with a two-day symposium in November 1985. The editors largeiy designed that conference, and except for Earl Ravenal's, the first drafts of these chapters were commissioned for that occasion. Thanks are also due to the Carnegie Endowment for International Peace, where Terry Deibel was on sabbatical as a resident associate during the period of his contributions to this publication. And of course, our authors deserve the greatest commendation; their hard thinking and skilled writing have provided a universe of contrasting yet authoritative commentary on the central foreign policy issue of our time. We trust our readers will find its exploration as challenging and thought-provoking as we have.

# 1 INTRODUCTION: THE EVOLUTION OF CONTAINMENT

*John Lewis Gaddis*

Biographers, as a rule, need to be very careful in speculating about what was in the minds of their subjects at any given point. Nevertheless, I think it safe enough to say that when George Kennan, more than forty years ago, sat down to draft his call for a "long-term, patient but firm and vigilant containment of Russian expansive tendencies,"[1] he had no idea of what he was letting himself in for. He himself has compared the experience to that of inadvertently loosening "a large boulder from the top of a cliff and now helplessly witness[ing] its path of destruction in the valley below, shudder- ing and wincing at each successive glimpse of disaster."[2] As this book indi- cates, the geopolitical landscape has yet wholly to stabilize itself, even after all these years. The boulder still bounces back and forth from time to time.

But biographers must also guard against exaggerating the influence of their subjects, and I suspect George Kennan would be the first to acknowl- edge that something like a strategy of containment would have evolved, in any event, even if he had chosen to devote his life to what he has ad- mitted he would really like to have been doing all this time — writing a long, leisurely biography of Anton Chekhov. After all, the breakdown of Soviet–American cooperation that followed World War II resulted not from the actions of any one man, or even any one nation, but from the work- ings of a political principle so ancient that Thucydides would have found it familiar: that great powers, separated only by power vacuums, tend not to get along. Nor would the old Greek have found it surprising that nations would seek, in such a situation, to "contain" one another. For "contain- ment" was just another way of restoring a balance of power in the world, and that idea would surely have developed in any event after World War II, even if Chekhov had had his biography.

George Kennan's importance lies not so much in the fact that he coined the term *containment*, but rather that he called for implementing it in a

1

particular way. As he himself has reminded us, that approach has not always found favor in official Washington or in the country at large; indeed, Kennan has spent more of the past four decades as a critic than as a defender of strategies that have nonetheless proceeded under the rubric he originated. This brings me to the major point I want to make here: that the idea of "containment" has taken on not just a life of its own, but several lives; that different people — indeed, different administrations — have understood it to stand for very different things over the years; and that even today, use of the term is more apt to start than to settle arguments.

What I would like to do in this essay is to set out — very briefly and in an admittedly oversimplified way — what seem, in retrospect, to have been the principal points at issue in this long debate over the meaning of "containment." My intent is by no means to try to resolve these arguments — an improbable task, in any event — but rather to introduce several of the issues that figure prominently in the more detailed discussions of containment that follow.

## THE QUESTION OF INTERESTS

Let us begin, as all good strategists should, with interests: just what is it that a strategy of "containment" is supposed to defend? The very term *containment* suggests defense rather than offense, and that in turn implies some conception of what is at stake in the first place. But not everyone has always agreed about that.

Kennan's own views were clear enough: the fundamental American interest throughout the twentieth century, he used to tell his students at the National War College, had been to keep key centers of military–industrial capability from falling under hostile control. It had been for that reason that the United States had twice gone to war to prevent the German domination of Europe; after 1945 the same interest required ensuring the defense of Western Europe and Japan against an ambitious but nervously insecure Soviet Union. Other parts of the world, most conspicuously China, did not fall within Kennan's list of interests to be defended for the simple reason that, lacking the requisite sources of industrial and military strength, their control by unfriendly regimes could pose no threat.

But Kennan's conception of interests proved easier to articulate than to implement. He himself acknowledged the need to defend Greece in 1947 and South Korea in 1950 — neither of them centers of industrial–military capability at the time — because the *psychological consequences* of their loss could be devastating to areas that *were* critical, like Western Europe and Japan. But this is where things get tricky, because once you introduce psychology into the equation, it becomes very hard to draw the line: if the loss of South Korea would be psychologically devastating, why not South Vietnam? Why not Quemoy and Matsu?

It was not all that difficult to slide from Kennan's insistence on distinguishing vital from peripheral interests to a very different approach, which in effect admitted no such distinction. The authors of NSC-68 expressed the second view very clearly in 1950 when they wrote that: "in the context of the present polarization of power a defeat of free institutions anywhere is a defeat everywhere."[3]

It followed from this that the fundamental American interest was not so much territory, or industrial–military capacity, but credibility: if the United States allowed itself to be challenged successfully in any part of the world, then its determination to resist aggression would be called into question everywhere else. "If we are driven from the field in Viet-Nam," Lyndon Johnson proclaimed in 1965, "then no nations can ever again have the same confidence in . . . American protection."[4] And it was left to an appalled Kennan to point out, the following year, that "there is more respect to be won in the opinion of this world by a resolute and courageous liquidation of unsound positions than by the most stubborn pursuit of extravagant and unpromising objectives."[5]

What was the problem here? How could containment evolve, in slightly over a quarter of a century, from a conception of interests so narrowly focused as to appear to require little more than the defense of Western Europe and Japan to one that seemed incapable of excluding any territory not already under communist control? Part of the answer, I suspect, has to do with the difficulty of defining security in the first place. It is, after all, a state of mind, and once you acknowledge that, you have rendered it subject to considerations that go beyond cool logic; you must take into account, whether within your own thinking or — more often — within that of allies, the illogical effect of anxieties, apprehensions, panics, phobias, and the fear of things that go "bump" in the night. Psychology provides the mechanism by which precise conceptions of interest become imprecise, and that creates a real problem for the strategist who is attempting to be clear on just what interests containment is supposed to be defending in the first place.

But this imprecision about interests is not altogether a matter of illogic: there is a very rational reason for it as well, and that has to do with what we might call the "Hobson's choice" of containment. If you differentiate between vital and peripheral interests, you retain the advantage of selecting how and where you will deploy your forces, but you also run the risk of inviting attacks on what may appear to be exposed and undefended flanks. Dean Acheson discovered this in the most painful way when he

attempted to delineate a "defensive perimeter" in the Western Pacific, only
to wind up inadvertently signaling the Russians that we would not defend
South Korea. But if you treat all interests as vital, you run into another
problem, which is relinquishing the initiative altogether: you then have to
be prepared to commit resources in places and at times chosen by your
adversary, not yourself. It was probably "no accident," as the Russians like
to say, that Moscow did so little to help us extricate ourselves from the Vietnam War; they even at one point — although in an unguarded moment —
advised the Johnson administration to *escalate* the American commitment
there.[6]

What this suggests, then, is that one should be sufficiently vague about
interests as to reassure allies and deter adversaries, but at the same time
sufficiently precise as to retain control over how, when and where one
might act to defend those interests. And that, I would be the first to admit,
is easier to say than to do.

## WHAT IS TO BE CONTAINED?

A second area of disagreement over containment has involved the question of who, or what, is to be contained. Once again, Kennan was very
precise about this: to pose a significant threat to American interests, he
argued, potential adversaries had to combine both hostility and capability.
It was not enough just to be unfriendly; one also had to be able to do something about it. In the immediate postwar years, only the Soviet Union met
this test; where communists were not under Moscow's control, as was
clearly the case in Tito's Yugoslavia and as seemed likely to be the case in
Mao Ze-Dong's China as well, Kennan's strategy looked to the possibility
of working with rather than against them to contain the Soviet Union.

That tradition of identifying adversaries in terms of capability rather
than ideology began to erode in 1949 and 1950, primarily as a result of the
victory of communism in China and the political repercussions set off at
home by that event. The Korean War — with which the People's Republic
had had little to do until overzealous American military action provoked
its intervention — only reinforced the public trend toward seeing all communists everywhere as equally dangerous. We now know from the documents that official perceptions were a good deal more sophisticated than
that: no less an ideologue than John Foster Dulles himself assumed an eventual split between Moscow and Beijing and sought, through his own policies, to bring that about.[7] Similar strategies existed within the Kennedy
and Johnson administrations as well. But what came across in public was
the rhetoric of ideological non-differentiation: containment came to be
understood as aimed at all communists, not just the Russians.

It is an indication of the strength of this sentiment that not until the coming to power of Richard Nixon and Henry Kissinger did an administration feel secure enough publicly to exploit Sino–Soviet differences that had been there for all to see for more than a decade: it did so by refocusing containment back toward its original target, the Soviet Union. But even then it confused the issue by continuing to regard indigenous Marxism outside of China and Yugoslavia — even, as in Chile, constitutionally legitimate Marxism — as a threat. Nor have our more recent policies in Central America provided any clearer answer to the question of just what it is we are seeking to contain.

One of the fundamental principles of strategy is to define enemies parsimoniously: never take on more than you need to at any given time.[8] And yet, the issue of what it is that containment is supposed to contain — whether it is a specific country, or an ideology, or simply patterns of behavior we don't much like — is one about which there has been, and still is, a surprising amount of disagreement.

## THE ISSUE OF MEANS

A third area of disagreement about containment relates to means: having identified interests to be defended and threats to be contained, what methods does one choose with which to implement containment? To say that the means chosen must be appropriate to the ends one has in view is axiomatic, but that does not make the task of selecting them any easier. Indeed, the strategy of containment confronts us with the perpetual dilemma of how, in seeking to contain our adversaries, we can avoid coming to resemble them.

George Kennan viewed the problem with uncharacteristic optimism in 1947: "to avoid destruction," he wrote in the "X" article, "the United States need only measure up to its own best traditions and prove itself worthy of preservation as a great nation."[9] We could, he seemed to be saying, contain the Russians, and still be true to ourselves. Certainly the first chosen instrument of containment — economic assistance to Western Europe through the Marshall Plan — provided a remarkably effective way to reconcile American geopolitical interests with American ideals.

But that coincidence of interests and ideals did not last very long. The Truman administration found it necessary to exaggerate the Soviet threat in order to win necessary appropriations from an economy-minded Congress: "we made our points clearer than truth," Dean Acheson later acknowledged, adding that this was a tactic in which "we did not differ from most other educators."[10] Kennan himself reluctantly supported development of a covert action capability for the Central Intelligence Agency on the grounds that the Russians already had and were using such a capability. And, of course, a strategy originally designed to contain a non-military threat by non-military means quickly became heavily militarized, not because Washington actually expected the Russians to invade Western Europe, but because the Europeans themselves demanded insurance, even against unlikely threats; it was a similar desire for insurance against uncertainty — not any identifiable military requirements at the time — that led to the decision to build the hydrogen bomb.

Reinhold Niebuhr liked to point out that it is sometimes necessary to do evil in order to accomplish good, and I suspect few practitioners of containment over the years would quarrel with that rather bleak proposition. The more difficult question is the one of degree: how many departures from the way one would like the world to be can one justify without bringing about the very conditions one hopes to avoid? Paul Nitze and the co-authors of NSC-68, drawing on Alexander Hamilton and the *Federalist Papers*, provided one answer: "the means employed must be proportioned to the extent of the mischief."[11] But this left unclear just what the proper proportion was, or how such matters were to be decided. Dwight Eisenhower, in one of those remarkably candid letters one finds in his papers, went a bit further in 1955: "Truth, honor, justice, consideration for others, liberty for all — the problem is how to preserve them, nurture them and keep the peace — if this last is possible — when we are opposed by people who scorn to give any validity whatsoever to these values. I believe we can do it, but *we must not confuse these values with mere procedures, even though these last may have at one time held almost the status of moral concepts.*"[12]

The procedural latitude that Eisenhower assumed with regard to means — and that was indeed granted strategists of containment throughout much of the history of the cold war — has in recent years been called into question. Kennan himself has seen it as leading to disproportionate excess, both in Vietnam and in the nuclear arms race: we can, he has been telling us, no longer afford to employ means that risk destroying the very ends we seek to secure. During the 1970s, spokesmen for human rights — from both liberal and conservative wings of the domestic political spectrum — made a point of assailing Nixon and Kissinger for compromising ideals in their search for geopolitical stability. New congressional restraints on executive authority, together with a print and electronic media not easily put off by appeals for discretion, have forced recent administrations to think more than their predecessors did about finding means that can be convincingly justified in terms of ends sought. The fact that we have spent several years now *overtly* debating the merits of *covert* aid to the contras in Nicaragua is only the most obvious example of how much more sensitive we have become to the way in which we implement containment — but, as that very example illustrates, this certainly has not made the task of implementing that strategy any easier.

## THE ISSUE OF COSTS

Yet another area of disagreement about containment — closely related to the one about means — has had to do with what it should cost: does one allow the requirements of containment to determine what one spends, or does one first consider what one can spend and then let that determine who, or what, one should contain? It makes a difference, and yet there has been little consistency on this point. Indeed the whole history of containment can be written in terms of oscillations between the belief on the one hand that means should be expanded to bring them into line with perceived interests, and the conviction on the other that interests should be restricted to keep them in line with perceived means.

It is often forgotten that the original strategy of containment proceeded from an assumption of severely limited resources: the atomic bomb was of little use short of an all-out war; American military forces had evaporated in the postwar rush to demobilize; President Truman was adamant in maintaining a $15 billion ceiling on military spending; and Kennan himself had profound doubts about the competence of Americans to manage any kind of global strategy in the first place. As a consequence, his view of containment was selective as to means — the emphasis would be almost entirely on economic assistance — and as to the places in which it would be implemented: Western Europe, the Mediterranean and Japan, but not China, not Southeast Asia, and definitely not what we would today refer to as the Third World. That skepticism about American capacity and competency has never really left him.

It was Paul Nitze and his colleagues who suggested the alternative approach in NSC-68: that when confronted by what appeared to be an all-out threat, it made no sense to restrict oneself to limited means, especially when the nation had unused productive capabilities. NSC-68 proposed a tripling of the defense budget; it also showed how this could be done — through the use of deficit spending to stimulate the economy — without setting off damaging inflation or unacceptable taxation. Whether in the absence of the Korean War President Truman would have accepted that argument is an interesting but academic question: as has happened time and time again, the Russians themselves provided the most convincing justification for a more expansive approach to containment, this time by authorizing the North Korean attack on South Korea.

President Eisenhower faced a dilemma with respect to this question of means: he agreed with Nitze's perception of a worldwide Soviet threat, but he emphatically did not accept the assumption that the nation could spend whatever was necessary to contain it. Convinced that deficit spending was just as dangerous as the communists, Eisenhower and Dulles sought ways to make containment work more effectively at less cost: the result was the first real integration of nuclear weapons into the strategy of containment. Deterrence would provide the mechanism by which global interests could be defended and, at the same time, budgets balanced.

There was, of course, a shift back to the doctrine of expandable means during the Kennedy and Johnson administrations—not least because of their desire to get away from Eisenhower's heavy dependence on nuclear weapons. But with Nixon, Ford and Kissinger, the pendulum swung back the other way again: the Nixon Doctrine, the opening to China, and indeed detente itself can all be seen as yet another attempt to make containment work more effectively at less cost—albeit this time without increased reliance on a nuclear superiority we no longer possessed. Carter, too, for all his differences with preceding administrations on moral issues, came into office determined to keep the lid on defense spending, at least until the Russians persuaded him otherwise by invading Afghanistan. And with the Reagan administration, we have come back to the opposite idea that the requirements of containment should determine what is spent on containment, even if that means spending a good deal less on everything else.

Why are these disagreements over costs important? They have an obvious bearing on how one allocates resources within a society, of course, but there is another less obvious consideration as well: there is reason to think that a linkage may exist between the perception of means available, on the one hand, and the perception of interests and threats, on the other. The history of containment suggests that when means have been perceived as expandable, conceptions of interests have tended to broaden; as conceptions of interests broaden, perceptions of threat tend to also. Conversely, perceptions of means as limited have forced differentiations between vital and peripheral interests, and, as a result, a somewhat less apocalyptic perception of threat.

All of which is to suggest a curious thing about containment: that it is as often a reflection of our internal state of mind at any given moment as it is a response to external reality. If this is true, then it would behoove us not to exclude from our considerations the internal roots as well as the external determinants of that doctrine.

## THE IMPACT OF DOMESTIC POLITICS

That brings me to the relationship between domestic politics and containment. George Kennan has never been noted for the enthusiasm with which he greets the intrusion of political considerations into the making of foreign policy. But there is a real problem here, and it has to do with the extent to which American foreign policy is capable of consistency. No competent strategist would allow his calendar to dictate when to switch from one strategy to another, and yet the domestic political process in the United States has imposed procedures very much like that upon the strategy of containment. Each new administration's approach to foreign policy tends to be determined, not by a calm and rational assessment of interests and threats, but rather by a desperate determination to do something — anything — new, something above all that will avoid association with the discredited policies of the preceding administration.

Thus, the Eisenhower administration's "New Look" was first worked out during the 1952 campaign, as a reaction to the Democrats' perceived vulnerability resulting from the "no-win" war in Korea. The "flexible response" strategy of Kennedy and Johnson grew out of the Democrats' campaign critiques of Eisenhower's excessive reliance on nuclear weapons. The Nixon Doctrine reflected the belief that the Johnson administration had overcommitted itself in Vietnam. The Carter "human rights" campaign was an obvious reaction to the perceived "amorality" of Henry Kissinger. And, of course, the Reagan administration's military buildup had been promised during the 1980 campaign as a means of closing the so-called "window of vulnerability" left open by Carter.

Now, no one would question the benefits of learning from the mistakes of one's predecessors. To the extent that the American system provides mechanisms for detecting and correcting failures in relatively short order, it has some advantages over, say, the Soviet system, where incompetence can be institutionalized for years without anyone being able to do anything about it. Our problem is that, because we depend upon our interminable and at times somewhat irrational presidential selection process to provide the occasion for evaluating past policies and suggesting new ones, we tend to distort reality by magnifying the errors of incumbents and by oversimplifying the necessary solutions. The effect is that each new administration faces a lengthy process — and it seems to get lengthier all the time — of adjusting its own rhetorical commitments to the circumstances of the real world.

This is one area in which the Russians have a legitimate complaint: how can they deal with the us, they ask, when we keep shifting our priorities in response to mysterious and unpredictable internal forces whose effects we ourselves seem unable to anticipate or to comprehend? In this sense, there is much to be said for what Kennan has been calling for all along: a greater insulation of the national security decision-making process from the whims and caprices of domestic politics. But how do we do this without violating the constitutional requirement of checks and balances? How do we secure the public support foreign policy needs to be effective without misleading the public as to what it can expect? How do we make new administrations see that it is really not necessary to throw out the baby with the bathwater every time?

## THE GOALS OF CONTAINMENT

The last point I wish to raise in this essay is, in many ways, the most fundamental: it is the question of what result, in the end, containment is supposed to produce. Having a strategy, after all, implies having an objective. It is supposed to lead to something; otherwise, as Clausewitz reminded us a century and a half ago, one's actions will have no meaning. George Kennan read Clausewitz while he was at the National War College, and partly as a result of that experience — but partly also because it is just plain common sense — he has always insisted that containment be viewed as a means toward a larger end, not as an end in itself.

Stated in this way, the point seems unexceptionable. But how often do you actually hear a discussion of what containment is supposed to lead to? The process of "containing," during these past four decades, has received far more attention than the question of where containment is supposed to take us, or of what might replace it if we ever get there.

One point is clear: containment has never implied the complete elimination of Soviet power, in the same way that we sought the unconditional surrender of Germany and Japan during World War II. Even if you could defeat the Soviet Union, Kennan used to ask his War College students, how would you occupy it? What kind of a regime would you replace it with? How could you be sure that such a regime would be any easier to live with than the old one? Containment, instead, sought a modification of Soviet behavior through a combination of deterrents and rewards — sticks and carrots, if you will. Disagreements about containment have focused largely on what the proper mix of these should be, and on precisely what kind of behavior they are supposed to produce.

Kennan's own criticism of the way containment has been implemented over the years has focused on what he considers to have been its neglect of the carrots: we have failed, he argues, to reward the Russians for the restraint they have shown, and hence have been unable to move to the next logical step beyond containment, which should be a negotiated resolution of differences looking toward stabilization of — and mutual respect for — our respective positions in the world. But others have been critical of containment for neglecting the sticks: we have failed, they assert, to deter the Russians from expanding their military power at home and their influence in the world at large, and hence have had to witness a corresponding and dangerous decline of our own.

Neither side has really made clear just what kind of behavior we expect from the Russians in the first place. Do we require an abandonment of world revolutionary ambitions? The relaxation of controls over Soviet satellites? A dismantling of the Soviet military machine? Liberalization of the Soviet internal system? Respect for our security interests and those of our allies? Participation in the international system by generally accepted rules of the game? Acknowledgment of what a war between our two countries would mean? Some of these objectives might be easier to achieve than others. And yet, because we so rarely talk about objectives in the first place, we provide ourselves few opportunities to think about which of them are feasible and which are not.

Strategy is largely a matter of getting from where you are to where you want to go. But if you don't know — or can't agree — on the intended destination, getting there is indeed likely to be a problem.

## GEORGE KENNAN: A PERSONAL NOTE

I cannot end this essay without including a word, in a more personal sense, about George Kennan. I first interviewed him thirteen years ago when he was setting up the Kennan Institute and was keeping an office in the old Smithsonian castle, the same building in which his namesake, the first George Kennan, had both lived and worked. I was intrigued to note that as the interview progressed, first his jacket came off, then he loosened his tie, then he rolled up his sleeves, then his shoes came off, and he finally wound up absolutely horizontal on the couch, feet propped up, hands behind his head, as wave after wave of eloquent "Kennanesque prose" came rolling forth. The more horizontal he got, the more eloquent he became. I have since learned — from Dorothy Hessman, his long-time secretary — that this is the standard Kennan dictating posture: that in fact the "long telegram" and several of the other great Kennan literary efforts were composed in precisely this manner.

I have not yet decided, as a biographer, just what to make of this. But I think it does illustrate at least one important point: that there is a personal side to great men, and that it may not always accord with their public image. It has been my privilege to learn that the Kennan who so often comes across as a man preoccupied with visions of decline, decay and catastrophe is in fact a man of generally optimistic temperament who takes great and vigorous delight in work, family, friends, and of course his farm, his sailing, his guitar, and even an occasional light-hearted or irreverent poem now and then.

He is also a man who understands — as few others would — the necessarily ambivalent relationship that must exist between a biographer and his subject. It is one that involves, on the part of the biographer, both sympathy and the ability to stand apart: the capacity to understand as well as the capacity to evaluate. On the part of the subject of the biography, it involves, above all else, great tolerance, and great trust. George Kennan has more than kept his part of that bargain; it is now up to me to keep mine.

## NOTES

1. "X" [George F. Kennan], "The Sources of Soviet Conduct," *Foreign Affairs*, 25 (July, 1947), 575.
2. George F. Kennan, *Memoirs: 1925–1950* (Boston: Atlantic Little, Brown, 1967), p. 356.
3. NSC-68, "United States Objectives and Programs for National Security," April 14, 1950, U.S. Department of State, *Foreign Relations of the United States: 1950* (Washington: Government Printing Office), I, 240.
4. Johnson press conference, July 28, 1965, *Public Papers of the Presidents: Lyndon B. Johnson, 1965* (Washington: Government Printing Office, 1966), p. 794.
5. U.S. Congress, Senate, Committee on Foreign Relations, *Supplemental Foreign Assistance Fiscal Year 1966 — Vietnam* (Washington: Government Printing Office, 1966), pp. 335–336.
6. See, on this point, John Lewis Gaddis, *Strategies of Containment: A Critical Appraisal of United States National Security Policy* (New York: Oxford University Press, 1982), p. 269.
7. *Ibid.*, pp. 142–143.
8. See Frederick H. Hartmann, *The Relations of Nations*, Fourth Edition (New York: Macmillan, 1973), p. 83.
9. "The Sources of Soviet Conduct," p. 582.
10. Dean Acheson, *Present at the Creation: My Years in the State Department* (New York: Norton, 1969), p. 375.
11. NSC-68, April 14, 1950, *Foreign Relations: 1950*, I, 244.
12. Eisenhower to Lewis Douglas, March 29, 1955, Dwight D. Eisenhower Papers, Ann Whitman File, "DDE Diary," Box 6, "Mar. 55(1)," Dwight D. Eisenhower Library, Abilene, KS. Emphases in original.

# PART 1

# PERSPECTIVES ON CONTAINMENT

# 2 REFLECTIONS ON CONTAINMENT*

*George F. Kennan*

The word "containment," of course, was not new in the year 1946. What was new, perhaps, was its use with relation to the Soviet Union and Soviet–American relations. And what brought it to public attention in this connection was its use in an article that appeared, in 1947, in the journal *Foreign Affairs*, under the title of "The Sources of Soviet Conduct," signed with what was supposed to have been an anonymous "X." This piece was not originally written for publication; it was written privately for our first Secretary of Defense, James Forrestal, who had sent me a paper on communism and asked me to comment on it. And it was composed, as I recall it, in December, 1946, in the northwest corner-room on the ground floor of the National War College building. So for the purpose of this volume I suppose it is fitting that I should try to explain something about how the word "containment" came to be used in that document, and what it was meant to signify.

I would ask you to try to picture, if you can, the situation that existed in that month of December, 1946. The Second World War was only a year and some months in the past. Our armed forces were still in the process of demobilization; so, too, though to a smaller extent (because they proposed to retain a much larger peacetime establishment than we did) were those of the Soviet Union.

In no way did the Soviet Union appear to me, at that moment, as a military threat to this country. Russia was at that time utterly exhausted by the exertions and sacrifices of the recent war. Something like 25 million of its people had been killed. The physical destruction had been appalling. In a large portion of the territory of European Russia the devastation had to be seen to be believed. Reconstruction alone was obviously going to take several years. The need for peace, and the thirst for peace, among the Rus-

*Copyright 1987 by George F. Kennan

sian people was overwhelming. To have remobilized the Soviet armed forces at that time for another war effort, and particularly an aggressive one, would have been unthinkable. Russia had then no navy to speak of, and virtually no strategic air force. She had never tested a nuclear weapon. It was uncertain when she would test one, and it was even more uncertain when, or whether, she would ever develop the means of long-range delivery of nuclear warheads. We ourselves had not yet developed such delivery systems.

In these circumstances, I reiterate, there was no way that Russia could appear as a military threat. It is true that even then she was credited with the capability of overrunning Western Europe with her remaining forces, if she wanted to do it. But I myself regarded those calculations as exaggerated (I still do); and I was convinced that there was very little danger of anything of that sort. So when I used the word "containment" with respect to that country in 1946, what I had in mind was not at all averting the sort of military threat people are talking about today.

What I *did* think I saw — and what explained the use of that term — was what I might call an ideological–political threat; and I will tell you why. Great parts of the northern hemisphere — notably Western Europe and Japan — had been seriously destabilized, socially, spiritually, and politically, by the experience of the recent war. Their populations were dazed, shell-shocked, uncertain of themselves, fearful of the future, and highly vulnerable to the pressures and enticements of communist minorities in their midst. The world communist movement was at that time a unified, disciplined movement under the total control of the Stalin regime in Moscow. Not only that, but the Soviet Union had emerged from the war with great prestige for its immense and successful military effort. The Kremlin was, for this and for other reasons, in a position to manipulate these foreign communist parties very effectively for its own interests. As for the intentions of the Stalin regime towards ourselves, I had no illusions. I had already served three tours of duty in Stalin's Russia, and had in fact just come home from the last of these tours in 1946. I had nothing but suspicion for the attitude of the Stalin regime towards us or towards the other recent Western allies. Stalin and the men around him were far worse — more sinister, more cruel, more devious, more cynically contemptuous of us — than anything we face today. I felt that if Moscow should be successful in taking over any of those major Western countries, or Japan, by ideological–political intrigue and penetration, this would be a defeat for us, and a blow to our national security, fully as serious as would have been a German victory in the war that had just ended.

Now, you must also remember that during that war, and to some extent into the post-hostilities period as well, our government had tried to win the confidence and the good disposition of the Soviet government by fairly

extensive concessions to Soviet demands with respect to the manner in
which the war was fought and to the prospect for the postwar international order. We had raised no serious objection to the extension of the
Soviet borders to the west. We had continued to extend military aid to
the Soviet Union even when its troops were overrunning most of the rest
of Eastern Europe. We had complacently allowed its forces to take Prague
and Berlin and surrounding areas even when there was a possibility that
we could arrive there just as soon as they did. They were refusing even to
give us a look inside their zone of occupation in eastern Germany, but were
demanding a voice in the administration and reconstruction of the Ruhr
industrial region in the west. There seemed to be a danger that communist
parties subservient to Moscow might seize power in some of the major
Western European countries, notably Italy and France, and possibly in
Japan as well.

What I was trying to say, in the "X" article, was simply this: "Don't
make any more unnecessary concessions to these people. Make it clear to
them that they are not going to be allowed to establish any dominant influence in Western Europe and in Japan if there is anything we can do to prevent it. When we have stabilized the situation in this way, then perhaps
we will be able to talk with them about some sort of a general political and
military disengagement in Europe and the Far East — not before." This, to
my mind, was what was meant by the thought of "containing" communism
in 1946.

Now, you may wish to compare that situation with the one we face
today, and to take account of the full dimensions of the contrast. Neither
of the two main features of what we confronted in 1946 — Soviet military
weakness, but also Soviet ideological–political strength — prevails today; on
the contrary, the situation is almost exactly the opposite.

I see no comparable ideological–political threat emanating from Moscow
at the present time. The Leninist–Stalinist ideology has almost totally lost
appeal everywhere outside the Soviet orbit, and partially within that orbit
as well. The situation in Western Europe and Japan has now been stabilized beyond anything we at that time were even able to foresee. Whatever
other dangers may today confront those societies, a political takeover by
their respective communist parties is simply not in the cards.

You may say: yes, but look at Soviet positions in such places as Ethiopia
or Angola. Fair enough. Let us look at them, but not exaggerate them.
Aside from the fact that these places are mostly remote from our own
defensive interests, what are the Russians doing there? With the exception
of Afghanistan, where their involvement goes much further, they are selling arms and sending military advisors — procedures not too different from
many of our own. Can they translate those operations into ideological
enthusiasm or political loyalty on the part of the recipient Third World

regimes? No more, in my opinion, than we can. These governments will take what they can get from Moscow — take it cynically and without gratitude, as they do from us. And they will do lip service to a political affinity with Moscow precisely as long as it suits their interest to do it and not a moment longer. Where the Russians acquire bases or other substantial military facilities, this has, of course, greater military significance. But it is not an ideological threat.

On the other hand, whereas in 1946 the military aspect of our relationship to the Soviet Union hardly seemed to come into question at all, today that aspect is of course of prime importance. I say this, not because I see the Soviet Union as threatening us or our allies with armed force. It is entirely clear to me that Soviet leaders do not want a war with us and are not planning to initiate one. In particular, I have never believed that they have seen it as in their interests to overrun Western Europe militarily, or would have launched an attack on that region generally even if the so-called "nuclear deterrent" had not existed. But I recognize that the sheer size of their armed force establishment is a disquieting factor for many of our allies. And, more important still, I see the weapons race in which we and they are now involved as a serious threat in its own right, not because of aggressive intentions on either side but because of the compulsions, the suspicions, the anxieties such a competition engenders, and because of the very serious dangers it carries with it of unintended complications — by error, by computer failure, by misread signals, or by mischief deliberately perpetrated by third parties.

For all of these reasons, I am free to admit that there is now indeed a military aspect to the problem of containment as there was not in 1946; but what most needs to be contained, as I see it, is not so much the Soviet Union as the weapons race itself. And this danger does not even arise primarily from political causes. One must remember that while there are indeed serious political disagreements between the two countries, there is no political issue outstanding between them which could conceivably be worth a Soviet–American war or which could be solved, for that matter, by any great military conflict of that nature.

And the weapons race is not all there is in this imperfect world that needs to be contained. There are many other sources of instability and trouble. There are local danger spots scattered about in the Third World. There is the dreadful situation in Southern Africa. There is the grim phenomenon of a rise in several parts of the world of a fanatical and wildly destructive religious fundamentalism, and there is the terrorism to which that sort of fundamentalism so often resorts. There is the worldwide environmental crisis, the rapid depletion of the world's non-renewable energy resources, the steady pollution of its atmosphere and its waters, and the general deterioration of its environment as a support system for civilized living.

And, finally, there is much in our own life, here in this country, that needs early containment. It could, in fact, be said that the first thing we Americans need to learn to contain is, in some ways, ourselves: our own environmental destructiveness; our tendency to live beyond our means and to borrow ourselves into disaster; our apparent inability to reduce a devastating budgetary deficit; our comparable inability to control the immigration into our midst of great masses of people of wholly different cultural and political traditions.

In short, if we are going to talk about containment in the context of the present, then I think we can no longer apply that term just to the Soviet Union, and particularly not to a view of the Soviet Union drawn too extensively from the image of the Stalin era, or, in some instances, from the even more misleading image of our Nazi opponents in the last great war. If we are going to relate that term to the Soviet Union of today, we are going to have to learn to take as the basis for our calculations a much more penetrating and sophisticated view of that particular country than the one that has become imbedded in much of our public rhetoric. But beyond that, we are going to have to recognize that a large proportion of the sources of our troubles and dangers lies outside the Soviet challenge, such as it is, and some of it even within ourselves. And for this reason we are going to have to develop a wider concept of what containment means — a concept more closely linked to the totality of the problems of Western civilization at this juncture in world history — a concept, in other words, more responsive to the problems of our own time than the one I so light-heartedly brought to expression, hacking away at my typewriter there in the northwest corner of the National War College building in December of 1946.

This — the development of this concept — is the task to which I hope future discussions will be devoted; and I wish only that I were young enough, and still enough of a citizen of this age, to be of greater use in getting on with that undertaking.

# 3 PUBLIC OPINION AND CONTAINMENT*

*Ole R. Holsti*

> To hell with public opinion. . . . We should lead, and not follow.
>
> — State Department
> official[1]

> Since the time when Thomas Jefferson insisted upon a "decent respect
> to the opinions of mankind," public opinion has controlled foreign
> policy in all democracies.
>
> — Cordell Hull[2]

## INTRODUCTION

It is relatively easy to identify the requirements for examining the relationship between public opinion and containment. They include survey data for the past four decades that touch upon at least some of the more basic elements of containment, including assessments of major threats to national security; the perceived intentions of the Soviet Union; the appropriate scope of American security commitments abroad; the various instruments of containment, including alliances, military and economic assistance; and specific undertakings by the United States in the conduct of its containment policy.[3] The questions should, of course, be carefully crafted in order to minimize biasing responses in one direction or another. Regular inclusion of the questions in surveys, and using identical wording each time would facilitate inferences about trends in public opinion.

*Research for this paper was supported in part by National Science Foundation grant No. SES-83-09036. The assistance of Daniel Harkins, Arturo Borja, Charles Sowards and Maija Holsti is gratefully acknowledged. For helpful comments on an earlier draft of this paper, the author is indebted to Robin Dorff, Daniel Harkins and Bruce Kuniholm.

Because we are likely to be interested in more than aggregate attitudes, information about the distribution of responses by various subgroups within the entire sample (for example, those defined by party, age, education, race, ideology, and gender) would be very useful. Because interest in and knowledge about foreign affairs is not evenly or randomly distributed throughout the population, at least occasional surveys should also distinguish between leaders and the mass public.

Even an accurate description of the state of public opinion on issues related to foreign and defense policy may not exhaust our needs, however. We may also wish to assess public opinion's impact on policy. In order to do so, it is essential to have information from decision-making groups to provide some insight into how various policymakers perceive public opinion, how (if at all) it enters into their calculations, and the extent to which it shapes or constrains their policy choices.

One might well assume that these requirements can be met rather easily. After all, containment is arguably the most persistent and important theme running through American foreign policy since World War II. Moreover, the past four decades have seen public opinion polling come of age.

Nevertheless, one must conclude that *not a single one* of the requirements spelled out above can be met in full. Among the more salient limitations are these:

- Many of the more important questions relating to containment have been included in surveys rather sporadically. Indeed, the public has rarely been questioned on the policy of containment itself even when it has come under attack, as it did from some quarters during the 1952 election. Questions on NATO have been asked rather infrequently, and it is even harder to find evidence on public attitudes toward such alliances as SEATO, CENTO, and ANZUS or bilateral defense agreements with Japan, South Korea, the Philippines and others. Some polls have, however, asked about the extent of American support for allied nations should they come under attack.
- At times, questions are worded in ways that are not wholly free from bias. Surveys on the appropriate level of defense spending have often been flawed in this respect.
- Even small changes in the wording of questions that are repeated at frequent intervals may pose problems for trend analyses. For example, after using a question on foreign aid for some years, in 1956 the Gallup organization tacked on the words "to prevent their going communistic" at the end of the question, giving it quite a different tenor.
- Although the situation has improved substantially during recent years, the major polls have not consistently provided information on

the distribution of responses by various strata and subgroups within the entire sample. Since Almond's seminal study of *The American People and Foreign Policy* (1950), it has been customary to distinguish between various strata of the public, typically between opinion leaders, the informed public, and the mass public, and there is reason to believe that this distinction is more important on foreign policy than on other issues. However, until the first of the Chicago Council on Foreign Relations surveys in 1974 there was relatively little information about leadership views on foreign affairs. Distinctions according to educational level—usually between those with college, high school and grammar school educations—are often reported, but a college education may not be a wholly satisfactory surrogate measure for leadership on foreign policy issues.[4]

These shortcomings pose a number of obstacles to valid and reliable descriptions of the public mood at a given time or across an extended period. There is also some truth in Mueller's observation that, because "the poll interview is a rather primitive stimulus–response social situation in which poorly thought-out answers are casually fitted to questions that often are overly ingenuous," one must be cautious in analyzing such data.[5]

These difficulties, however, pale in comparison to those posed by the other requirements. In particular, information on the impact of public opinion on foreign policymaking is very scanty. Cohen has shown that the constraining role of public opinion is often asserted but rarely demonstrated or even put to a systematic test.[6] For example, a classic study of the public–legislator relationship revealed that the attitudes of constituents had less impact on members of the House of Representatives on foreign policy than they did on other issues.[7] Cohen's research on the foreign policy bureaucracy indicates that State Department officials have a rather modest interest in public opinion and, to the extent that they even think about the public, they see it as an entity to be "educated" rather than by which to be guided. With some exceptions,[8] case studies of key foreign policy decisions make no references to public opinion. But we do not know whether that is because public opinion was irrelevant in the case under analysis, because it was excluded from the research design, or because disproportionate attention to crisis decisions tends to exclude cases in which public opinion might be expected to have a greater impact.

Given this state of affairs, it is hardly surprising that there is little agreement about the impact of public opinion. Is it a constraint that, over the intermediate-to-long run, effectively sets limits upon policymakers? Or is public opinion (to the extent that it can be said to exist at all) essentially a shapeless, malleable lump that can readily be molded through public relations activities and compliant media to meet the immediate needs of policymakers?[9] One has little difficulty in finding experts who will confidently espouse either position, as well as many in between. Or, is the relationship too complex to be described adequately by theories which assume a simple, direct, and one-way flow of influence between leaders and the public on foreign affairs? More complex models of the process are also available.[10]

There is scarcely more agreement on the important normative question about the impact of public opinion. If it does have an effect on foreign policy, is it a force for enlightenment — indeed, a necessary if not sufficient condition for sound foreign policy — as celebrated by the Wilsonians and others in the liberal tradition? Or are Walter Lippmann, Hans Morgenthau, George Kennan and others of the "realist" school correct in describing public opinion as a barrier to thoughtful and coherent diplomacy, hindering efforts to promote national interests that transcend the moods and passions of the moment? This issue is of more than passing interest to the student of containment because, as articulated so clearly by Kennan in his seminal "X" article, effective containment requires "caution, circumspection, flexibility and deception," as well as patience, firmness, vigilance, and a long view. He also emphasized that "such a policy has nothing to do with outward histrionics: with threats or blusterings or superfluous gestures of outward 'toughness.'" Are these qualities for which the American public is noted? Indeed, are they attributes that can often be found among leaders? Once again, even a cursory search will uncover advocates for virtually every position on this issue. Indeed, the same Walter Lippmann who considered public opinion "dangerous" in 1955 had, a decade later, come to regard the public as more enlightened than the White House on the Vietnam issue.

Do these difficulties then suggest that "public opinion and containment" is a non-topic that is unworthy of serious inquiry? Not really. As long as foreign policy encompasses the most important issues facing the United States, as long as Soviet–American relations are the dominant question on the nation's diplomatic agenda, and as long as the nature and channels of influence and accountability between leaders and the public (which is the very nature of democratic society) are of vital concern, the issue of public opinion and foreign policy will be important. In short, this introduction is not intended to dismiss the relevance of the topic but, rather, to serve as an explicit reminder of the limitations on the analysis that follows.

## INTERNATIONALISM IN PUBLIC OPINION

The public mood following the end of World War II was of considerable concern to policymakers and many others who worried that it might trace out a pattern resembling the period after World War I: wartime

idealism and internationalism, followed soon by cynicism and disenchantment with active American involvement in efforts to create a more stable international order. This concern is reflected in the frequency with
which polling organizations asked respondents a variety of questions about
whether it would be better for the United States to "take an active role"
or to "stay out" of world affairs.

When confronted with that choice, a majority of the public has selected
the "take an active role" option in every poll conducted since the end of
World War II, as Table 3.1 shows. During and immediately after World
War II, those favoring àn active role usually exceeded 70% of respondents. The onset of the cold war and the Korean War witnessed some
reduction of approval for internationalism, but approximately two respondents in three still rejected isolationism. Public support for an active
international role increased again following the Korean armistice, reaching a zenith of 79% in June 1965. Such data have been cited as evidence
that public opinion is characterized by "a strong and stable 'permissive
mood' toward international involvement."[12] Moreover, opinion polls

Table 3.1. Should the United States Play an Active Role in World Affairs,
or Should It Stay Out? American Leaders and the Public, 1943–1982*

| | | Public (%) | | | Leaders (%) | | |
|---|---|---|---|---|---|---|---|
| Date | Poll** | Active Role | Stay Out | No Opinion | Active Role | Stay Out | No Opinion |
| March 1943 | Gallup | 76 | 14 | 10 | | | |
| February 1944 | Gallup | 69 | 21 | 10 | | | |
| May 1944 | Gallup | 73 | 18 | 9 | | | |
| October 1945 | Gallup | 71 | 19 | 10 | | | |
| February 1946 | Gallup | 72 | 22 | 6 | | | |
| November 1946 | Gallup | 77 | 19 | 4 | | | |
| 1947 | NORC | 68 | 25 | 7 | | | |
| October 1947 | Gallup | 65 | 26 | 9 | | | |
| November 1948 | Fortune | 62 | 30 | 8 | | | |
| January 1950 | NORC | 67 | 24 | 9 | | | |
| March 1951 | NORC | 66 | 25 | 9 | | | |
| March 1955 | NORC | 72 | 21 | 7 | | | |
| 1956 | NORC | 71 | 25 | 4 | | | |
| June 1965 | NORC | 79 | 16 | 5 | | | |
| March 1973 | NORC | 65 | 31 | 4 | | | |
| December 1974 | CCFR | 66 | 24 | 10 | | | |
| December 1978 | CCFR | 59 | 29 | 12 | 97 | 1 | 2 |
| December 1982 | CCFR | 53 | 35 | 12 | 98 | 1 | 1 |

*The exact wording of the questions and response options varied somewhat from survey to survey.

**NORC = National Opinion Research Center; CCFR = Chicago Council on Foreign Relations.

have consistently demonstrated that respondents with a higher level of education are more likely to favor internationalism, and this relationship has usually carried over to views on more specific policies, for example, in substantially greater support for foreign aid, liberalization of trade, and assistance to allies.

However, since 1965, when public opposition to American policy in Vietnam was quite limited, there has been a rather steadȳ decline in support for international activism, reaching lows in 1978 and 1982 surveys that have not been seen since before Pearl Harbor. It is important to point out, however, that the same surveys revealed overwhelming support by leaders—97% and 98%, respectively—for an active American role in world affairs. Although internationalism has never been evenly distributed throughout the population, this bifurcation of attitudes between leaders and the general public is almost surely greater now than at any time since 1945.

## COMMITMENTS AND INTERVENTIONS

Because an "active role in world affairs" can encompass a wide array of specific undertakings, not all of which are part of containment, the figures in Table 3.1 can only provide the broad opinion background against which American policy has developed. In order to gain a more precise sense of public attitudes toward containment, it is necessary to examine public responses to the specific external commitments and interventions — actual and hypothetical — that have given shape to the policy of containment during the past four decades.

Although George F. Kennan's seminal analysis of the sources of Soviet foreign policy and their implications for relations between Moscow and Washington had reached the State Department a year earlier, 1947 marks a convenient starting point for analyzing public attitudes toward containment. The first of the three major undertakings that defined the American response to Soviet policy—the program of economic and military aid to Greece and Turkey known as the Truman Doctrine—was announced in March, followed soon by the Marshall Plan. Two years later the North Atlantic Treaty Organization was formed. Taken together, these actions constituted a significant part of what has been called "the revolution in American foreign policy."

The domestic context in early 1947 was one of rapidly changing attitudes about the prospects of cooperation with the Soviet Union. Planning for the postwar period during the Roosevelt administration had assumed that continued collaboration between the major wartime allies (the "Four Policemen") would serve as a major pillar of peace, and public attitudes tended to be consistent with that premise. Less than two years before the

Truman Doctrine speech, the public was optimistic about postwar relations with the Soviet Union. In a Gallup poll taken a month after Japan's
surrender, the public agreed by a margin of almost two-to-one (54% –
30%) that Russia could be trusted to cooperate with the United States. As
late as December 1946, Gallup reported that 43% of the public believed
that Moscow could be expected to cooperate, whereas 40% disagreed.
Polls also indicated that the more highly educated respondents tended to
be more optimistic in this respect.

Public opinion surveys revealed moderately strong but growing support
for the Truman Doctrine, the Marshall Plan and NATO (Table 3.2). Two
days after President Truman's address to Congress requesting aid to Greece
and Turkey, a Gallup poll revealed that those approving outnumbered
opponents by a margin of 56% –32%. At that time public faith in the ability of the United Nations to deal with major international problems was
rather high; indeed, much of the domestic criticism of the Truman Doctrine focused on the charge that the Greek–Turkish aid program would
unilaterally bypass the newly created international organization. A month
after Secretary of State Marshall's June 1947 speech at Harvard, the margin in support of the economic assistance program for Europe was better
than two-to-one (57% –21%), and within eighteen months that margin
had grown to five-to-one (65% –13%) — the postwar high point of support
for foreign assistance. NATO elicited even more substantial and consistent approval. Polls in 1949 and 1950 showed that between two-thirds
and three-quarters of respondents favored the NATO pact, whereas the
opposition never reached the 20% level.

But if the kinds of programs that constituted the core of containment
during the late 1940s had substantial public approval, not all of the real
and hypothetical projects undertaken in the name of containment have
garnered automatic support. Questions about sending American troops
abroad have typically elicited much more varied patterns of response.
The Korean and Vietnam Wars are, of course, the most important instances of American armed intervention. In both instances, initial bipartisan public support eroded as the prospects for early victory declined and
as American casualties increased. The highly educated were most likely to
approve American intervention, whereas those with only a grade school
education were most critical.[13]

Reservations about deployment of American forces abroad, especially
in unstable Third World areas, have persisted. Several examples will illustrate this point:

- Whereas a 1950 Gallup poll indicated a 74% –17% margin of support
  for NATO, another survey by the same organization only a year later
  showed that only 55% approved sending American troops to Europe,

whereas 35% preferred to have them remain at home to protect this
hemisphere. Once forces are deployed, however, opinion often shifts.
For example, a 1959 survey revealed overwhelming (81%) public support for keeping troops in Berlin even at the risk of war, rather than
withdrawing them in the face of Premier Khrushchev's threat to alter
the status of that divided city.

- As the French effort to maintain control in Indochina was reaching its
climactic phase in 1953–1954, Gallup polls reported that as much as
85% of the public opposed sending American troops there. Despite
various "trial balloons" about American intervention that were being
floated in Washington during the spring of 1954, overwhelming public
opposition to intervention persisted. Two polls in May indicated that
opponents outnumbered supporters of such an undertaking by margins of more than three-to-one. Even the proposal to deploy only naval and air forces to Indochina was opposed by a substantial majority.

- Following the tumultuous events of 1956 in the Middle East, the public was rather evenly divided on the question of sending American
troops should the Soviet Union attack the area, with 50% approving,
and the remainder opposing (34%) or expressing no opinion (16%).

- Less than a month before the Cuban missile crisis in 1962, less than
one-quarter of the public favored using armed force to overthrow the
Castro regime in Cuba.

- Even though a 1975 survey indicated fairly strong support for continuing the policy of containment (the margin of approval was 53% to
37%), a roughly comparable majority also favored a *reduction* of
American forces in Europe. Support for using American troops to
defend major allies should they be attacked has also tended to fluctu-
ate rather sharply since the early 1970s (Table 3.3). Although wording
differences no doubt account for at least some of the variation in responses during a specific year, there is a discernible pattern of declining support in the immediate wake of the war in Vietnam, followed
by rising approval for defending Western Europe and Japan. The
most recent Chicago Council survey in 1982 also reported, however,
that should South Korea, Taiwan, Israel, El Salvador or Saudi Arabia
be attacked, an overwhelming majority of the public would oppose
sending American troops to help them.[14]

- During the post-Vietnam period, public support for American interventions in the Third World has been decidedly lukewarm. Even the
successful and low-cost invasion of Grenada elicited less than overwhelming approval from either the public (59%) or leaders (62%).[15]
Repeated surveys during the 1980s have revealed strong and growing
resistance to deploying American troops or military advisers in Central America. The past few years have witnessed vigorous debates

Table 3.2. Public Opinion on Various Actual and Proposed
Containment-Related Undertakings Abroad, 1947–1985

| Date | Poll | Issue* | %<br>Favor** | %<br>Oppose*** | % No<br>Opinion |
|---|---|---|---|---|---|
| March 1947 | Gallup | Aid to Greece<br>(Truman Doctrine) | 56 | 32 | 12 |
| July 1947 | Gallup | Marshall Plan | 57 | 21 | 22 |
| November 1948 | Gallup | To continue the<br>Marshall Plan | 65 | 13 | 22 |
| May 1949 | Gallup | North Atlantic<br>Treaty Organization | 67 | 12 | 21 |
| May 1950 | Gallup | North Atlantic<br>Treaty Organization | 74 | 17 | 9 |
| July 1950 | Gallup | Military supplies to<br>Chiang Kai-shek<br>government on<br>Formosa | 48 | 35 | 17 |
| August 1950 | Gallup | Support for U.S. en-<br>try into Korean War | 66 | 19 | 15 |
| January 1951 | Gallup | Sending troops to<br>Europe or keeping<br>them at home to<br>defend the Americas | 55† | 35‡ | 10 |
| October 1952 | Gallup | Support for U.S. en-<br>try into Korean War | 37 | 43 | 20 |
| January 1953 | Gallup | Support for U.S. en-<br>try into Korean War | 50 | 36 | 14 |
| May 1953 | Gallup | Sending troops to<br>Indochina | 12 | 78 | 10 |
| August 1953 | Gallup | Sending troops to<br>Indochina | 8 | 85 | 7 |
| May 1954 | Gallup | Sending troops to<br>Indochina | 20 | 72 | 8 |
| December 1956 | Gallup | Foreign aid to help<br>stop communism | 58 | 28 | 14 |
| January 1957 | Gallup | U.S. promise to send<br>troops to Middle<br>East if Russians<br>attack there | 50 | 34 | 16 |
| March 1959 | Gallup | Keeping troops in<br>Berlin even at risk<br>of war | 81 | 11 | 8 |
| September 1962 | Gallup | Using armed force<br>to overthrow Castro | 24 | 63 | 13 |

*continued*

Table 3.2. (continued)

| Date | Poll | Issue* | % Favor** | % Oppose*** | % No Opinion |
|------|------|--------|-----------|-------------|--------------|
| March 1966 | Gallup | Support for U.S. entry into Vietnam War | 59 | 25 | 16 |
| February 1973 | Gallup | Support for U.S. entry into Vietnam War | 29 | 60 | 11 |
| September 1973 | Gallup | Reduce U.S. troops in Europe | 57 | 33 | 10 |
| February 1975 | Gallup | Additional aid to South Vietnam and Cambodia | 12 | 78 | 10 |
| April 1975 | Gallup | Continue policy of helping governments that might be overthrown by communist-backed forces | 53 | 37 | 10 |
| June 1977 | Gallup | Withdrawal of U.S. troops from South Korea | 40 | 38 | 22 |
| March 1981 | Gallup | U.S. support for government in El Salvador | 44 | 47 | 9 |
| July 1983 | Gallup | Increasing military advisers in El Salvador from 55 to 125 | 24 | 63 | 13 |
| July 1983 | Gallup | Military assistance to friendly governments in Central America | 35 | 55 | 10 |
| October 1983 | Gallup | Sending Marines to Lebanon | 37 | 51 | 12 |
| May 1985 | Gallup | Trade embargo on Nicaragua | 46 | 37 | 17 |
| May 1985 | Harris | Invasion of Nicaragua | 20 | 75 | 5 |
| May 1985 | Harris | Military aid to anti-Sandinista rebels in Nicaragua | 23 | 73 | 4 |

*Summary of issue rather than exact wording of question asked.

**Includes such responses as "yes," "agree," "support," "good idea," "right thing."

***Includes such reports as "no," "disagree," "wrong thing," "poor" or "fair idea."

†Send to Europe.

‡Keep at home to defend only North and South America.

Table 3.3. Willingness to Come to the Defenses of Western Europe
and Japan if They are Attacked*

| | | Public | | Leaders | |
|---|---|---|---|---|---|
| Date | Poll** | Western Europe | Japan | Western Europe | Japan |
| 1972 | PA | 52 | 43 | | |
| 1974 | CCFR | 39 | | 77 | |
| | PA | 48 | 37 | | |
| 1975 | PA | 48 | 42 | | |
| 1976 | PA | 56 | 45 | | |
| 1978 | CCFR | 54 | 42 | 92 | 81 |
| | PA | 62 | 50 | | |
| | Roper | 43 | | | |
| 1979 | PA | 64 | 54 | | |
| 1980 | AP/NBC | 67 | | | |
| | PA | 70 | 57 | | |
| 1981 | PA (Feb.) | 51 | | | |
| | PA (July) | 53 | | | |
| 1982 | CCFR | 65 | 51 | 92 | 78 |

*Percentage of respondents who favor having the United States come to the defense of allies.

**PA = Potomac Associates; CCFR = Chicago Council on Foreign Relations; AP/NBC = Associated Press/National Broadcasting Corporation. Surveys within a single year are listed in alphabetical order.

about whether perceived parallels between American involvement in Vietnam and Central America illustrate a proper appreciation of "the lessons of Vietnam" or a simplistic misapplication of them, but public opinion surveys repeatedly demonstrate that between two-thirds and three-fourths of the public fear that the situation in Central America will witness a repetition of the Vietnam War. The public also opposed the deployment of American Marines in Lebanon, with many (64%) expressing the fear that the situation there would turn into another Vietnam.[16]

## DEFENSE SPENDING

Because a substantial part of defense spending is allocated for containment, attitudes toward the Pentagon's budget provide another relevant indicator of the public mood. Questions on the issue were included in surveys rather sporadically until the late 1960s; for example, between 1953 and 1969, the Gallup poll asked about the defense budget only in 1960. In contrast, that organization polled the public at least three times on defense spending in 1983 alone.

The few surveys on the appropriate level of defense spending during the Truman and Eisenhower periods indicated an absence of public dissatisfaction (Table 3.4). In each of three Gallup polls — in 1950, 1953, and 1960 — a majority of those with an opinion on the issue judged the budget to be "about right," and of the rest, slightly more favored raising rather than lowering allocations to the Pentagon.

The absence of poll data on defense spending during the Kennedy and Johnson years makes it impossible to pinpoint a shift in mood, but it is a reasonable guess that the sharp changes in sentiment were linked to disenchantment with the Vietnam War.[17] Gallup polls in 1969, 1971, and 1973 revealed that respondents who felt that Pentagon spending was "too much" exceeded the combined total of those who judged it "too little" or "about right." Although the margin in favor of reduced defense spending varied somewhat from poll to poll during the Nixon and Ford administrations, the overall results point to substantial support for reduced defense spending.

The erosion of détente and growing concern about the magnitude of Soviet military programs during the later 1970s were reflected in a strong shift back toward support for greater defense spending, reaching a zenith during the 1980 election and the first year of the Reagan administration. Surveys of leaders and the general public revealed substantial majorities in favor of increasing allocations to the Pentagon.

The "defense consensus" was short-lived, however, despite repeated statements by President Reagan and Defense Secretary Weinberger that the job of "rebuilding America's defenses" has only begun. Evidence of a dramatic change in opinion is overwhelming; the polls since 1982 differ only on the magnitude of the shift toward a preference for reduced defense spending. Perhaps even more importantly, surveys of American leaders reveal that they also experienced a sharp shift in sentiment. Among the driving forces behind the change in mood may be a belief that the military build-up has been completed — views of the president and defense secretary to the contrary notwithstanding — but follow-up questions in a 1985 Harris survey also document some other reasons, including massive budget deficits, perceived waste, cost overruns in defense procurement, and weapons that often seem to function poorly.

## LEADERS AND THE GENERAL PUBLIC

Although the distinction between various strata of the public has been a standard part of the literature on public opinion and foreign policy for at least three and a half decades, until recently opinion surveys have rarely distinguished between leaders and the general public in their surveys.[18] This difficulty has been substantially reduced during the post-Vietnam

Table 3.4. Net Attitudes Favoring an Increase or Decrease
in U.S. Defense Spending, 1950–1985*

| Year | Surveys of the General Public** | | | | | | Surveys of Leaders** | |
|------|--------|--------|------|---------|-------|------|--------|------|
|      | Gallup | Harris | NORC | NYT/CBS | Roper | CCFR | CCFR | FPLP |
| 1950 | 8 | | | | | | | |
| 1953 | 3 | | | | | | | |
| 1960 | 2 | | | | | | | |
| 1969 | (44) | | | | | | | |
| 1970 | (41) | | | | | | | |
| 1971 | (39) | (34) | (27) | | | | | |
| 1972 | (28) | | | | | | | |
| 1973 | (34) | | | | | | | |
|      | (33) | | | | | | | |
| 1974 | (32) | | (14) | | | (19) | (48) | |
| 1975 | | | (14) | | | | | |
| 1976 | (14) | (2) | (3) | | | | | |
| 1977 | 4 | | 1 | | | | | |
| 1978 | | 18 | 5 | | 8 | 16 | | 3 |
|      | | 41 | | | | | | |
| 1979 | | | | | 25 | | | |
| 1980 | 35 | | 45 | 58 | 44 | | | 39 |
| 1981 | 36 | 42 | | 54 | 2 | | | |
|      | | | | 43 | | | | |
| 1982 | (17) | | (1) | | (19) | (3) | (21) | |
|      | (25) | | | | | | | |
| 1983 | (31) | (14) | | | | | | |
|      | (28) | (11) | | | | | | |
|      | (16)*** | 21*** | | | | | | |
|      | | 8 | | | | | | |
| 1984 | | | | (7) | | | | (63) |
| 1985 | (35) | (29) | | | | | | |

*Percent favoring an increase minus percent favoring a reduction; or percent stating budget is "too small" minus percent stating budget is "too large."

**Numbers in parentheses indicate net support for reducing the defense budget. NORC = National Opinion Research Center; NYT/CBS = New York Times/Columbia Broadcasting System; CCFR = Chicago Council on Foreign Relations; FPLP = Foreign Policy Leadership Project.

***Surveys taken immediately after the USSR shot down Korean Airlines flight 007.

Note: As Russett (1974) has demonstrated, questions on the defense budget are not uniformly free of bias (usually in an anti-defense direction). Moreover, differences in wording or context (for example, whether the defense budget is appraised alone or within a cluster of other government programs) can have an impact on responses. Thus, the data here should be viewed with some caution. Nevertheless, they would appear adequate for tracing out broad shifts in public sentiments. [Bruce M. Russett, "The Revolt of the Masses: Public Opinion on Military Expenditures," in John P. Lovell and Philip S. Kronenberg, eds., *New Civil-Military Relations: The Agonies of Adjustment to Post-Vietnam Realities.* New Brunswick, N.J.: Transaction Books, 1974.]

period, however, as surveys of leaders have been undertaken by the Chicago Council on Foreign Relations, the Foreign Policy Leadership Project, Allen Barton, Bruce Russett and Elizabeth Hanson, and Barry Sussman.[19] The CCFR also surveyed the general public at the same time.

Many of the questions posed in recent leadership surveys are not precisely the same as those asked of the general public, but they do provide some opportunities to compare mass and leadership attitudes on a number of questions pertaining to containment. For example, Table 3.1 already revealed the huge gap between leaders and the public in support for an active American role in world affairs.

The post-Vietnam leadership surveys make it possible to draw more precise comparisons of public and leadership attitudes on containment. Table 3.5 summarizes responses from six surveys to two central questions — the importance of "containing communism" and of "defending our allies' security" since the end of the Vietnam War. Responses to the first item reveal a good deal of consistency during the 1974–1984 period concerning the importance of containment among both leaders and the general public. Just under one half of the leaders described containment as "somewhat important," while slightly smaller proportions rated that goal as "very important." Although the general public has been more skeptical than leaders about foreign commitments on most issues, concern for containing communism is an exception, as majorities ranging from 54% to 60% described that goal as "very important."[20]

Reversing the finding on containing communism, results for the question on "defending our allies' security" indicate a substantially greater sense of importance among leaders than among the general public in each of the three Chicago Council surveys. But in another respect, the data are somewhat harder to interpret because of the sharp, repeated, and inexplicable differences in the Chicago and Leadership Project surveys. The one important similarity in the two surveys is that each reveals growing support over time for protecting allies.

Containment and defending allies were only two of more than a dozen foreign policy goals which respondents were asked to rate in Chicago Council and Leadership Project surveys. These clusters of questions provide an opportunity to examine assessments of containment within the context of a richer menu of foreign policy goals. Table 3.6 presents responses to nine goals, combining answers into a single summary index.

Several important points emerge from these results. Although containment was not rated by leaders or the general public as a trivial goal, it did not emerge as the dominant or superordinate goal of American foreign policy. Indeed, of the five items dealing with military/strategic issues, arms control was consistently given a higher priority by leaders and the public in both surveys — even in 1980, when strong majorities favored

Table 3.5. The Importance of "Containing Communism" and "Defending Our Allies' Security" as Foreign Policy Goals: American Leaders and the General Public, 1974–1984

| | | Leaders (%) | | | | The General Public (%) | | | |
|---|---|---|---|---|---|---|---|---|---|
| | | Very Important | Somewhat Important | Not important at all | Not Sure | Very Important | Somewhat Important | Not important at all | Not Sure |
| *Containing communism* | | | | | | | | | |
| 1974 | CCFR* | 34 | 49 | 16 | 1 | 54 | 27 | 13 | 6 |
| 1976 | FPLP* | 39 | 42 | 14 | 5 | | | | |
| 1978 | CCFR | 45 | 47 | 7 | 1 | 60 | 24 | 10 | 6 |
| 1980 | FPLP | 41 | 46 | 11 | 2 | | | | |
| 1982 | CCFR | 44 | 46 | 8 | 2 | 59 | 27 | 8 | 6 |
| 1984 | FPLP | 38 | 47 | 13 | 1 | | | | |
| *Defending our allies' security* | | | | | | | | | |
| 1974 | CCFR | 47 | 49 | 2 | 2 | 33 | 50 | 9 | 8 |
| 1976 | FPLP | 37 | 55 | 4 | 4 | | | | |
| 1978 | CCFR | 77 | 21 | 1 | 1 | 50 | 35 | 7 | 8 |
| 1980 | FPLP | 44 | 52 | 3 | 1 | | | | |
| 1982 | CCFR | 82 | 16 | 1 | 1 | 50 | 39 | 5 | 6 |
| 1984 | FPLP | 47 | 49 | 3 | 1 | | | | |

*CCFR = Chicago Council on Foreign Relations; FPLP = Foreign Policy Leadership Project.

34

Table 3.6. The Importance of Several Goals of American Foreign Policy: American Leaders and the Public, 1974–1984*

| Goals | Leaders** | | | | | | The Public | | |
|---|---|---|---|---|---|---|---|---|---|
| | 1974 (CCFR) | 1976 (FPLP) | 1978 (CCFR) | 1980 (FPLP) | 1982 (CCFR) | 1984 (FPLP) | 1974 (CCFR) | 1978 (CCFR) | 1982 (CCFR) |
| Containing communism | .59 | .63 | .69 | .65 | .68 | .63 | .72 | .77 | .77 |
| Defending our allies' security | .73 | .67 | .88 | .71 | .91 | .73 | .63 | .73 | .74 |
| Protecting weaker nations against foreign aggression | .60 | .53 | .63 | .58 | .70 | *** | .53 | .63 | .63 |
| Matching Soviet military power | *** | *** | *** | *** | *** | .63 | *** | *** | .69 |
| Maintaining a balance of power among nations | .73 | .69 | *** | .76 | *** | .68 | .65 | *** | *** |
| Worldwide arms control | .93 | .82 | .89 | .74 | .92 | .83 | .82 | .82 | .81 |
| Securing adequate supplies of energy | .88 | .85 | .94 | .88 | .86 | .92 | .88 | .90 | .85 |
| Combatting world hunger | .88 | .72 | .83 | .73 | .82 | .76 | .79 | .78 | .78 |
| Helping to improve the standard of living in LDCs | .81 | .65 | .81 | .68 | .77 | .78 | .66 | .62 | .63 |

*Responses scored as follows: "Very important" = 1.00; "Somewhat important" = 0.50; "Not at all important" = 0.00; "Not sure" not scored. The index ranges from 0.00 to 1.00.

**CCFR: Chicago Council on Foreign Relations; FPLP = Foreign Policy Leadership Project.

***Question not included in that survey.

35

increasing the defense budget (see Table 3.4). This view was shared by those who stated that "matching Soviet military power" is a "very important" foreign policy goal; 84% of them favored arms control agreements with the Soviet Union.[21] It is also evident that a variety of economic issues including energy, hunger and Third World poverty, have come to be viewed as of at least equal, if not greater importance than containment.[22] In the absence of directly comparable data from the period between the Truman Doctrine and the end of the war in Vietnam it is impossible to offer confident assessments about changes and continuities in leadership attitudes on containment, but the evidence in Tables 3.5 and 3.6 strongly suggests that both leaders and the public perceive a richer set of challenges to and opportunities for American diplomacy than did their counterparts during much of the Truman–Eisenhower–Kennedy–Johnson era.

Finally, and perhaps most importantly, there is substantial evidence of deep cleavages on foreign policy issues that encompass, but also go beyond, attitudes on containment (Table 3.7). Surveys of both the general public and leaders have revealed the existence of at least three very distinct ways of thinking about international relations and America's proper role in world affairs. Although the labels used to describe these belief systems vary from study to study,[23] their essential characteristics are quite similar:

- The cold war internationalists — also described as "conservative internationalists" and "the security culture" — are inclined to believe that the international system remains bipolar. A relentless Soviet drive for international supremacy, buttressed by a rapid military buildup which exceeds any reasonable defensive needs, is thus the primary threat. In order to meet the Soviet challenge, it is vital that the United States and the West maintain a high level of military capabilities, a determination to match or exceed increases in Soviet force levels, and a willingness to use military power if needed to forestall Soviet adventures and to maintain the credibility of containment and deterrence.
- Variously described as "liberal internationalists," "the equity culture," and "post–cold war internationalists," a second group tends to view the international system and primary threats to American interests with substantial emphasis on non-military/strategic issues, including the growing gap between rich and poor nations, threats to the environment, population, resources, racial conflict, Third World debts, and similar issues. Although not unmindful of East–West tensions, they are inclined to view problems between Moscow and Washington as tractable. Détente, arms control agreements and similar arrangements are seen as offering the prospect for stabilizing relations between the superpowers; they may also permit some resources that

have gone into arms races to be used for coping with non-military threats to national security.

- Whereas the first two schools of thought locate the primary threats to the national interest in the international system, a third group—the "semi-isolationists" or "non-internationalists"—are skeptical. They tend to doubt America's responsibility for and ability to cope with a wide range of international problems; indeed, they believe that the excessive global agenda pursued by the United States is itself a major threat to American security. By taking on the roles of the world's policeman, "do-gooder," or conscience, the United States has squandered its material and other resources without commensurate success. America's vital international interests are finite, as are the resources that can be expended to protect them.

Two important points emerge from these findings. In a superficial sense, internationalists no doubt continue to constitute a majority, but differences between the two schools of internationalism are so fundamental and are rooted in such significant ideological differences that barring a major international crisis, the chasm is not likely to be bridged in the near future. Second, semi-isolationism has achieved a position of respectability probably not seen since before Pearl Harbor. Indeed, on some issues (such as trade) the isolationist position may represent the majority view.

## PARTISANSHIP IN PUBLIC OPINION ON CONTAINMENT

Speculation about partisanship, a gender gap, or a generation gap reflects an interest in how the public's attributes affect its attitudes on foreign policy. The relationship of party and age to foreign policy views may be of special interest. Information on party trends may provide some clues about the extent to which major aspects of containment might be a source of partisan conflict, with the prospect that containment might be more difficult to sustain when one party replaces another in control of the White House or Congress. Thus, the composition of an opinion majority may be almost as important as its size. A 60%–40% poll on a containment issue in which Republicans and Democrats are similarly divided is likely to have different long-run consequences than a 60%–40% split that is composed of a 90%–10% division in one party and a 30%–70% split in the other. The distribution of attitudes across age groups may provide hints, not only about generational differences, but also about the likelihood of change as one age cohort replaces its predecessors.

During the formative years of America's containment policy, the bipartisan cooperation between the White House and Congress (which made

Table 3.7. Some Elements of Three Foreign Policy Belief Systems

| | Cold War Internationalism | Post-Cold War Internationalism | Semi-Isolationism |
|---|---|---|---|
| **Nature of the international system** | | | |
| Structure | Bipolar: Tight links between issues and conflicts. | Complex and interdependent: Moderate links between issues and conflicts. | Multipolar: Weak links between issues and conflicts. |
| World order priorities | A world safe from aggression and terrorism. | International regimes for coping with a broad range of issues. | Top priority should be to reduce linkages, dependencies, and interdependencies. |
| Conception of interdependence | Encompasses security issues ("domino theory"). | Encompasses economic/social issues. | Exaggerated by internationalists. |
| Primary threats to the United States | Soviet and Soviet-sponsored aggression and terrorism. Military imbalance favoring the USSR. | Danger of nuclear war; North-South issues (e.g. rich-poor gap). | Danger of war by miscalculation; Domestic problems. |
| **The Soviet Union** | | | |
| Nature of the system | A model totalitarian state. | A great power. | A great power with manifest domestic problems. |
| Driving force of foreign policy | Aggressive expansionism inherent in the Soviet system. | Seeks parity with U.S.; Defensiveness (exaggerated view of defense needs may create further tensions). | Fear |

| | | | |
|---|---|---|---|
| *Soviet-American relations* | | | |
| Nature of the conflict | Conflicts of interest are genuine; Largely zero-sum. | Some conflicts of interest, but these are exaggerated by hard-liners on both sides; Largely non-zero sum. | Few if any genuine conflicts of interest; Largely non-zero sum. |
| *The Third World* | | | |
| Role in present international system | Primary target of Soviet and Soviet-inspired subversion and aggression. | Primary source of unresolved social/economic problems that must be resolved to create a viable world order. | With a few exceptions, largely peripheral and irrelevant, especially to U.S. interests. |
| Primary U.S. obligations | Help provide security from aggression and terrorism. | Economic and other forms of non-military assistance; Play a leading role in structural systemic changes. | Few, if any obligations for either security or economic development. |
| *Prescription for American foreign policy* | Rebuild military strength to regain a position of parity with the U.S.S.R.; Rebuild collective security system. | Stabilize relations with U.S.S.R., in order to free resources for dealing with North-South and other priority issues. | Stabilize relations with U.S.S.R. and reduce commitments and dependencies abroad. |

possible aid to Greece and Turkey, the Marshall Plan and the North Atlantic Treaty Organization) was reflected in public opinion on these undertakings. As indicated earlier (Table 3.2), each of these striking departures from traditional foreign policy had rather solid public support. Equally important is the fact that Democrats and Republicans differed little with respect to any of these key elements of containment (Table 3.8). Issues relating to the Far East tended to be more contentious and placed greater strains on bipartisan cooperation, especially after the Truman–MacArthur dispute. The president's decision to fire MacArthur, culminating a conflict that reflected some fundamental differences in the appropriate conduct of containment, was not popular among Democrats (opposed 53%–30%), independents (51%–30%), or (especially) Republicans (72%–17%).[24] But surveys on other issues found limited partisan differences; for example, the decision to resist aggression in Korea, the move to aid the Chinese government in Taiwan, and the proposal to send American forces to Indochina as the French effort there was collapsing, found Republicans and Democrats about equally supportive or critical. To be sure, by 1952 polls revealed that the Korean War—"Truman's War" as it was often called by critics—had lost far more support among Republicans than among Democrats, but sharp partisan divisions did not persist into the Eisenhower years. Even though the defense budget had become a controversial issue in 1960 (with charges that a complacent administration had permitted a dangerous "missile gap" to develop), a Gallup poll revealed that differences attributable to party loyalties were insubstantial. The absence of strong partisan cleavages extended into the early years of the Vietnam War, majorities within both parties expressing strong support for the policies of the Johnson administration.[25]

For two and a half decades spanning the Truman, Eisenhower, Kennedy and early Johnson administrations, then, whatever differences divided the American public on foreign policies rarely fell along a cleavage defined by partisan loyalties. Indeed, during the pre-Vietnam period the distribution of attitudes among supporters of the two major parties was sufficiently similar that the self-identified political "independents" usually stood on one side or another of the Democrats and Republicans, rather than in between them.

The decade since the end of the Vietnam War has witnessed a striking revival of partisan differences on a broad range of issues relating to containment. During the years immediately following the 1975 withdrawal of the last Americans from Saigon, pollsters generally concentrated on domestic issues (inflation, unemployment and crime) because these appeared to be of the most immediate public concern. Even the controversial question of how the United States should respond to events in Angola did not elicit a probe by the Gallup organization. Table 3.8

Table 3.8. Partisanship on Selected Foreign and Defense Policy Issues: The General Public, 1946–1984

| Date/Poll | Issue* | | Responses by Party Affiliation (%) | | |
|---|---|---|---|---|---|
| | | | Republican | Democrat | Independent |
| February 1946 Gallup | Role U.S. should play in world affairs | Active | 72 | 72 | NR† |
| | | Stay Out | 23 | 22 | NR |
| | | No Opinion | 5 | 6 | NR |
| March 1947 Gallup | Aid to Greece (Truman Doctrine) | Approve | 56 | 56 | NR |
| | | Disapprove | 31 | 32 | NR |
| | | No Opinion | 13 | 12 | NR |
| July 1948 Gallup | U.S. policy toward the Soviet Union | Too Soft | 73 | 70 | NR |
| | | Too Tough | 3 | 4 | NR |
| | | About Right | 14 | 14 | NR |
| | | No Opinion | 10 | 12 | NR |
| February 1950 Gallup | Defense budget | Too Much | 16 | 12 | 18 |
| | | Too Little | 22 | 25 | 24 |
| | | About Right | 46 | 46 | 40 |
| | | No Opinion | 16 | 17 | 18 |
| July 1950 Gallup | Military supplies to Chiang Kai-shek government on Taiwan | Should | 48 | 50 | NR |
| | | Should Not | 39 | 32 | NR |
| | | No Opinion | 13 | 18 | NR |
| July 1951 Gallup | Sending U.S. troops to Europe or keeping them at home to defend the Americas | Europe | 53 | 61 | 49 |
| | | At Home | 39 | 30 | 38 |
| | | No Opinion | 8 | 9 | 13 |
| May 1954 Gallup | Sending U.S. troops to Indochina | Approve | 18 | 22 | 17 |
| | | Disapprove | 76 | 70 | 72 |
| | | No Opinion | 6 | 8 | 11 |
| December 1956 Gallup | Approve foreign aid to help stop communism | Yes | 59 | 58 | 58 |
| | | No | 28 | 28 | 28 |
| | | No Opinion | 13 | 14 | 14 |

(continued)

Table 3.8. (continued)

| Date/Poll | Issue* | Responses by Party Affiliation (%) | | |
| --- | --- | --- | --- | --- |
| | | Republican | Democrat | Independent |
| January 1957 Gallup | Promise to send U.S. troops to Middle East in case of Russian attack there | | | |
| | Approve | 53 | 47 | 52 |
| | Disapprove | 34 | 36 | 32 |
| | No Opinion | 13 | 17 | 16 |
| March 1960 Gallup | Defense budget | | | |
| | Too Much | 19 | 20 | 16 |
| | Too Little | 15 | 24 | 23 |
| | About Right | 51 | 42 | 44 |
| | No Opinion | 15 | 14 | 17 |
| January 1963 Gallup | Foreign aid | | | |
| | For | 54 | 59 | 61 |
| | Against | 35 | 28 | 28 |
| | No Opinion | 11 | 13 | 11 |
| January 1973 Gallup | Was U.S. policy in Vietnam a mistake? | | | |
| | Yes | 54 | 64 | NR |
| | No | 35 | 26 | NR |
| | No Opinion | 11 | 10 | NR |
| September 1973 Gallup | Reduction of U.S. troops in Europe | | | |
| | Should | 54 | 61 | 56 |
| | Should Not | 36 | 31 | 34 |
| | No Opinion | 10 | 8 | 10 |
| June 1977 Gallup | Withdrawal of U.S. troops from South Korea | | | |
| | Favor | 32 | 47 | 36 |
| | Oppose | 51 | 30 | 41 |
| | No Opinion | 17 | 23 | 23 |
| March 1981 Gallup | U.S. role in El Salvador conflict** | | | |
| | Help Government | 44 | 19 | 25 |
| | Stay Out | 19 | 33 | 34 |
| | Don't Know | 6 | 6 | 5 |
| September 1981 Harris | Defense budget | | | |
| | Increase | 73 | 49 | 57 |
| | Decrease | 9 | 20 | 15 |
| | Keep Same | 15 | 25 | 26 |
| | Not Sure | 3 | 6 | 2 |

| Date / Source | Issue | Response | | | |
|---|---|---|---|---|---|
| March 1982 Gallup | Defense budget | Too Much | 18 | 43 | 39 |
| | | Too Little | 27 | 16 | 18 |
| | | About Right | 46 | 32 | 36 |
| | | No Opinion | 9 | 9 | 7 |
| July 1983 Gallup | Is El Salvador likely to turn into a situation like Vietnam? | Very | 27 | 48 | 41 |
| | | Fairly | 33 | 30 | 32 |
| | | Not Very | 26 | 13 | 14 |
| | | Not At All | 8 | 3 | 6 |
| | | No Opinion | 6 | 6 | 7 |
| October 1983 Gallup | On sending Marines to Lebanon | Yes, Mistake | 36 | 61 | 50 |
| | | No | 53 | 29 | 36 |
| | | No Opinion | 11 | 10 | 14 |
| January 1985 NYT/CBS | Defense budget† | Increase | 21 | 19 | 16 |
| | | Decrease | 16 | 32 | 27 |
| | | Keep Same | 60 | 47 | 52 |
| | | No Opinion | 3 | 2 | 5 |
| January 1985 Gallup | Defense budget | Too Much | 29 | 60 | 49 |
| | | Too Little | 15 | 7 | 10 |
| | | About Right | 49 | 27 | 35 |
| | | No Opinion | 7 | 6 | 6 |
| April 1985 Gallup | Proposal to reduce defense spending as a way of reducing the deficit | Approve | 56 | 76 | 65 |
| | | Disapprove | 36 | 19 | 30 |
| | | No Opinion | 8 | 5 | 5 |
| May 1985 Gallup | Trade embargo against Nicaragua | Approve | 65 | 26 | 45 |
| | | Disapprove | 16 | 58 | 38 |
| | | No Opinion | 19 | 16 | 17 |

*Summary statement of the issue rather than the exact wording of the question asked. Response options are given in parentheses below the issue and in abbreviated form to the left of the percentage distribution of responses.

**Percentages exclude those who have not heard of the situation in El Salvador.

†NR = Not reported.

includes relatively little evidence about issues relating to containment during the Ford and Carter years.

Data on foreign policy attitudes have become more plentiful during the 1980s, however, and they reveal clearly that partisan differences are sharp and persistent, and that these differences encompass most containment-related issues. Moreover, the cleavages are not limited to the public but are equally pronounced among American leaders (Table 3.9), with Republican support for containment roughly double that of Democrats. The bifurcation along partisan lines is sufficiently great that, unlike during the pre-Vietnam period, recent responses of political independents typically fall between those of Democrats and Republicans. With the possible exception of some agreement on the need to reduce defense spending, evidence neither from leaders nor from the general public suggests that a convergence of foreign policy views across political parties will be easily achieved. Not the least reason for this diagnosis is evidence that partisan differences are buttressed by hardening ideological cleavages. The evidence on this score at the leadership level is rather strong,[26] and the same dynamics may also be found among the general public.[27]

## GENERATIONS AND CONTAINMENT

A generational interpretation of American foreign policy views appears to offer an attractive way to account for periodic shifts in public attitudes on foreign affairs. It seems to provide an explanation for the long-term cycles in which public moods have been described as swinging between internationalism and isolationism at intervals of approximately a generation in length throughout the history of the republic.[28] It is also consonant with the observation that members of each generation view the world in the light of the critical events that marked their coming to maturity.

The generational hypothesis seemed especially pertinent in the aftermath of the Vietnam War, giving rise to several analyses that depicted domestic cleavages on the war in generational terms.[29] Among the earliest and most visible opponents of the war were students at Berkeley, Harvard and other campuses. These and other critics rejected many of the intellectual underpinnings of containment, notably the relevance for the conflict in South East Asia of the "lessons" of the pre-World War II era about the futility of appeasement and the premise that the war in Indochina presented a threat similar to that posed by Stalinist Russia during the late 1940s. Hence, several analysts depicted the foreign policy debates of the late 1960s and early 1970s as pitting the theories and values of the "Munich generation" against those of the "Vietnam generation." Former

National Security Adviser Zbigniew Brzezinski summarized the argument in this way:

> There is a tendency in America to be traumatized by international difficulties. The generation of the Nineteen-forties was always thinking about the failure of the League of Nations. I'm talking about leadership groups now. The leadership of the sixties was always thinking about Munich. Now there is a generation worried by Vietnam, with consequences of self-imposed paralysis, which is likely to be costlier in the long run.[30]

Finally, the generational hypothesis seems particularly pertinent to the present topic because the policy of containment seems to evoke more of the putative differences between age groups than other foreign policy issues. For these reasons, it appears especially appropriate to ask whether the "successor generation" — those for whom Vietnam was the great foreign policy drama (or trauma) of their formative years, and who are assuming increasingly important responsibilities in various American institutions — differs significantly with older groups in viewing the international arena and America's proper role in it.

The major problem with the generational thesis is that hard evidence to support it is rather scarce. Even during the midst of the Vietnam War, the allegedly "dovish" younger generation provided stronger support than other age groups for the George Wallace–Curtis LeMay ticket. Public opinion polls of the post-Vietnam period also reveal few if any striking age-based differences on foreign and defense issues (Table 3.10). Even when small differences appear, they do not consistently fit the pattern implied by the "Munich generation versus Vietnam generation" thesis. For example, a Gallup poll in 1975 asked respondents whether the United States should continue a policy of protecting other nations against communist takeovers. There were virtually no differences in levels of support among the three youngest age groups, and respondents over the age of 50 expressed somewhat more, rather than less, skepticism. Surveys during the 1980s dealing with such controversial issues as the proper level of defense spending and the appropriate American role in Central America also fail to reveal any sharp age-based discontinuities.

Perhaps the search for age group cleavages among leaders rather than the general public might prove more fruitful. Vietnam protests were more often found at the "elite" universities than at state and community colleges or non-educational settings. As revealed in Table 3.11, however, responses by American leaders to three central questions — on the importance of containing communism, on using force to do so if necessary, and on defending allies — reveal relatively minor differences across four age groups. Again, those differences which do emerge do not always conform to the pattern of "young doves" versus "old hawks." For example, mem-

Table 3.9. Partisanship on Containment: American Leaders, 1976–1984

| Date/Poll | Issue | | Responses by Party Affiliation (%) | | |
|---|---|---|---|---|---|
| | | | Republican | Democrat | Independent |
| March 1976 FPLP* | Containing communism (as a foreign policy goal) | Very Important | 58 | 24 | 39 |
| | | Somewhat Important | 34 | 46 | 43 |
| | | Not At All Important | 5 | 21 | 11 |
| | | Not Sure | 2 | 8 | 7 |
| March 1976 FPLP | Defending our allies' security (as a foreign policy goal) | Very Important | 46 | 28 | 37 |
| | | Somewhat Important | 49 | 61 | 53 |
| | | Not At All Important | 3 | 5 | 5 |
| | | Not Sure | 3 | 6 | 5 |
| March 1976 FPLP | The U.S. should take all steps including the use of force to prevent the spread of communism | Agree | 50 | 20 | 35 |
| | | Disagree | 50 | 78 | 64 |
| | | No Opinion | 0 | 1 | 1 |
| March 1980 FPLP | Containing communism (as a foreign policy goal) | Very Important | 57 | 30 | 40 |
| | | Somewhat Important | 37 | 54 | 47 |
| | | Not At All Important | 5 | 14 | 11 |
| | | Not Sure | 1 | 2 | 2 |

| | | | | |
|---|---|---|---|---|
| March 1980 FPLP | Defending our allies' security (as a foreign policy goal) | Very Important | 52 | 40 | 41 |
| | | Somewhat Important | 46 | 56 | 54 |
| | | Not At All Important | 1 | 2 | 4 |
| | | Not Sure | 1 | 2 | 1 |
| March 1980 FPLP | The U.S. should take all steps including the use of force to prevent the spread of communism | Agree | 53 | 24 | 36 |
| | | Disagree | 46 | 74 | 62 |
| | | No Opinion | 2 | 2 | 2 |
| March 1984 FPLP | Containing communism (as a foreign policy goal) | Very Important | 63 | 23 | 33 |
| | | Somewhat Important | 34 | 56 | 53 |
| | | Not At All Important | 3 | 20 | 13 |
| | | Not Sure | 0 | 1 | 1 |
| March 1984 FPLP | Defending our allies' security (as a foreign policy | Very Important | 57 | 45 | 44 |
| | | Somewhat Important | 42 | 52 | 53 |
| | | Not At All Important | 2 | 3 | 2 |
| | | Not Sure | 0 | 1 | 1 |
| March 1984 FPLP | The U.S. should take all steps including the use of force to prevent the spread of communism | Agree | 56 | 19 | 30 |
| | | Disagree | 43 | 81 | 69 |
| | | No Opinion | 1 | 1 | 1 |

*FPLP = Foreign Policy Leadership Project.

Table 3.10. Generations on Containment: The American Public, 1973–1985

| Date/Poll | Issue* | Responses by Age of Respondents (%) | | | |
| | | 18–29 | | 30–49 | 50 & over |
| | | 18–24 | 25–29 | | |
|---|---|---|---|---|---|
| March 1971<br>Gallup | Defense budget<br>Too Much<br>Too Little<br>About Right<br>No Opinion | <br><br><br><br> | <br>57<br>10<br>27<br>6 | <br>49<br>11<br>33<br>7 | <br>46<br>11<br>31<br>12 |
| January 1973<br>Gallup | Was U.S. policy in Vietnam a mistake?<br>Yes<br>No<br>No Opinion | <br>55<br>36<br>9 | <br>49<br>44<br>7 | <br>56<br>32<br>12 | <br>68<br>20<br>12 |
| September 1973<br>Gallup | Reduction of U.S. troops in Europe<br>Should<br>Should Not<br>No Opinion | <br>58<br>33<br>9 | <br><br><br> | <br>60<br>28<br>12 | <br>60<br>28<br>12 |
| April 1975<br>Gallup | Should U.S. maintain its policy of containment?<br>Should<br>Should Not<br>No Opinion | <br>57<br>35<br>8 | <br>58<br>31<br>11 | <br>57<br>35<br>8 | <br>47<br>41<br>12 |
| November 1982<br>Gallup | Defense budget<br>Too Much<br>Too Little<br>About Right<br>No Opinion | <br>49<br>15<br>25<br>11 | <br>45<br>19<br>29<br>7 | <br>41<br>16<br>32<br>11 | <br>35<br>17<br>34<br>14 |
| July 1983<br>Gallup | Proposal to increase U.S. military advisers in El Salvador<br>Favor<br>Oppose<br>No Opinion | <br>23<br>68<br>9 | <br>27<br>63<br>10 | <br>24<br>63<br>13 | <br>25<br>59<br>16 |

| Survey | Question / Item | Response | | | | |
|---|---|---|---|---|---|---|
| July 1983 Gallup | Should U.S. provide military aid to friendly governments in Central America? | Provide Aid | 36 | 32 | 40 | 32 |
| | | Not Become Involved | 57 | 58 | 51 | 57 |
| | | No Opinion | 7 | 10 | 9 | 11 |
| July 1983 Gallup | Is El Salvador likely to turn into a situation like Vietnam? | Very Likely | 33 | 37 | 43 | 42 |
| | | Fairly | 39 | 41 | 31 | 25 |
| | | Not Very | 16 | 15 | 14 | 18 |
| | | Not At All | 6 | 4 | 4 | 7 |
| | | No Opinion | 6 | 3 | 8 | 8 |
| September 1983 Gallup | Defense budget | Too Much | 42 | 43 | 35 | 36** |
| | | Too Little | 24 | 16 | 23 | 21 |
| | | About Right | 29 | 33 | 39 | 38 |
| | | No Opinion | 5 | 8 | 3 | 5 |
| October 1983 Gallup | On sending Marines to Lebanon | Yes, Mistake | | 56 | 51 | 50 |
| | | No | | 35 | 37 | 37 |
| | | No Opinion | | 9 | 12 | 13 |
| January 1985 Gallup | Defense budget | Too Much | | 49 | 46 | 44 |
| | | Too Little | | 13 | 11 | 8 |
| | | About Right | | 34 | 36 | 38 |
| | | No Opinion | | 4 | 7 | 10 |
| May 1985 Gallup | Trade embargo on Nicaragua | Approve | | 40 | 48 | 46 |
| | | Disapprove | | 36 | 36 | 38 |
| | | No Opinion | | 24 | 16 | 16 |

*Summary of the issue rather than exact wording of the question asked. Response options are given in parentheses below the question.

**50–64 age group. Respondents 65 and over responded as follows: Too much (32%); Too little (19%); About right (38%); and No opinion (11%).

Table 3.11. Generations on Containment: American Leaders, 1976–1984

| Date/Poll | Issue | | Responses by Generations* (%) | | | |
|---|---|---|---|---|---|---|
| | | | Vietnam | Interim | Korea | WWII |
| March 1976 FPLP | Containing communism (as a foreign policy goal) | Very Important | 39 | 37 | 38 | 40 |
| | | Somewhat Important | 44 | 43 | 44 | 40 |
| | | Not At All Important | 12 | 15 | 13 | 14 |
| | | Not Sure | 5 | 6 | 5 | 6 |
| March 1976 FPLP | Defending our allies' security (as a foreign policy goal) | Very Important | 45 | 39 | 32 | 33 |
| | | Somewhat Important | 50 | 55 | 61 | 56 |
| | | Not At All Important | 3 | 4 | 4 | 6 |
| | | Not Sure | 2 | 3 | 4 | 6 |
| March 1976 FPLP | The United States should take all steps including the use of force to prevent the spread of communism | Agree | 44 | 39 | 27 | 28 |
| | | Disagree | 55 | 60 | 72 | 71 |
| | | No Opinion | 1 | 2 | 1 | 1 |
| March 1980 FPLP | Containing communism (as a foreign policy goal) | Very Important | 36 | 39 | 42 | 43 |
| | | Somewhat Important | 48 | 50 | 49 | 44 |
| | | Not At All Important | 15 | 10 | 8 | 11 |
| | | Not Sure | 1 | 2 | 1 | 2 |

| | | | | | |
|---|---|---|---:|---:|---:|---:|
| March 1980<br>FPLP | Defending our allies' security (as a foreign policy goal) | Very Important | 44 | 45 | 40 | 44 |
| | | Somewhat Important | 51 | 52 | 55 | 53 |
| | | Not At All Important | 3 | 2 | 4 | 3 |
| | | Not Sure | 1 | 1 | 1 | 1 |
| March 1980<br>FPLP | The United States should take all steps including the use of force to prevent the spread of communism | Agree | 34 | 40 | 37 | 33 |
| | | Disagree | 65 | 58 | 61 | 65 |
| | | No Opinion | 1 | 2 | 2 | 2 |
| March 1984<br>FPLP | Containing communism (as a foreign policy goal) | Very Important | 37 | 41 | 40 | 36 |
| | | Somewhat Important | 50 | 48 | 45 | 51 |
| | | Not At All Important | 13 | 11 | 14 | 13 |
| | | Not Sure | 1 | 1 | 2 | 2 |
| March 1984<br>FPLP | Defending our allies' security (as a foreign policy goal) | Very Important | 51 | 51 | 47 | 41 |
| | | Somewhat Important | 46 | 47 | 50 | 56 |
| | | Not At All Important | 4 | 2 | 2 | 2 |
| | | Not Sure | 0 | 1 | 2 | 2 |
| March 1984<br>FPLP | The United States should take all steps including the use of force to prevent the spread of communism | Agree | 38 | 35 | 34 | 27 |
| | | Disagree | 60 | 65 | 64 | 72 |
| | | No Opinion | 2 | 0 | 1 | 1 |

*Generations: Vietnam (born since 1940); Korean (born 1933–1940); Interim (born 1924–1932); World War II (born before 1924).

bers of the World War II generation were *least* prone to agree with the proposition that "the U.S. should take all steps including the use of force to prevent the spread of communism." Three leadership surveys taken at four-year intervals yielded essentially similar negative evidence; this evidence adds to skepticism about the generational thesis.[31]

In summary, there is little in these survey results to indicate that the inevitable replacement of one generation by its successor will yield significant changes in public opinion toward containment policy. Attitudes toward containment are unlikely to remain frozen over any extended period of time, but generational differences may not be the most fruitful place to look for the dynamics of change.

## CONCLUSION

"Realist" foreign policy analyses place primary emphasis on the nature of the international system and the challenges emanating from it. In this respect, Kennan's "X" article was fully within the realist tradition as it focused on the Soviet challenge and the forces driving Russian foreign policy. But in his superb analysis of containment, John Lewis Gaddis demonstrates that changes in doctrine and strategy have been sensitive also to domestic factors, especially beliefs about the resources available for defense.[32] To the extent that public opinion enters into his analysis, it is often in connection with leaders' efforts to shape public attitudes; for example, he cites with sympathy George Kennan's strong objections to the open-ended commitments of the "Truman Doctrine" speech, rhetorical excesses allegedly arising from a need to arouse emotional support in a recalcitrant Congress and an apathetic and ill-informed public.

Two areas suggest themselves for some summarizing and concluding observations about public opinion and containment. The first relates to trends that might provide some clues to the future of containment, the second to the impact of public opinion on containment policy during the past four decades.

The first area is the easier of the two because conclusions are imbedded within the survey data themselves. Although this discussion has not begun to exhaust either the substantive issues or the types of analyses that might lead to useful generalizations, at least several tentative conclusions about the future of containment may be offered:

1. Although such general values as "peace" and "strength" have usually evoked positive and relatively stable responses, *general public support for international activism has declined.* Because leaders continue to approve of internationalism, there is a substantial split between the general public and leaders in this respect.

2. Public attitudes toward the *means* of implementing containment have been much more volatile because means always imply costs. Foreign assistance, once quite popular, has in recent years consistently been rated as the least popular and most expendable government program. Security commitments to allies, interventions (especially in Third World areas), and other specific undertakings to implement containment have also brought forth quite varied responses. Currently the public also favors reduced defense spending.

3. Support for *means and ends* among leaders and the general public is reversed, with *leaders more means-oriented* (because they know that ends are elusive and they often have vested interests in means), and the *public more ends-oriented* (since means often involve highly specific and technical issues that have little meaning for the public).[33]

4. *Containment is no longer viewed as a superordinate goal* today, as several other foreign policy goals compete for that position.

5. Survey data seem to show that the past two decades have witnessed a *significant breakdown in consensus* on many important elements of containment, among both the general public and leaders. There are at least *three broad orientations* on foreign and defense policy today, two rather different varieties of internationalism and a third which indicates a revived respectability for a more isolationist perspective on America's proper role in the world. However, the sources, dynamics, and even the existence of a change with respect to a foreign policy consensus have generated spirited debates. Hence, the core question is not whether the nation is currently divided on many key foreign issues but, rather, whether this condition represents a significant change from earlier periods of the post-World War II era. Is it appropriate to describe the two decades following World War II as "the age of consensus,"[34] or is that merely an exercise in nostalgia? Was the Vietnam War the primary source of dissension, or was a post-World War II consensus breaking down well before Vietnam became a controversial issue? Did changes in public opinion originate primarily from disillusionment with (and perhaps an excessive tendency to generalize about) the containment policies that were perceived as having ultimately led to the Vietnam quagmire, or were attitudes among the general public essentially reflecting a collapse in consensus first at the leadership level and then among the attentive public?[35] These questions illustrate rather than exhaust some of the controversies concerning continuity and change in public attitudes toward foreign and defense policy.

6. Differences in foreign policy attitudes are becoming increasingly rooted in *partisanship. Ideological cleavages* are also becoming more apparent. These trends would appear to make the prospects for the early emergence of a post-Vietnam foreign policy consensus rather

dim. Similar bases of disagreement among leaders are especially significant in assessing the prospects for forging a consensus, at least in the near future. However, age difference on these issues seems largely irrelevant.

Any assessment of public opinion and containment would be incomplete unless some attention was directed to the thorny question of public opinion's ultimate impact on policy. As indicated in the introduction to this chapter, the impressive range of views on the matter is not matched by systematic evidence linking foreign policy leaders, the bureaucracy, the attentive public, and the media to public opinion.[36] Indeed, it is probably the paucity of hard evidence on the question that sustains such diverse conclusions.

There is no shortage of evidence that most post-World War II presidents have followed Theodore Roosevelt in thinking that the White House is "a bully pulpit," whether it is used "to scare the hell out of them" in order to gain support for aid to Greece and Turkey, to warn against the dangers of "unwarranted influence, whether sought or unsought, by the military-industrial complex," or to drum up support for assistance to the contras in Nicaragua. It is equally evident that such efforts have not been equally successful. Perhaps Yankelovich is correct in asserting that the relationship between leaders and the public has changed—"farewell to 'the President knows best,'" as he put it[37]—but it is far from clear that this new relationship represents a permanent change in the equation.

The more difficult question concerns the influence, if any, in the other direction, where the evidence is even skimpier and more anecdotal.[38] Did President Kennedy genuinely believe that he would be impeached should he fail to force removal of Soviet missiles from Cuba, as he said, or was he merely seeking to bolster decisions arrived at for reasons that had nothing to do with public opinion? How much did growing public impatience lead the Carter administration to embark on the ill-fated effort to free American hostages in Iran, or the Reagan administration to withdraw U.S. Marines from Lebanon?

In the absence of substantial evidence, it is probably appropriate to maintain a posture of skepticism about public opinion strongly influencing foreign policy decisions. Perhaps part of the reason for the shortage of data on the question of impact arises from the differing concerns of the public and the policymakers noted earlier, with the public mostly interested in the *ends* of foreign policy while policymakers focus primarily on *means*. Thus, the public may express strong support for preventing further Soviet expansion while, at the same time, having little interest or knowledge of strategies and tactics for pursuing that goal. (That may, of course, change when American casualties are at issue.) On the other hand, most policymakers have probably accepted containment as a "given" and are actively involved in debating the means.

Finally, one might ask to what extent the anticipation of public disapproval has acted to *prevent* action. There is substantial evidence that during the 1980s a majority of the public has consistently opposed American military involvement in Central America. Would the Reagan administration have intervened more directly in El Salvador or Nicaragua in the absence of such attitudes? Solid evidence about contemporary non-events is, to understate the case, rather hard to come by. Yet it is precisely such hard-to-answer questions that lie at the heart of this topic. Unfortunately, while this essay has explored some interesting issues on public opinion and containment, the most compelling questions must be left unanswered.

## NOTES

1. Quoted in Bernard Cohen, *The Public's Impact on Foreign Policy* (Boston: Little, Brown & Co., 1973), p. 62.
2. Speech at Pan American Conference, Buenos Aires, December 5, 1936, text in *New York Times* (December 6, 1936): 47.
3. The term "containment" means different things to different people. Thus, there is still an active debate about "what Kennan *really* meant" in 1946–1947, to say nothing of the much more acrimonious debate about the appropriate scope of containment today. Participation in those controversies is beyond the scope of this chapter; the discussion that follows will take a broad view of containment as involving commitment by the United States to sustain the security of other nations. Restrictions on what containment entails are imposed by limits on relevant public opinion data rather than by definition.
4. William C. Rogers, Barbara Stuhler, and Donald Koenig, "A Comparison of Informed and General Public Opinion on U.S. Foreign Policy," *Public Opinion Quarterly* 31 (1967): 242–252.
5. John E. Mueller, *War, Presidents, and Public Opinion* (New York: Wiley, 1973), p. 265.
6. Cohen, *The Public's Impact.*
7. Warren E. Miller and Donald E. Stokes, "Constituency Influence in Congress," *American Political Science Review* 57 (1963): 45–46.
8. James N. Rosenau, *National Leadership and Foreign Policy* (Princeton: Princeton University Press, 1963); Bernard Cohen, *The Political Process and Foreign Policy: The Making of the Japanese Peace Settlement* (Princeton: Princeton University Press, 1957); Raymond A. Bauer, Ithiel de Sola Pool, and Lewis A. Dexter, *American Business and Public Policy: The Politics of Foreign Trade*, 2nd Ed. (Chicago: Aldine, 1972).
9. David Paletz and Robert Entman, *Media Power Politics* (New York: Free Press, 1981).
10. Elihu Katz, "The Two-Step Flow of Communication: An Up-to-Date Report on an Hypothesis," *Public Opinion Quarterly* 21 (1957): 61–78; James N. Rosenau, *Public Opinion and Foreign Policy* (New York: Random House, 1961).

11. X. [George F. Kennan], "The Sources of Soviet Conduct," *Foreign Affairs* 25 (1947): 575.
12. William R. Caspary, "The Mood Theory: A Study of Public Opinion and Foreign Policy," *American Political Science Review* 64 (1979): 546. Although Caspary's study was published in 1970, he reports data on international-ism/isolationism only through 1953.
13. Mueller, *War, Presidents, and Public Opinion.*
14. John E. Rielly, ed., *American Public Opinion and U.S. Foreign Policy 1983* (Chicago: Chicago Council on Foreign Relations, 1983), p. 31.
15. Gallup poll in November 1984 and the FPLP survey in March 1984. As early as 1965, according to Gallup, only 52% of the public supported the Ameri-can intervention in the Dominican Republic.
16. Gallup polls in March 1981; March, June and July 1983; and May 1984 on Central America; and October 1984 on Lebanon.
17. For more evidence on the persisting effects of the Vietnam War, see Ole Hol-sti and James N. Rosenau, *American Leadership in World Affairs: Vietnam and the Breakdown of Consensus* (London: Allen & Unwin, 1984), and Rielly, ed., *American Public Opinion, 1975*, p. 17, and *1983*, p. 31. A differ-ent interpretation of the breakdown in the foreign policy consensus is devel-oped by John Mueller, "Cold War Consensus: From Fearful Hostility to Wary Contempt," mimeo 1984. Mueller emphasizes the correlation between perceptions of Soviet threat and consensus, arguing that the latter was the adhesive that maintained the consensus.
18. Herbert McCloskey, Paul J. Hoffman, and Rosemary O'Hara, "Issue Conflict and Consensus Among Party Leaders," *American Political Science Review* 54 (1960): 406–427, is a notable exception.
19. Rielly, *American Public Opinion, 1975, 1979, 1983*; Allen H. Barton, "Con-sensus and Conflict Among American Leaders," *Public Opinion Quarterly* 38 (1974–75): 507–530; Bruce M. Russett and Elizabeth C. Hanson, *Interest and Ideology: The Foreign Policy Beliefs of American Businessmen* (San Fran-cisco: Freeman, 1975); Barry Sussman, *Elites in America* (Washington: Washington Post, 1976).
20. This is one of the many questions on which wording might make a significant difference. Specifically, would respondents have attributed greater impor-tance to containment had the question been worded differently: "Containing Soviet expansion"? By 1974 the United States was well on the way to nor-malizing relations with the largest communist nation (China), and by 1980 leaders who were most "hawkish" in their assessments of the Soviet Union were calling for an alliance between Beijing and Washington to counter Moscow. Holsti and Rosenau, *American Leadership in World Affairs*, p. 215.
21. Rielly, ed., *American Public Opinion 1983*, pp. 14–15.
22. The importance attached to "combatting hunger" and "helping to improve the standard of living of LDCs" by the public may seem startling in view of the finding in poll after poll that for some time a great majority of Americans have wanted to reduce if not eliminate foreign aid programs. Perhaps the answer to this seeming anomaly is that many in the public see little connec-tion between foreign economic aid and these two goals. In this respect, leaders are strikingly different since they are overwhelmingly in favor of eco-nomic assistance programs.
23. Michael Mandelbaum and William Schneider, "The New Internationalisms: Public Opinion and Foreign Policy," in Kenneth A. Oye, Robert J. Lieber,

and Donald Rothchild, eds., *Eagle Entangled: U.S. Foreign Policy in a Complex World* (New York: Longman, 1979); Holsti and Rosenau, *American Leadership in World Affairs*: and Michael A. Maggiotto and Eugene Wittkopf, "American Attitudes Toward Foreign Policy," *International Studies Quarterly* 25 (1981): 601–31.

24. H. Schuyler Foster, *Activism Replaces Isolationism* (Washington: Foxhall Press, 1983), p. 112. For evidence of partisan differences on foreign policy during the period immediately following Truman's dismissal of MacArthur, see George Belknap and Angus Campbell, "Political Party Identification and Attitudes Toward Foreign Policy," *Public Opinion Quarterly* 55 (1951–52): 601–623.

25. For the most detailed assessment of public support for the Korean and Vietnam Wars, see Mueller, *War, Presidents, and Public Opinion*. Sidney Verba, *et al.*, "Public Opinion and the War in Vietnam," *American Political Science Review* 61 (1967): 317–333 report that even after the Vietnam War became controversial, party identification was not an important determinant of attitudes on the war.

26. Holsti and Rosenau, *American Leadership in World Affairs*, pp. 151–153, 209.

27. William Schneider, "Conservatism, Not Interventionism: Trends in Foreign Policy Opinion, 1974–1982," in Kenneth A. Oye, Robert J. Lieber, and Donald Rothchild, eds., *Eagle Defiant: United States Foreign Policy in the 1980s* (Boston: Little, Brown & Co., 1983).

28. Frank L. Klingberg, "Cyclical Trends in American Foreign Policy Moods and Their Policy Implications," in Charles W. Kegley, Jr., and Patrick J. McGowan, eds., *Challenges to America: United States Foreign Policy in the 1980s* (Beverly Hills, California: Sage, 1979); Klingberg, "The Historical Alternation of Moods in American Foreign Policy," *World Politics* 4 (1952): 239–273; and Jack E. Holmes, *The Mood/Interest Theory of American Foreign Policy* (Lexington, Kentucky: University Press of Kentucky, 1985).

29. Graham T. Allison, "Cool It: The Foreign Policy of Young Americans," *Foreign Policy* 1 (Winter 1970–71): 144–60; Michael Roskin, "From Pearl Harbor to Vietnam: Shifting Generational Paradigms and Foreign Policy," *Political Science Quarterly* 89 (1974): 563–588; Bruce M. Russett, "The Americans' Retreat from World Power," *Political Science Quarterly* 90 (1975): 1–21.

30. Elizabeth Drew, "A Reporter at Large (Brzezinski)," *New Yorker* (May 1, 1978): 116–117.

31. The negative evidence on the impact of generation is not confined to the issues identified in Tables 10 and 11. For evidence on other foreign policy issues, see Holsti and Rosenau, *Amerian Leadership in World Affairs*, pp. 153–163, 209.

32. John Lewis Gaddis, *Strategies of Containment* (New York: Oxford University Press, 1982).

33. Adam Yarmolinsky, "Confessions of a Non-User," *Public Opinion Quarterly* 27 (1963): 543–548.

34. Stanley Hoffmann, *Primacy or World Order* (New York: McGraw-Hill, 1978).

35. William Schneider, "Public Opinion," in Joseph S. Nye, Jr., ed., *The Making of America's Soviet Policy* (New Haven: Yale University Press, 1984).

36. In addition to the studies cited in the Preface, others which have tried to assess the impact of public opinion include Richard Fagen, "Some Assess-

ments and Uses of Public Opinion in Diplomacy," *Public Opinion Quarterly* 24 (1960): 448–457, and Leila Sussman, "FDR and the White House Mail," *Public Opinion Quarterly* 20 (1956): 5–16.

37. Daniel Yankelovich, "Farewell to 'President Knows Best'," *Foreign Affairs* 57 (1979): 670–693.

38. The Chicago Council on Foreign Relations surveys reveal that neither the public nor leaders believe that public opinion plays a very significant role in policy making. In three surveys undertaken at four-year intervals, between 19% and 26% of the public rated public opinion as a "very important" factor, whereas even fewer leaders (15% to 20%) gave it that rating. On the other hand, both the public and leaders consistently ranked public opinion at the top of factors that *should* be more important in policy making.

# 4 ECONOMIC CONTAINMENT

*Angela E. Stent*

The conviction that it is both desirable and possible to contain the Soviet Union by retarding its economic development has been a key element of American policy since the end of World War II. The logic is as follows: The Soviet Union is weaker economically than the United States and wants to import Western manufactures to improve its economic performance. Denying it advanced industrial goods will slow development of its industry (and therefore its military–industrial complex), enhancing America's national security by ensuring a weaker Soviet economy. A secondary aspect of economic containment has been the belief that economic leverage can be used in the pursuit of political ends.

These two premises and the policies they have produced have been a subject of constant controversy, not only in the United States but also within the NATO alliance. One part of the controversy centers on the effectiveness of economic containment: Since the Soviet Union has managed to attain military parity with the United States, can economic containment claim to have worked? Another aspect arises out of the rather confused way economic measures have been used for both political and economic ends: Since the goals of American economic containment policy are multiple and sometimes unclear, how can one ascertain whether they have been achieved?

Despite the controversy, economic containment retains a distinct attraction for policymakers. After all, the United States is the mightiest economic nation on earth and produces goods that the Soviets need. In the rather meager arsenal of levers available for us to use in dealing with our chief antagonist, this one seems an effective means of influencing Soviet developments. Moreover, when the militarily powerful Soviets take actions that outrage us morally or seem to threaten Western security, the economic weapon is one of the safe and acceptable means of reacting that we have.

Economic containment in the postwar era has three major components. The first, no longer totally operative, is *economic warfare*, the attempt to weaken the overall economic performance of the Soviet Union both in civilian and military sectors. The second is the *strategic embargo*, designed to

59

deny goods (increasingly in high technology areas) that could be used specifically to build up the Soviet military. The third element of U.S. policy has been *economic leverage*, the use of economic means to restrain Soviet political behavior.[1]

This chapter focuses on how America's economic containment policy has evolved since 1945 and what economic and political effects that policy has had on the U.S.S.R.

## THE EVOLUTION OF
## U.S. ECONOMIC CONTAINMENT

Prior to World War II, American economic policy toward the U.S.S.R. was mixed. Initial government opposition to the Bolshevik seizure of power, with its cancellation of czarist debts and withdrawal from World War I, was followed by a period of enthusiastic business participation in the Russian economy in the 1920s. It was Stalin's policy of autarky, rather than U.S. reservations, that reduced U.S. economic ties with the Soviets during the 1930s.

There has always been a belief on the part of some U.S. businessmen that the Soviet Union offered a vast potential market to U.S. entrepreneurs. As *Fortune* argued in 1945,

> Our businessmen are both perplexed by the thought that Russia's huge economic potential will bring it neck-and-neck with us in another twenty years, and bemused with the business possibilities in helping it reach that point. . . . Russia holds for us a fascination that engages our respect. . . . Russians are remarkably like us in recognizable traits — our common expansiveness as heirs to a spacious land, our kindred feelings for machines.[2]

Although the article in *Fortune* was written a few months before the end of wartime collaboration between Washington and Moscow, these sentiments have been echoed many times in subsequent business discussions. The U.S. government was always more skeptical than the private sector about the possibilities for trade, largely because there seemed little that the United States wanted to purchase from the U.S.S.R.

At the end of World War II, there was a debate about whether or not the United States should pursue a policy of economic cooperation with the Soviet Union. Behind this debate were disagreements over whether trade could be used as a political lever and whether the United States was threatened with a postwar economic depression that Russian orders would help avert. While Averell Harriman, the U.S. ambassador in Moscow, favored offering postwar economic aid to the U.S.S.R., his counselor, George F. Kennan, disagreed. Kennan was unconcerned about a U.S. depression and skeptical of the value of extending trade and credits to the Soviets; he supported the cutoff of Lend-Lease in May 1945.[3] His position was that economic assistance to the Soviets would not elicit political concessions and that the U.S.S.R. would use U.S. trade and credits to build up its military–industrial infrastructure to the detriment of U.S. national security. Kennan advocated a long-term strategy of economic denial to the U.S.S.R. on security grounds. Yet he was well aware of the difficulties of securing agreement in Washington on such a policy. In 1949, he criticized some government officials who "have an idea that if you can only lure the Russians . . . into some sort of a flexible free trade system, you will thereby put salt on the feathers of the Russian tail and the bird will appear to be much more tame and amenable."[4]

The debate about whether to pursue a policy of economic inducement or denial continued until late 1947, when both the executive branch and Congress endorsed restrictions on economic ties with the U.S.S.R. in view of the Soviet takeover of Eastern Europe and the growing tensions in U.S.–Soviet relations. Since the government feared that the United States might soon be involved in a war with the Soviet Union, economic warfare seemed appropriate. Obviously, nothing should be done to strengthen overall Soviet war-making capacity. The key decision was taken in 1947, when the National Security Council decided that "U.S. national security requires the immediate termination, for an indefinite period, of shipments from the United States to the U.S.S.R. and its satellites of all commodities which are critically short in the United States or which would contribute to the Soviet military potential."[5] The following month, the order was expanded to cover items of indirect military significance. The U.S. military, favoring economic warfare, linked the granting of Marshall Plan aid to an embargo against the Soviets.[6] But even then, there was agreement that trade controls should not be so stringent as to cause the Soviets to limit their supply of strategic materials to the United States.[7]

Until the Nixon era, U.S. economic containment was formalized in two pieces of legislation. The first was the Export Control Act of 1949, which emphasized the danger to U.S. national security of exporting materials without regard to their potential military significance and empowered the president to exercise trade controls. It was the first comprehensive system of export controls ever adopted by Congress in peacetime.[8] The second was the Mutual Defense Assistance Control Act of 1951 (known as the Battle Act), which recognized that economic warfare would only succeed if American allies cooperated. It empowered the president to terminate all forms of military, economic, and financial assistance to any nation that knowingly sold embargoed goods to a prohibited destination, thereby providing for potential U.S. sanctions against NATO allies. In order to multilateralize and coordinate the strategic embargo aspect of economic warfare, the United States formed the Consultative Group–Coordinating

Committee (CoCom) in 1949, an organization of NATO states minus Iceland and plus Japan.[9]

By 1951, therefore, American economic warfare policy was enshrined in various pieces of legislation. The premise was that any assistance in building up the Soviet economy by the sale of Western goods with direct or indirect military application represented a danger to U.S. national security. The essence of U.S. policy was the desire to weaken the Soviet economy through denial and to contain Soviet power by retarding the growth of the military–industrial infrastructure that would permit Soviet foreign expansion. Moreover, Washington recognized that its policy would be ineffective if it did not secure allied cooperation. The United States therefore used a mixture of positive (Marshall Plan aid) and negative (Battle Act) incentives to achieve this cooperation. There was little attempt during these years at the height of the cold war to use trade as a political weapon to moderate either Soviet domestic or foreign policy. The overriding importance of denial for national security reasons took precedence over more carefully calibrated attempts at linkage.

Despite various liberalizations of the CoCom lists in the 1950s, U.S. policy remained essentially unchanged until the Kennedy administration began to retreat from economic warfare. After 1963, economic containment policy moved toward mixing the strategic embargo with agricultural sales and positive economic–political linkage as the administration reconsidered the entire premise of U.S. economic warfare policy. Walt Rostow, then head of the Policy Planning Staff in the Department of State, wrote:

> The major issues of our trade control policy are political — not strategic, economic or commercial. From the standpoint of the USSR, the political significance of the U.S. restrictive policies has been out of all proportion to their impact on the Soviet economy or strategic position. . . . They serve as a symbol of U.S. unwillingness to grant the USSR full respectability as an equal in the postwar world order. . . . Trade denial has also come to be an important symbol of our cold war resolve and purpose and of our moral disapproval of the USSR.[10]

Here was a recognition, echoed in other documents from the Kennedy administration, that economic warfare had had a limited economic effect.

Nevertheless, in 1962 the Kennedy administration had decided to risk a major allied confrontation by seeking to prevent its alliance partners from selling the U.S.S.R. large-diameter pipe — a commodity not on the CoCom list — for the construction of the Soviet-East European Friendship Oil pipeline. This effort echoed earlier economic warfare policies, and in many ways foreshadowed the 1982 gas pipeline sanctions. The official motivation was to bolster Western security by preventing the construction of a pipeline that would enhance the Soviet military posture in Eastern Europe. Another reason was the desire to retard the growth of the Soviet energy industry, under the fear that a flood of Soviet oil would "drown" the West and make it too dependent on Soviet supplies.[11] In addition, there may have been concern on the part of the Western oil industry that Soviet competition would threaten its business. Also, because the United States was angry that its European allies had begun to increase their trade with the Soviets, the administration sought to arrest this new economic flow. The effort partly succeeded, in that it forced West Germany to comply with the embargo. But other NATO allies refused to cancel contracts, and the embargo may have forced the Soviets to improve their capacity to produce large-diameter pipe. Certainly, though the Friendship pipeline was completed, the West did not drown in Soviet oil.

Ultimately, in fact, Kennedy's broader policies were moving away from economic warfare. A few weeks before his assassination, he announced the first wheat sale to the U.S.S.R. in the postwar era, justifying it as good for "the American farmer, the American exporter, [and] the American citizen concerned with the strength of our balance of payments."[12] Suddenly, domestic economic interests seemed to have superseded national security. There was, however, also some attempt to justify wheat sales on political grounds. The State Department argued that a wheat sale "would advertise the superiority of our agricultural system over the communist system in a most dramatic fashion. . . . It would be a further step toward reduction of East–West tensions."[13] Thus, it was claimed that wheat could be used as a political lever, whereas large-diameter pipe could not; American wheat sales apparently did not threaten national security, whereas European industrial equipment sales did. Although wheat did not in fact help directly to build up Soviet industry, this argument was greeted with skepticism by America's allies, who argued that grain was, if anything, more important than large-diameter pipe for the survival of the Soviet economy.

The dual policy of the Kennedy administration — combining strategic embargoes with grain sales and the use of trade for political purposes — continued in the Johnson administration. In 1965, President Johnson created a Special Committee on U.S. Trade Relations with East European countries and the Soviet Union, instructing it to explore "all aspects of expanding trade" in support of the President's policy of bridge building. Although the main elements of policy did not change in this period, there was increased emphasis on the use of "peaceful" trade as a positive political lever.

The major change in American economic policy toward the U.S.S.R., downplaying the strategic embargo and emphasizing the political and economic significance of trade, came during the Nixon presidency. Although the strategic embargo remained in force, there was considerable liberalization of export controls. In 1969, the Export Control Act was renamed the Export Administration Act, symbolizing the movement away from embargoes to a cautious expansion of exports. The assumption was that trade should be encouraged unless it could affect U.S. security detrimentally, with the burden of proof on the opponents of East–West trade rather than its proponents.

The policy of the United States changed because Europe had recovered and was no longer receiving Marshall Plan aid; it was much harder for the U.S. to exercise leverage over its allies on East–West trade questions. The Europeans and Japanese had begun to expand their trade with the U.S.S.R, and there was fear that U.S. business was losing opportunities in the East.

Another major reason for the change, however, lay in the requirements of détente. In his memoirs, Henry Kissinger claims that initially both he and the president opposed liberalizing trade with the Soviets until they showed foreign policy restraint. Indeed, he criticizes those in the State Department who believed that more trade would lead to better Soviet behavior.[14] Kissinger's grand design involved linking trade and politics, using trade incentives to reward Soviet behavior after rather than before Soviet policies were implemented.[15] Nevertheless, despite Kissinger's insistence that trade be linked only to Soviet foreign policy, he did discuss the question of Jewish emigration with the Soviets. According to his account, he secured an informal agreement that the U.S.S.R. would permit a certain number of Jews to emigrate in return for a trade treaty that included Most Favored Nation (MFN) status. From Kissinger's point of view, the Jackson-Vanik amendment torpedoed his attempts at linkage by denying the Soviets MFN status until they made the promise formal.[16] Senator Jackson and his supporters disagreed.

Whatever the precise sequence of events, the Nixon–Kissinger linkage strategy was never given a chance to work. The Stevenson amendment, which set a limit of $300 million on official credits for the Soviets, may have been more important than Jackson-Vanik in torpedoing the U.S.–Soviet trade treaty. Although there was some liberalization of trade and the Soviets were able to secure a few major gains like the notorious 1972 grain deal, the administration's inability to secure congressional support of the new policy hampered any major trade expansion. By 1974, therefore, U.S. economic containment (with the exception of the strategic embargo) had been diluted. The principle of economic–political linkage was partially implemented, but executive-legislative battles made impossible a consistent set of new guidelines.

President Carter, therefore, inherited a mixed situation. Trade had been liberalized, but it had also been more directly linked to Soviet political behavior. Carter continued along both of these lines, first encouraging economic relations and later hinting that the issue of a U.S.–Soviet trade treaty might be revived in Congress.[17] On the other hand, since human rights was a cornerstone of his administration's foreign policy, Carter was committed to linking trade to Soviet internal behavior far more broadly than was Nixon. Samuel Huntington of the National Security Council developed a sophisticated plan for the use of both economic "carrots" and "sticks" in dealing with the Soviets. Where Nixon and Kissinger had favored positive linkage, the Carter White House believed in using both positive incentives and trade denial.[18] Indeed, Carter imposed trade sanctions on the Soviets for their treatment of dissidents (Shcharansky and Ginzburg) as well as for their invasion of Afghanistan. Yet the Carter sanction policy was erratic, as its fluctuating policies on energy technology transfer show,[19] and its inconsistencies caused problems with both allies and the American business community.

After the Soviet invasion of Afghanistan, the Carter administration began to move U.S. policy back toward economic warfare. It took a more consistent stand on East–West trade, imposing a grain and technology embargo on the U.S.S.R. and trying to enlist NATO allies in this cause. It also secured an agreement within CoCom for a "no exceptions" policy for the U.S.S.R.[20] Although most U.S. officials agreed that these sanctions would not lead to the withdrawal of Soviet forces, they wanted to show the U.S.S.R. that there could be no more business as usual.[21] In some ways, these U.S. actions marked a return to the idea that economic warfare should be used to express the United States' "moral disapproval" of the Soviets, even if it did not retard their economic development.

The inconsistencies of U.S. economic containment have hardly been resolved in the Reagan era. During the 1980 election campaign, Ronald Reagan argued both for a tougher technology transfer policy toward the Soviets and for removal of the grain embargo, claiming that the embargo had hurt U.S. farmers while not affecting the Soviets because they had merely purchased grain elsewhere. In fact, there is evidence that the grain embargo *did* impose considerable economic costs on the U.S.S.R., and that the main reason for the Reagan pledge was domestic politics, just as had been true of John F. Kennedy's initial grain agreement. And like Kennedy's, the dualism of Reagan's economic containment has caused problems both domestically and abroad.

The argument for selling grain to the U.S.S.R. while restricting a wide variety of technology has been two-fold: "Grain, the Soviets can get in other places, if they want it. . . . The other element is that grain [sales] will result in the Soviet Union having to pay out hard cash."[22] This justification has been greeted with skepticism. American grain sales may save the Soviet economy $30 billion annually by enabling Moscow to avoid costly new investments.[23] But at the same time, the Reagan administration has returned more fully than any of its predecessors to an economic warfare policy reminiscent of the cold war years. It has broadened the definition of military relevance by including certain items which, it argues, could make an indirect contribution to Soviet warfighting capability. Domestically, technology transfer laws and procedures have been tightened, and the United States has sought, though with only limited success, to secure CoCom agreement on larger embargo lists.

Another feature of Reagan's partial economic warfare policy has been the use of economic coercion against American allies who do not share Washington's approach to East–West economic relations. In 1982, the administration imposed extraterritorial sanctions on European states that had contracted to sell compressor components for the Urengoi natural gas pipeline from western Siberia to Western Europe.[24] The sequence of events was similar to that in 1962, but this time a more independent West Germany did not comply. The United States put forward familiar arguments: that the Europeans would become dangerously dependent on Soviet gas supplies, and that the Soviets would gain hard currency enabling them to purchase technology from the West to build up their military–industrial infrastructure. Europe rejected the arguments and cited U.S. grain sales as proof of American double standards.

In the end, the conflict was resolved by Secretary of State George Shultz, and a series of allied studies was carried out to harmonize East–West trade policies.[25] Although the United States failed to prevent the construction of the Urengoi pipeline and did not change its allies' policies on East–West trade, Washington retained strict controls on energy trade with the U.S.S.R. Moreover, the U.S. sanctions, by delaying some of the gas contracts, were partially successful. Because the gas market softened, Europe contracted to take only 26 billion cubic meters (bcm) of Soviet gas as opposed to the 40 bcm originally envisaged.[26]

Reagan has avoided the use of trade inducements to alter Soviet political behavior. Considering the Kissinger–Nixon linkage policy naive, administration officials express skepticism that trade carrots could ever affect Soviet behavior. Instead, the administration has pursued trade denial as the only acceptable means of deterring future Soviet behavior or reacting to Soviet moves.    —

Thus, by 1984, the United States had come almost full circle from the early years of the Export Control Act and the Battle Act. There was partial economic warfare, in that the administration wanted to weaken the entire Soviet economy rather than only its military sector, and arguments against economic ties with the Soviets were based on national security grounds as well as political disapproval. In 1985, it appeared that the United States might be moving away from this tougher policy of economic containment in its efforts to seek a dialogue with the new Soviet leadership; but many inside the Reagan administration still opposed any liberalization.

## THE DOMESTIC POLITICS OF U.S. EAST–WEST
## TRADE POLICY

Since the early cold war years, the United States has not been able to formulate or implement a consistent long-term economic policy toward the
Soviet Union because of the cacophony of officials, politicians, and interest
groups who have an input into policymaking. Often, these individuals and
the institutions they represent have disagreed on matters of principle. At
other times, they have used the question of economic ties with the Soviet
Union to fight domestic political battles that have nothing to do with
East–West trade. Either way, the ability of the United States to conduct
a rational, consistent, and effective policy has been impaired.

The first major problem that has beset East–West trade policy has been
rivalry within the executive branch for policy control. The National Security Council and the Departments of Defense, Commerce, State, Energy,
Agriculture, and the Treasury have all had a hand in policymaking and
have increasingly disagreed over what U.S. policy should be. Traditionally,
the Departments of Commerce and Agriculture have taken the most forthcoming attitude toward trade with the Soviets; the State Department and
National Security Council have been concerned with the political implications of such trade as part of overall diplomacy toward the U.S.S.R.; and
the Defense Department has taken a much more restrictive attitude, focusing on the danger to national security of such commerce.[27] The Department of Defense has taken a stronger role in the Reagan administration,
but it has not always been able to tighten restrictions on economic relations
with the U.S.S.R. Moreover, in recent years, there have been conflicts
*within* these various departments over East–West trade, further complicat-
ing the procedure. Because of the cumbersomeness of policymaking and the
inherent rivalries between various parts of the executive branch, economic
policy toward the U.S.S.R. is often hostage to bureaucratic squabbles, frustrating those affected by that policy — the American business community,
America's allies, or the Soviet Union — and leaving loopholes from which
the U.S.S.R. can and does benefit. The question of who has ultimate
responsibility for trade policy remains unanswered.

Another problem is the role of Congress. Sometimes, Congress and the
administration have agreed on economic policy toward the U.S.S.R.; but
at other times, Congress has blocked administration attempts either to
liberalize or tighten policy. During the 1950s, the executive branch and
Congress agreed on East–West trade policy, but as presidential authority
weakened and Congress became more assertive, problems like those posed
by the Jackson-Vanik and Stevenson Amendments increased. In those cases,
a Democratic Congress that had previously criticized the executive branch
for too restrictive a policy toward the U.S.S.R. decided to thwart White

House policy. Yet the Democrats also opposed a policy of détente that paid no attention to human rights. Moreover, since trade is one of the few available weapons, Congress has often been quick to impose economic sanctions as a response to Soviet actions. To some extent, congressional actions were a product of opposition to the administration's handling of the Vietnam War, making U.S.-Soviet trade hostage to struggles that had little to do with the merits of economic ties.

Interest groups have also had some influence on the evolution of U.S. policy, although they have had far less impact than the executive or legislative branches of government. The business community has occasionally lobbied for increased East-West trade, but with surprising reticence compared to lobbying efforts on other aspects of U.S. foreign trade policy. American business groups have been deterred from vigorous lobbying for U.S.-Soviet trade because of the political stigma attached to such advocacy and the risk of provoking consumer boycotts of their products at home. In addition, the cost of doing business with the cumbersome Soviet bureaucracy has dampened the pursuit of Soviet markets. The farm lobby has been less reluctant to campaign for exports to the U.S.S.R. because its activities generally have received official encouragement — the Carter grain embargo being the one exception. Finally, organized labor — particularly the AFL-CIO — has consistently opposed a policy of liberalized trade with the U.S.S.R. and has enthusiastically supported boycotts and sanctions against Moscow.

## ECONOMIC CONTAINMENT AND AMERICAN ALLIES

Since the beginning of postwar economic containment, it has generally been assumed that such a policy could only be effective if the United States secured its allies' cooperation. Since the era of détente, it has become equally clear that America's allies do not share Washington's belief in the desirability or efficacy of economic containment apart from the limited strategic embargo. Some people within this country have argued that failing allied agreement, Washington should impose an economic containment policy unilaterally.[28] But most experts recognize that without allied cooperation, a restrictive policy is impossible, so they continue to seek European and Japanese consent.

European willingness to support the U.S. attitude toward economic ties with the U.S.S.R. ended when the continent recovered from economic devastation and ceased its reliance on Marshall Plan aid. The last European statesman to support across-the-board restrictions was Konrad Adenauer, who complied with the 1962 pipe embargo but criticized Kennedy for selling grain to the USSR.[29] Western Europe and Japan are far more trade-dependent than the United States, and even though trade with the Soviets

constitutes only a small percentage of the total, it is disproportionately
important for certain sectors of their economies (particularly the steel,
machine-tool, and chemical industries).[30] Moreover, the Europeans and
Japanese see a healthy economy as vital to national security, whereas
American officials have traditionally given security a much narrower military definition. Thus, from our allies' perspectives, the contribution to
national security that comes from a healthy export sector — including non-
military exports to the U.S.S.R. — outweighs the potential danger to
national security that machinery exports to the Soviets might involve. All
of the United States' allies agree that no explicitly military technology
should be exported to the U.S.S.R., but they favor all other industrial
exports.

There is a political dimension to this approach. Most European nations
view the détente era as successful. Tending to judge Soviet behavior by
what the Kremlin does in Europe, not by its activities in Afghanistan or
Nicaragua, they argue that the Soviets have abided by their agreements in
Western Europe despite the deployment of SS-20 missiles. Moreover, they
believe that economics and politics are linked and that a cooperative economic relationship can reinforce political ties. The West Germans particularly believe that trade incentives can bring political results, as shown by
the development of the inter-German relationship. The French, British,
Italians, and Japanese are more skeptical about positive economic levers,
but they all agree that sanctions are not an acceptable means of responding to Soviet behavior because they hurt the countries involved without
affecting what Moscow does.

Furthermore, although Europe and Japan accept the necessity for a strategic embargo and have been willing to cooperate in CoCom's tightening
of technology transfers, they have been unwilling to accept the broad, U.S.-
backed definition of indirect contributions to Soviet military prowess. There
have been endless disagreements about the relevance of the "militarily critical" technologies concept enshrined in U.S. law.[31] CoCom works surpris-
ingly well, considering that it is an informal organization with no power
to impose sanctions against violators; yet it will not restrict the flow of civilian goods to the U.S.S.R. unless they can be proved to have direct application to Soviet military capabilities.

Europe and Japan have particularly resisted U.S. attempts to use industrial trade sanctions to punish the Soviets for their actions in Afghanistan
or Poland or for their human rights abuses. The 1982 extraterritorial pipeline sanctions, for instance, affected companies in Europe and Japan much
more than in the United States; indeed, they were seen as sanctions against
Western Europe rather than the U.S.S.R. The Europeans sold pipeline
equipment to the Soviets, even under threat of American countersanctions
against European goods coming into the United States. Arguably, America's

economic containment policy in the last few years has had more effect on
Western Europe than on the U.S.S.R. Certainly, those in the White House
and Defense Department who favor a restrictive policy are willing to apply
it to Western Europe as much as to the East, unless Western Europe is willing to alter its stance. These administration officials have already sought
to limit contact among Western scientists working in what the government
considers sensitive areas.

Europe and Japan reject the idea of an across-the-board policy of economic containment, apart from CoCom, arguing that it is unworkable and
counterproductive. This position will probably not change, since Conservative and Socialist governments alike share it. As a consequence, it is possible to achieve only the lowest common denominator of allied cooperation
in CoCom, and this only with considerable pressure.

## THE ECONOMIC EFFECT
## OF ECONOMIC CONTAINMENT

What effect have such fitful economic containment policies had on the
Soviet economy? A careful examination of Soviet writings on Western trade
restrictions reveals a dual message. On the one hand, the Soviets have always criticized them as a manifestation of the cold war and contrary to
"normal" international practice.[32] Countless articles have pointed out that
U.S. restrictions violate the Helsinki principles and are opposed by America's allies, citing particularly the pipeline embargo of 1982.[33] Soviet authors have also emphasized the clash between U.S. business interests, who
favor trade with the U.S.S.R., and those in Congress who oppose trade.[34]
Since an acute consciousness of technological inferiority is a major element
in Russian political culture, the Soviets go out of their way to say that they
favor economic ties because trade will help the American economy. They
rarely admit their own economic needs.

On the other hand, Soviet writers have always been quick to stress that
American restrictions have not affected the U.S.S.R. economically, even if
they have complicated the political atmosphere. Soviet articles point to the
U.S.S.R.'s economic progress, its economic links with other capitalist states,
and its rosy prospects for future economic growth. And yet, their level of
invective against U.S. restrictions belies that tone of indifference. Moreover,
the fact that the Soviets have acquired so much American technology ille-
gally (and appear to have a special section for that purpose in the KGB)
suggests that they are very interested indeed in obtaining it by whatever
means possible.[35]

The policy of economic warfare—to the extent that it has been implemented since 1949—has not prevented the U.S.S.R. from experiencing impressive rates of growth in the postwar era or becoming the world's largest

producer of a number of key commodities, including oil and steel. Despite current difficulties, Soviet economic achievements and potential should not be dismissed. Moreover, it is likely that Soviet economic problems are more the product of the Soviet domestic system than the result of Western economic denial.

But if economic warfare has proved ineffective, most Western experts agree that the strategic embargo has had a greater impact. It may well have contributed to slower rates of technological development, and although it has not prevented the U.S.S.R.'s military buildup in the conventional or nuclear spheres, it may have made the buildup more costly in terms of resource diversion from other sectors.

Despite such basic agreement that CoCom restrictions have had an impact, the more difficult question is how much they have retarded Soviet growth. Some analysts contend that the Western embargo, particularly in the strategic sphere, has had a smaller impact on Soviet development than Americans would like to believe. On one end of the political spectrum, Anthony Sutton has argued in an exhaustive examination of Western technology exports to the Soviet Union that all items — even those of strictly civilian equipment — have fueled Soviet military growth:

> We cannot make any meaningful distinction between military and civilian goods. Every industrial plant directly or indirectly affords some military capability. It is the availability of Western technology that makes Soviet industry more efficient. . . . The Soviet Union and its socialist allies are dependent on the Western world for technical and economic viability. . . . We have constructed and maintain a first-order threat to Western society.[36]

Sutton's argument — that America's strategic embargo has failed (partly due to misguided U.S. policies) and that the West has built up the Soviet economy — has been taken up by opponents of trade with the Soviets.[37] At the other end of the political spectrum, Gunnar Adler-Karlsson's study of CoCom concludes that the Western strategic embargo did little to halt Soviet economic growth because it was not supported by the American allies or neutral countries and because the Soviets did not need Western technology to develop their economy or their military sector.[38]

More recent analyses of the impact of Western technology and trade — and their denial — on the Soviet economy suggest that it has been marginal but not irrelevant. One detailed analysis of the Soviet economy, sector by sector, shows that Western equipment has made a very modest, even minimal contribution to the development of Soviet industry and the Soviet military.[39] However, it may have reduced bottlenecks in some sectors like energy. Morris Bornstein's study for the OECD emphasizes the U.S.S.R.'s difficulty in absorbing and diffusing Western technology, suggesting that such imports have a net resource-demanding effect on the Soviet economy.[40] Recent developments indicate that the Soviet Union is becoming more technologically "chauvinistic," with key officials stressing the need for the U.S.S.R. to rely on its own technology.[41] Moreover, some have argued that "U.S. denials of strategic products may galvanize [the U.S.S.R.] to overcome its problems in the longer run."[42] This theory stresses that the Soviets carefully study the U.S. embargo lists and then put all their resources into producing embargoed items, with the result that U.S. restrictions ultimately have a counterproductive effect.

The message that has recently emerged from most Western writing on this issue — one that is supported by some U.S. government estimates — is that Western equipment and technology imports have made only a very modest contribution to Soviet economic growth. Moreover, the Soviets have cut back their imports of Western technology since 1977. The West, most scholars argue, has a very limited impact on a Soviet economy that is large, self-sufficient, and deliberately insulated from the effects of Western restrictions. Just as a strategy of trade denial has not succeeded in retarding Soviet *military* growth, so a strategy of across-the-board trade promotion would probably not have much impact on Soviet *economic* growth. The overcentralized, neo-Stalinist Soviet economic system, and not Western restrictions, is the major barrier here, a view Mikhail Gorbachev has all but acknowledged. If so, the United States' ability to influence Soviet economic developments has probably been exaggerated.

## THE POLITICAL EFFECT
## OF ECONOMIC CONTAINMENT

Economic containment has, therefore, had only a marginal effect on the Soviet economy. But has it had any political effects? The evidence suggests not, largely because of asymmetries in the economic and political stakes involved. Because trade with the West has never played an important macroeconomic role in Soviet economic development, the United States has often found itself using relatively insignificant economic ties in attempts to force changes in Soviet behavior on core political issues (such as treatment of dissidents or actions in Poland or Afghanistan). Quite simply, the ends demanded have been out of all proportion to the means used.[43]

There are two major forms of economic linkage: negative and positive. Negative linkage, or trade denial, uses the stick retroactively.[44] Usually, the United States has used it to punish the Soviets for domestic or foreign policy actions, without demanding specific concessions in return. As a result, it is difficult to find any examples in the postwar era when American sanctions have led to a modification of Soviet policies, even when (like the grain embargo) they may have had an economic impact. Moreover, a major problem in using negative linkage is devising a timetable that will send consistent signals. For example, President Carter imposed technology sanctions on the Soviets to punish them for their treatment of dissidents, but then removed the sanctions even though Shcharansky and others were still imprisoned. Similarly, President Reagan lifted the grain embargo when the Soviets were still in Afghanistan. These kinds of inconsistencies — largely the product of domestic politics — call into question the entire rationale of the exercise and lessen American credibility.

Positive linkage, using trade incentives to elicit more desirable behavior from the U.S.S.R. domestically or internationally, is the other available option. Any trade carrot is, of course, a potential stick, because the Soviets realize that the incentive can be withdrawn if the requisite concessions are not forthcoming. Although the Soviets have always argued that they will never make political concessions in return for trade, postwar experience indicates that they have sometimes done so, providing the stakes were roughly commensurate and the concessions demanded did not involve core values or major questions of national security. There are examples of such trade-offs in the Soviet–West German economic relationship, involving humanitarian concessions on emigration in return for increased trade,[45] and Moscow also proved willing to liberalize Jewish emigration until the Jackson-Vanik and Stevenson Amendments were passed.[46] Although the United States has rarely tried to implement a policy of positive linkage, the record suggests some reason to believe that a trade inducement strategy might produce humanitarian concessions on marginal issues.

## IMPLICATIONS FOR THE FUTURE

Economic containment has been only partially implemented since the mid-1950s, and its economic and political impact has been questionable. While it may have retarded Soviet economic development in some areas, it has not prevented an impressive Soviet military buildup or considerable economic achievements in heavy industry and energy. In some ways, a refusal to sell grain to the Soviets might have been a more effective form of pressure, but since 1963 this means of leverage has not been politically acceptable in the United States. The strategic embargo has prevented the transfer to the U.S.S.R. of technology with direct military application, but only at the cost of constant struggles to agree on dual-use technologies, and CoCom's effectiveness has been hampered by inconsistencies in U.S. and allied policies.

Similarly, using economic levers to produce political results has been disappointing. Yet one can still argue that sanctions have a deterrent effect. It is impossible to prove the contrary, because that would involve knowing what Soviet behavior would have been without the threat of sanctions. Moreover, it is undeniable that if American politicians feel it necessary to react to Soviet misconduct, then the trade weapon is one of the few safe and domestically popular ones—as long as grain is left out. Nevertheless, recent sanctions have done more harm to the West than to the East. In the pipeline case, the economic costs imposed on the U.S.S.R. may not have been worth the damage done to the Western alliance and therefore to Western security. Positive linkage may be more productive, but trade inducement is not containment, whatever its utility to a more cooperative U.S.-Soviet relationship.

The United States has three options for the future. The first would be to return to a policy of economic warfare, including a total grain embargo as envisaged in 1949. The assumptions behind this policy would be that a weak Soviet economy is good for U.S. security and that American policy can affect how weak the Soviet economy is. Both propositions are, of course, debatable. Should the United States decide to return to such a confrontational policy, it would provoke even more dissension within the NATO alliance and further jeopardize Western cooperation, resulting in a unilateral (and therefore ineffective) policy. It is safe to say that Washington would never be able to secure European or Japanese cooperation for economic warfare unless the U.S.S.R. were to invade Western Europe or Japan. Thus, it is difficult to envision any future American administration returning to economic warfare. Moreover, the broad crackdown on high technology trade between the East and the West and within the alliance demanded by such a policy would be detrimental to U.S. research and development.

The second option would be to continue the current mixed policy, encouraging grain sales, cautiously promoting exports of some manufactures, maintaining the strategic embargo, tightening up on high technology exports, and periodically using trade for foreign policy purposes. Acceptable domestically, this policy will secure only grudging allied cooperation. It will also provoke continued complaints from the U.S. business community that Washington is giving business to Western Europe while not preventing the Soviets from acquiring Western technology. A Democratic administration might lean somewhat more toward encouraging trade, but in either case this mixed scenario is the most likely one for the foreseeable future.

A third option would be to assume that it is in the interest of the United States to have a stronger Soviet economy, on the premises that a fat communist is less belligerent than a thin one and that the United States could help to improve Soviet economic performance through a policy of trade inducement. Again, both propositions are debatable. A policy of encouraging grain and manufacture exports while retaining necessary strategic controls would give more business to the United States, would lead to less political conflict with U.S. allies, and would increase cooperative channels of communication with the Soviets. To be consistent, this kind of trade promotion strategy would have to eschew economic linkage, but trade and politics might more generally reinforce each other in a policy of revived détente. It is questionable, however, whether Congress or the executive branch would be willing to forego totally economic sanctions for foreign policy reasons.

The sobering reality is that none of these three strategies would have an appreciable *economic* effect on the U.S.S.R. They would, however, make a difference domestically and in ties between the United States and Western Europe. The major influence on Soviet economic performance in the future will be Gorbachev's economic policy, and whether he is willing and able to reform the ossified Soviet system. The economic policy of the United States can certainly affect the *political* relationship between the two nations, but it cannot determine Soviet economic policy. Some observers may continue to argue that if only we could get our allies and all the neutral countries to agree to a total economic blockade of the U.S.S.R., we could bring it to its knees. Perhaps, but the premise is based on fantasy. There has never been, nor will there ever be, worldwide agreement on economic warfare against any nation in peacetime. The best the United States can do is to reconsider whether what is achievable in economic containment is worthwhile, balancing as best it can the East–West, West–West, and domestic economic and political dimensions of the issue.

## NOTES

1. For a fuller discussion of these three strategies, see Michael Mastanduno, "Strategies of Economic Containment," *World Politics* 38 (No. 4, 1985): 503–529.
2. "What Business with Russia?" *Fortune* (January 1945): 204.
3. John Lewis Gaddis, *The United States and the Origins of the Cold War* (New York: Columbia University Press, 1972), Ch. 6; George F. Kennan, *Memoirs (1925–1950)* (Boston: Atlantic Little, Brown, 1967), pp. 280–284.
4. Lecture by George Kennan and Lewellyn G. Thompson at the National War College, September 17, 1949, p. 24. George F. Kennan papers, Princeton University Library.
5. Report by the National Security Council, "Control of Exports to the USSR and Eastern Europe," December 17, 1947, in *Foreign Relations of the United States, 1948*, Vol. IV, p. 512.
6. Department of the Army, memorandum, "National Security Interest in East-West Trade," December 8, 1947, Spaatz Papers, Box 28; Secretary of the Navy, memorandum, "U.S. Government organization for Conducting Economic Warfare," April 9, 1948; Spaatz Papers, Box 29, Library of Congress.
7. State Department, "Control of Exports to the Soviet Bloc," March 26, 1948. Harry S Truman Library, Independence, MO. President's Secretary's Files.
8. See Harold Berman and John Garson, "United States Export Controls — Past, Present and Future," *Columbia Law Review* 57 (No. 5, 1967): 791–890, for more details.
9. See Office of Technology Assessment, *Technology and East-West Trade* (Washington, D.C.; Government Printing Office, 1979), ch. VII.

10. W. W. Rostow, Memo to the Policy Planning Council, "U.S. Policy on Trade with the European Soviet Bloc," July 26, 1963, pp. 2, 5. Box 223, National Security Files, John F. Kennedy Library, Boston.
11. See Angela Stent, *From Embargo to Ostpolitik: The Political Economy of West German-Soviet Relations, 1955–1980* (Cambridge: Cambridge University Press, 1981), Ch. 5.
12. Letter from John F. Kennedy to Mike Mansfield, November 15, 1963; Box 314, National Security Files, John F. Kennedy Library, Boston.
13. Comments on Question 17, "U.S. Benefit from Sale to USSR of Wheat," State Department Memorandum, September 25, 1963. Box 314, National Security Files, John F. Kennedy Library, Boston.
14. Henry A. Kissinger, *White House Years* (Boston: Little, Brown, 1979), pp. 152–154.
15. *Ibid*, pp. 1270–1271.
16. Henry A. Kissinger, *Years of Upheaval* (Boston: Little, Brown, 1982), pp. 985–988.
17. Bruce Jentleson, "Pipeline Politics: The Complex Political Economy of East-West Energy Trade," Unpublished Ph.D. dissertation, Cornell University, 1984, Ch. 5.
18. Samuel P. Huntington, "Trade, Technology and Leverage: Economic Diplomacy," *Foreign Policy* 32 (Fall, 1978): 63–80.
19. Office of Technology Assessment, *Technology and Soviet Energy Availability* (Washington, D.C.: Government Printing Office, 1981).
20. CoCom operates by having weekly meetings where exceptions to the embargo lists are discussed. Before 1979, the United States always requested the largest number of exceptions in order to export items to communist nations. After 1979, there was a general agreement that, apart from items necessary to keep pipelines to the West operating, there would be no more exception requests for the U.S.S.R.
21. According to National Security Adviser Zbigniew Brzezinski, "We had no illusions that sanctions in themselves would force the Soviets out, but we felt that the Soviet Union had to pay some tangible price for its misconduct." *Power and Principle* (New York: Farrar, Straus, Giroux, 1983), p. 43.
22. President Ronald Reagan, quoted in the *New York Times*, July 29, 1982.
23. Jan Vanous, *Washington Post*, October 10, 1982.
24. Angela E. Stent, *Soviet Energy and Western Europe*, The Washington Papers, no. 90. (New York: Praeger, 1982).
25. See Angela E. Stent, "Technology Transfers in East-West Trade: The Western Alliance Studies," in *AEI Foreign Policy and Defense Review* 5 (No. 2, 1985): 44–52.
26. Angela Stent, "The Geopolitics of Soviet Energy," Cambridge Energy Research Associates Private Report (Cambridge, MA), November 1985.
27. See "East–West Commercial Policy: A Congressional Dialogue with the Reagan Administration," a study prepared for the use of the Joint Economic Committee, Congress of the United States. February 16, 1982.
28. Statement of Charles Wolf in Senate Foreign Relations Committee and CRS, *The Premises of East–West Commercial Relations: A Workshop*, Dec. 14–15, 1982 (Washington, D.C.: Government Printing Office, 1983), p. 145.
29. See Stent, *From Embargo to Ostpolitik*, pp. 121–124.
30. For a detailed discussion of European views, see Angela E. Stent, *Technology Transfer to the Soviet Union: A Challenge for the Cohesiveness of the West-*

*ern Alliance.* Arbeitspapiere zur Internationalen Politik no. 24 (Bonn: Europa-Union Verlag, 1983).

31. The concept of "militarily critical technology" was first developed in a 1976 Department of Defense Report known as the Bucy Report. An unclassified version of the militarily critical technologies list (which in its classified versions runs over 700 pages) can be found in Department of Defense, *The Militarily Critical Technologies List*, October 1984 (Washington: Office of the Under Secretary of Defense Research and Engineering).

32. For instance, see A. Kozyrev, "Torgovlya Oruzhiem Kak Instrument Vneshneii Politiki SShA," *SShA: Ekonomika, Politika, Ideologiia* no. 5, 1980, pp. 19–30.

33. O. Ye. Tishelenko, "Soviet-American Trade Today," in *USA: Economics, Politics, Ideology* (FBIS Translation) no. 11, 1984; V. Shemyatenkov, "'Ekonomicheskaia Voina' ili Ekonomicheskoe Sorevnovanie?" *Mirovaia Ekonomika i Mezhdunarodnye Otnosheniia*, no. 3, 1985, pp. 30–40.

34. G. Bazhenov, "USSR–USA: Businesslike Cooperation," *International Affairs* (Moscow) August 1974, pp. 15–21.

35. See the new DoD study, "Soviet Acquisition of Militarily Significant Western Technology: An Update" (September 1985).

36. Anthony Sutton, *Western Technology and Soviet Economic Development, 1945 to 1965* (Stanford: Hoover Institution Publications, 1973), pp. 399–400.

37. Carl Gershman, "Selling Them the Rope," *Commentary* (April 1979): 35–45.

38. Gunnar Adler-Karlsson, *Western Economic Warfare 1947–1967* (Stockholm: Almquist and Wiksell, 1968).

39. See Bruce Parrott, ed., *Technology and Soviet-American Relations* (Bloomington: Indiana University Press, 1985), for a detailed sector-by-sector analysis.

40. Morris Bornstein, "West–East Technology Transfer: Impact on the USSR," *The OECD Observer* 136 (September 1985): 18–22. See also, Thane Gustafson, *Selling the Russians the Rope* (Santa Monica: The RAND Corporation, 1981).

41. See Philip Hanson, "Technological Chauvinism in the Soviet Union," *Radio Liberty Research*, April 30, 1985.

42. Marshall Goldman and Raymond Vernon, "Economic Relations," in Joseph S. Nye, Jr., ed., *The Making of America's Soviet Policy* (New Haven: Yale University Press, 1984), p. 169.

43. See Stent, *From Embargo to Ostpolitik*, pp. 7–12.

44. For a fuller discussion see Ellen Frost and Angela Stent, "NATO's Troubles with East–West Trade," *International Security* 8 (Summer 1983): 179–200.

45. See Stent, *From Embargo to Ostpolitik* for details.

46. In the later Carter years, when the promise of a trade treaty was revived, the numbers of Jewish emigrants reached an all-time high of 51,320 in 1979.

# 5 CONTAINMENT AND THE STRATEGIC NUCLEAR BALANCE

*George H. Quester*

Having completed four decades of the nuclear age, we are also approaching four decades since the doctrine of containment was enunciated as American foreign policy. It is altogether natural for analysts to see important connections between the two, hypothesizing that the ratios of U.S. to Soviet nuclear arsenals somehow explain the successes or failures of American efforts to keep Soviet political domination from spreading. But the relationship of containment to the nuclear balance is very complicated; recent shifts to "parity" or "Soviet superiority" hardly suffice to explain the apparent opening of holes in our barriers of containment. Even the very origin of the policy of containment, in years when the United States alone had nuclear weapons and had just used them at Hiroshima and Nagasaki, demands some quite complicated explanations.

## AMBITION, OR A LIMIT TO AMBITION?

The most elementary question about containment goes to its very essence: Was this a doctrine expanding America's role in the world, or modestly limiting it?

Compared to earlier historical periods of American "isolation," periods when the United States was benefiting from a global balance of power arranged by others, the commitment implied by containment to holding the line against Soviet expansionism looks very ambitious. Indeed, if one thinks of the traditional American aversion to war and international commitments, the decisions required by containment were a greater departure for the Republic than even Woodrow Wilson's involvement in World War I. However, compared to the unconditional surrender imposed on Germany and Japan, containment amounted to a major restraint and reduction of ambitions.[1] The United States had not been content merely to "contain" Nazism or Japanese militarism, to demand simply that German

78

armies retreat once again across the Rhine or that Japanese armies be withdrawn back to their home islands. Rather, the American logic in World War II was that there was no point to winning the war unless a politically democratic form of government could be established in Germany and Japan, as well as in Italy. In the Japanese case, this ambition was admirably served by the sudden U.S. monopoly of nuclear weapons; the message of Hiroshima and Nagasaki was that Japanese cities would be destroyed one by one unless Japan surrendered and submitted to the establishment of free elections. Americans had been willing and prepared to fight on into 1947 or 1949 to impose this kind of surrender on Tokyo; the atomic bomb facilitated the surrender in a shorter time and at lower cost. But if Americans were willing to go to such lengths to impose political democracy in Japan and Western Germany (in retrospect, with great success despite all the cliches about how the "American model" cannot be transplanted abroad), should we not have expected much more ambitious plans for imposing free elections on Warsaw and Bucharest, or perhaps even on Moscow?

In short, which of the following two is the proper question: "Why did we do as much as containment?" or "Why did we settle for as little as containment?" And directly relevant to the theme of this chapter, "What role did the state of the nuclear balance play in whatever change occurred?"

## KENNAN'S OWN PERSPECTIVE

How containment is to be differentiated from alternative foreign policies is closely linked to the continuing question of what George F. Kennan himself meant by the word, and whether his meaning was somehow immediately misinterpreted by the American government and people.

Various interpreters of Kennan's thinking[2] (and indeed Kennan's own retrospective interpretation of what he meant[3]) suggest that containment was not intended to be a radical alteration of American foreign policy and that the doctrine did not require manning a perimeter around the globe to hold in Soviet power. In this view, containment was not very different from the balance of power diplomacy that had been second nature to Britain in the nineteenth century, a policy that watched for threats from abroad and sought to check them by building up other rival power centers.

Even as Britain would build up France when Spain was too powerful, and Spain when France was too powerful, so the United States would want to build up Western Europe once the Soviet Union had become too powerful. Just as Britain would never have allowed France or Spain to swallow too much of the continent's sources of economic and military power (lest the result pose a threat to England itself), so the United States would work to keep Western Europe from coming under Moscow's control. Containment, by this interpretation, was simply a ringing of an alarm bell within a traditional alarm system, an identification of a threat coming from a new direction. Moscow now needed to be "contained," or checked from becoming too powerful, just as other threats would have had to be checked or contained in the past.

But a considerably different view of the uniqueness of Kennan's message might have seen it instead as proposing a new and necessary *alternative* to the old balance of power.[4] Since the older major states (Germany, Japan, Britain, and France) had become so weakened by World War II, it was now necessary for the United States actively to man the frontiers against the menace to American interests. Since more than American interests were threatened — indeed, communism threatened all political democracy around the globe, as did the earlier spread of Fascism — many supporters and critics of Kennan's containment message saw it as a call for a uniquely active, continuous, and multifaceted American involvement in world affairs. The traditional balance of power formulation promised some rest periods, when inherent checks and balances were operating, and thus seemed a moderate commitment of American energies. Containment offered little opportunity for rest and demanded more continuous commitment of resources.

The recent history of international politics had involved two states, Nazi Germany and imperial Japan, which apparently would never give up hopes of conquest and could not be checked short of war. A power-politics view of Kennan's thinking would characterize them as unusual and special threats to other nations' vital interests that had required total defeat rather than a mere checking. Kennan's analysis of the Soviet Union was that no such total defeat would be needed to keep Moscow from attacking the outside world, that the U.S.S.R. was less threatening in practical terms than the Axis powers had been.

Yet was the only reason for pursuing the unconditional surrender of Germany and Japan the likelihood of further aggression from these powers? After Germany had been driven back to the Rhine again, and after the Japanese had lost even Okinawa, was it not plausible that Hitler or the Japanese army would have accepted being contained for a while? As suggested earlier, was it not the obnoxious internal nature of the Nazi and Japanese regimes, rather than the prospect of renewed aggression in 1946 or 1947, that had made the Allies ready to go further? Or was it instead a fear in Washington that the Nazis or the Japanese might soon possess nuclear weapons that led to the demand for unconditional surrender and a total territorial occupation? But if this was the reason to go beyond the dictates of the balance of power — even to destroy the balance by destroying Germany and Japan as military entities — what then of the fact that Stalin would get atomic bombs sooner or later, and that the West had to look forward to this precisely as Kennan was composing his analysis?

## PRE-1949: "WHY DID WE SETTLE FOR CONTAINMENT?"

If we consider the containment doctrine as an embodiment of restraint, it can hardly be explained solely by nuclear factors, because the United States was as safe against nuclear retaliation in 1947 as in 1945. Indeed, from 1945 to 1949, nuclear considerations should have worked *against* (rather than for) something so limited as containment. A few years later, by 1949 to be exact, the nuclear monopoly had definitively ended, but the initial limits of the containment doctrine have to be traced to a form of discouragement other than "mutual assured destruction." If Hitler had possessed nuclear weapons, would not the United States have been forced to give up its goal of unconditional surrender in exchange for something more like containment? Conversely, since Stalin did not have nuclear weapons in 1946, why was containment postulated rather than something more ambitious? Why, in other words, did Kennan seem to endorse a different treatment for the U.S.S.R. than for Germany and Japan?

Kennan's analysis was tied importantly to his sense of American unwillingness to "pay the price" and make the sacrifices for any venture in international politics. His analysis does not seem to allow the possibility that the new nuclear arsenal could make a war with the Soviet Union as inexpensive for the United States as had been the last week of World War II against Japan. Utterly repulsed by the damage conventional bombings had done to cities like Hamburg and Dresden, Kennan considered nuclear weapons so destructive as to be useless for political or even military purposes, justifiable only to deter the use of similar weapons against the United States.[5] His analysis was thus that the U.S. nuclear monopoly did not offer any special opportunities; i.e., he accepted, at a time when the Soviets had no nuclear weapons, restraints on U.S. behavior that otherwise might have been accepted, with resignation, only after the Soviets acquired them. (Yet we all understand today that nuclear proliferation makes a tremendous difference. Was there ever a greater difference than that between the U.S.–Japanese confrontation of 1945 and the U.S.–Soviet confrontation of 1950? And why does Kennan's interpretation make so little of this difference?)

If the containment doctrine had been published by George Kennan in the immediate aftermath of the Soviet nuclear test, we would all be analyzing it today as a sensible, inevitable resignation to the limits imposed on U.S. foreign policy by a totalitarian dictator's ability to destroy American cities. In military terms, containment makes perfect sense when a dictator already has nuclear weapons. He might not dare to use them when he is simply trying to grab another piece of territory, but he would have no incentive not to use such weapons if we were trying to depose him and free his people. But containment was not a response to Soviet nuclear weapons potential, or even to their imminence, at least as far as we can tell from the documents and the memories of the doctrine's drafters.

One might perhaps attempt to reconcile the nuclear issue with the inception of containment, to dispel the apparent paradox, by assuming some degree of temporal discounting in Kennan's views. Perhaps he was assuming that the Soviets would have the bomb very quickly, say by 1948, or perhaps he assumed more generally that any aggressive American policy (foregoing some kind of galvanizing Soviet conventional sneak attack) would take longer than Soviet nuclear technology to fall into place. If Kennan, subliminally or more consciously, was thus already resigned to Soviet possession of the nuclear ultimate-veto weapon, then his endorsement of containment might be regarded as illustrating the determining impact of the nuclear factor right from the start.

Yet there are problems with this interpretation. The typical forecast by American experts was that it might be 1955 before the Soviets acquired nuclear weapons. The commitment and urgency of the original American effort to develop atomic bombs was based on 1940 reports that Hitler's dictatorship might be seeking such weapons. Should not similar forecasts about Stalin's dictatorship have called for attaching some greater significance to an interim of another two or three years? Just as the American commitment to "unconditional surrender" and the total occupation of Germany was premised in part on worries about possible German nuclear capability, so the as-yet-unrealized Soviet nuclear capability might have amounted to an argument to move beyond containment rather than accept it.

## COMPARING STALIN WITH THE AXIS

Kennan would afterward contend that minor ambiguities in the wording of his "X" article caused major misunderstandings and mistakes in policy.[6] He states that phrases like "counterforce" led to too much emphasis on military confrontation rather than non-military checks against the Soviets.

Yet in making these arguments, Kennan seems to ignore the differences between conventional and nuclear military power. Once the Soviets had detonated their first atomic bombs, the drafters of NSC-68 feared the possibility that the Soviet bomb might now check the threats and influence of the U.S. bomb.[7] Following what they believed to be the logic of Kennan's NSC-20 as it applied to the end of the U.S. nuclear monopoly, the drafters of NSC-68 called for substantial offsetting increases in conventional military preparations.

But what then of the logical obverse of NSC-68, an analysis of how the United States could handle Soviet threats when Moscow had no nuclear weapons? Should the logic not have been that more could be made of the

potential of the U.S. nuclear stockpile? In his criticisms of NSC-68's deri-
vations from his own premises, Kennan criticized all of the arms buildup,
nuclear and conventional, that resulted from the implementation of containment. Yet this ignores the nuclear jolt that NSC-68 was responding to.

Consistent with the retrospective interpretation that Kennan was advocating not an expansion of American commitments but their moderation,
we must note his belief that Stalin could not be as total or immediate a
threat as Hitler had been.[8] Moscow, with its Marxist–Leninist ideology
and world view, was seen by Kennan as much more cautious and patient.
Firm resistance might suffice here, where it had not sufficed for the Japanese and Germans.

The differences between Hitler and Stalin were real enough, and very
much along the lines that Kennan outlined, but one still wonders whether
they were the sole explanation for the American shift from "unconditional
surrender" to "containment." Assuming that without the atomic bomb the
United States would have been expending nearly 100,000 American lives
storming the beaches of Japan in the months when Kennan was instead
analyzing the postwar Soviet Union, was imperial Japan really so qualita-
tively different from Stalin's Russia that Tokyo needed to be occupied while
Moscow only needed to be fenced in at some distance? Such reasoning suggests that the early history of containment was much more directly affected
by nuclear weapons than Kennan tends to admit. But for the bomb, we
very plausibly would still have been fighting against Japan in 1946 and
1947, with the Soviets overrunning all of Manchuria and Korea, and with
Moscow and Washington jointly worrying about the casualties incurred in
an invasion of the Japanese home islands. Under such circumstances, would
Kennan have gotten the same attention for his analysis of Soviet behavior?

The differences between Japan's situation and Russia's, each facing an
American nuclear monopoly, still requires more analysis than Kennan was
willing to provide, for Kennan's "X" article was in part an explanation
of why the United States would not do as much against the U.S.S.R. as
against Japan. What could the U.S.S.R. have threatened to do in retaliation if President Truman had ordered U.S. nuclear weapons into action in
response to the violations of the Yalta pledges? As Soviet cities were being
destroyed and the death toll mounted from 20 to 40 or 50 million, con-
joined with some American demand for a Soviet surrender, no U.S. cities
could have been similarly destroyed. But the cities of Western Europe could
indeed have been occupied by the Soviet Army in revenge.[9] The rapidity
of the U.S. demobilization after the German surrender, along with the
demobilizations of British and French forces, ensured that there would be
nothing except Russian exhaustion to halt such an advance. The Soviets had
also demobilized their forces after the summer of 1945, but not nearly so
completely.

By comparison, the Japanese already were in occupation of many Chinese cities (and had already done their worst to Nanking). The means of retaliation available to Japan were not sufficient to counterweight the threat demonstrated at Hiroshima and Nagasaki, but the means were available to the Soviets, given their geographical access to Western Europe and the advanced deployment of Soviet forces after the defeat of the Germans.

This difference in retaliatory options, which may explain the differing vulnerabilities of Japan and the U.S.S.R. to the U.S. nuclear monopoly, may also explain Kennan's failure to accord any significance to that monopoly. Yet the difference in these options is only explained in part by geography. It is also largely explained by American attitudes — attitudes that Kennan interpreted as already formed rather than malleable.

Why indeed did the United States not maintain at least enough of a conventional defense of Western Europe so that some use could have been made of the nuclear monopoly? In part, Americans were tired of war, eager to get their sons home regardless of what this did to the combat effectiveness of the military units from which they were being released. They were unwilling to pay the costs of the necessary conventional forces auxiliary to a use of nuclear power.[10] But in larger part, Americans were incapable of launching a war against a state like the U.S.S.R., no matter how many pledges it had broken about respecting systems of free elections in Eastern Europe, unless Moscow first attacked the United States, just as Japan had attacked at Pearl Harbor. If Hitler had not declared war on the United States on December 11, 1941, it might even have been difficult for President Roosevelt to get the United States committed to taking part in the European war.

The American attitude of never beginning wars but then fighting them through to unconditional surrender is hardly explained by any astute commitment to the considerations of power politics. Neither is it explained by ideological considerations of the importance of supporting democracy against totalitarianism.

"War fatigue" thus has to be put into context. Almost no Americans would have guessed at the beginning of August 1945 that World War II was to end within the month. However fatigued they may have been with the costs of that war, very few would have considered any kind of negotiated peace whereby Japan would escape occupation and democratization. Americans disarmed after August 1945 in the face of the Russians, but they would not have disarmed in the face of the Japanese if Japan had continued to resist.

Perhaps what was missing, in ways Kennan sought to correct, was a full awareness that Stalin's regime could be just as dictatorial as Tojo's had been. Yet the wartime naivete which had convinced some Americans that Stalin's Russia was really a government by the consent of the governed was rapidly fading. What was more crucially missing was any sense of an enemy's having brought a war on himself, an enemy's having started the war in question. Kennan indeed advised that Russia was unlikely to start such a war. And he recognized that the United States could not start such a war, even if one might have been appropriate from the standpoint of the balance of power or concerns about the spread of political democracy.

## CHANGES IN THE NUCLEAR BALANCE

Everything changes, it is being argued here, with the Soviet tests of nuclear weapons detected in 1949. From that point the question of "Why did we settle for as *little* as containment?" has a simple answer, rather than a complicated one. Stalin and his successors now had the means for destroying major American cities in a last-gasp nuclear retaliatory attack, so we could never eliminate the Soviet menace in the way we had eliminated the Nazi and the Japanese menace. But at the same time the question of "How can we do as *much* as containment?" becomes much more complicated.

Skeptics might intervene here to question the significance of 1949. Wasn't the United States still very much "superior" to the Soviets in nuclear weaponry, even after the first Soviet atomic bomb was detonated? If the lack of ambition in containment requires an explanation before 1949, would not some of the same puzzle remain as long as the U.S. Air Force and nuclear weapons stockpiles continued to be far larger than those of the Soviet Union?

It is not uncommon for surveys of the evolution of the Soviet–American nuclear balance to settle into a phraseology of "superiorities," listing steps in the progression as follows:

| | |
|---|---|
| American monopoly | 1945–1949 |
| American "superiority" | 1949–1968 |
| "parity" or "essential equivalence" | 1969–1979 |
| Soviet "superiority" | 1980–? |

Yet there are too many misleading inferences that tend to be drawn from such a list, and even the historical pacing of this sequence can be questioned.

A first misleading inference is the implied next step of the logical chain, which an elementary sense of symmetry reveals as "Soviet monopoly." On reflection, it seems unlikely that the pendulum would ever swing so far. Moscow and Leningrad will never be as secure against an American retaliatory attack as Washington and New York were in 1947 against Soviet retaliation (or in 1945 against a Japanese nuclear strike). Neither the worst-case scenarios put forward by the Committee on the Present Danger before 1980 nor the cases examined by the Scowcroft Commission in 1983, often labelled "the window of vulnerability," come even close to offering Moscow the kind of safety from retaliation that the United States had in 1945 or 1948.[11]

Any pendulum model of the evolution of the Soviet–American nuclear confrontation also misleads us in a second way: in how we reconstruct history. How were American analysts looking forward to the period we now remember as one of the "U.S. superiority" in the 1950s? In fact, this "superiority" had already been functionally discounted into a mutual deterrence parity in the writings of Brodie and Kissinger and others, including the authors of NSC-68. Perhaps Americans were always inclined to be pessimistic, indulging in a prudential worst-case analysis, and thus were unable to sense whatever advantages the nuclear balance was offering.

Yet the pessimism at that time was hardly limited to a dismissal of U.S. advantage, for the dominant worry after the mid-1950s was something far worse. An effective Soviet *monopoly* loomed if the U.S.S.R. succeeded in passing the United States in the development of intercontinental ballistic missiles (the "missile gap"). Because bombers were so vulnerable on their bases, and because the U.S.S.R. could be so secretive, the scenario of a Soviet first strike catching all U.S. bombers before any retaliation could be inflicted did not seem unreal or impossible in those years.

As presented in the writings of professional analysts like Generals Taylor, Gavin, and Medaris,[12] Moscow by the early 1960s might well have had what Washington possessed in the mid-1940s: the ability to use nuclear weapons and escape all nuclear retaliation. What would have happened to containment then? Would the Soviets have been content with "containing" the United States, or would they have elected to strike while they held such a new monopoly, imposing the same kind of change of government on the United States that the United States had imposed on Japan? Kennan, for his part, feared that they might.

As we try to plot possible links between the U.S.–Soviet nuclear balance and the failures of containment, we might instead outline the progression of the more important, *anticipated* balance as follows:

|  | seen in: | looking forward to: |
| --- | --- | --- |
| U.S. monopoly | 1947 | 1955 |
| U.S. "superiority" | 1949 | 1960s |
| Soviet monopoly!! | | |
|    (bomber gap, missile gap) | 1957 | 1959 |
| U.S. monopoly? | | |
|    (missile gap in reverse) | 1961 | 1970 |
| U.S. "superiority" | 1963 | 1970s |
| parity | 1968 | 1970s |
| Soviet "superiority"? | 1974 | 1980s |

The third, most relevant point obscured by conventional retrospectives on the nuclear balance is that there is only one tremendously important transition here, and it is not the shift from one side's nuclear superiority to another's. Rather, it is the shift from U.S. monopoly to anything else, the point when New York, Washington, and other U.S. cities could no longer be assured against Soviet retaliation. Once the Soviet possession of even Hiroshima-sized bombs had been established—however many fewer bombs the Soviets had and however primitive their means of delivery—the U.S. Air Force could not have been certain of protecting all U.S. cities against attack, even in the most "splendid" of preemptive first strikes. If a resignation to containment did not make nuclear sense before 1949, it did so immediately thereafter.

When one looks at the analysis offered of nuclear weapons in the late 1940s and the 1950s, it is indeed remarkable how little weight is attached to "U.S. superiority" as compared with "U.S. monopoly." Any U.S. superiority where the Soviets have nuclear weapons with which to strike at American cities is repeatedly rounded down to very little advantage for the West, with the immediate prospect, therefore, of conventional wars and failures of containment.

Bernard Brodie suggested this outcome as early as 1946, in his chapters of *The Absolute Weapon*:

> The bomb cannot but prove in the net a powerful inhibition to aggression. It would make relatively little difference if one power had more bombs and were better prepared to resist than its opponent. It would in any case undergo incalculable destruction of life and property.[13]

The authors of NSC-68 worked from a similarly pessimistic premise when asked to respond to the 1949 discovery that the Soviets had tested an atomic bomb:

> In the event of a general war with the U.S.S.R., it must be anticipated that atomic weapons will be used by each side in the manner it deems best suited to accomplish its objectives. In view of our vulnerability to Soviet atomic attack, it has been argued that we might wish to hold our atomic weapons only for retaliation against prior use by the U.S.S.R. To be able to do so and still have hope of achieving our objectives, the non-atomic military capabilities of ourselves and our allies would have to be fully developed and the political weaknesses of the Soviet Union fully exploited.[14]

The North Korean attack on South Korea in June of 1950, repulsed only by the introduction of substantial U.S. and allied conventional ground forces, illustrated this hypothetical scenario only too clearly. The United States could not use nuclear weapons to get the North Koreans out of Seoul (as it had used such weapons, in part, to get the Japanese out of Seoul), for the North Koreans were now shielded by a patron who had nuclear weapons of his own.

A number of authors in the mid-1950s developed the argument of limited war more fully, contending that nuclear forces (even if quite different in total size) basically cancelled each other out because each side would fear for the safety of its cities. William Kaufmann outlined such a conclusion clearly enough in *Military Policy and National Security*:

> If the Communists should challenge our sincerity, and they would have good reasons for daring to do so, we would either have to put up or shut up. If we put up, we would plunge into all the immeasurable horrors of an atomic war. If we shut up, we would suffer a serious loss of prestige and damage our capacity to establish deterrents against further Communist expansion. Indeed, given existing conditions, there is no escaping the conclusion that the doctrine of massive retaliation would be likely to confront us continually with having to choose between one or the other of these two most distasteful alternatives.[15]

Henry Kissinger's first book, *Nuclear Weapons and Foreign Policy*, developed at length the case that strategic nuclear forces had already cancelled each other out, though he went on to argue that nuclear weapons could somehow be used profitably, within the restraints of a limited war, to defend Western Europe.

> The growth of the Soviet nuclear stockpile has transformed massive retaliation from the least costly into the most costly strategy. With the end of our traditional invulnerability . . . [a]ll-out war has turned into a strategy which inevitably involves trading a life for a life; it has become the war of attrition par excellence.[16]

As noted, the United States may have earlier been kept from using its nuclear monopoly for anything more than containment by the counterweight of the Soviet conventional military advantage. Washington's ability to drop atomic bombs on Minsk was balanced by the Soviet army's ability to occupy Frankfurt. But what, then, when the Soviets also had atomic bombs? What would hold back a Soviet conventional attack if the two nuclear forces deterred each other's nuclear attack?

Before 1949, any war between the two post–World War II superpowers would have seen a monopoly of nuclear capability for the United States, but a great preponderance of conventional military force for the Soviets. As Soviet nuclear forces joined such a conventional imbalance, one again has to ask how the United States could be so ambitious as to aspire to containment. Just as Mao's communist armies overwhelmed those of Chiang to take over China, would not Stalin's communist hordes be able to sweep over Western Europe sooner or later? If the United States did not feel able to aspire to liberate Poland from Stalin, as it had liberated Belgium from Hitler, could it even hope to defend Belgium against Stalin?

The relationship of containment to this comparison of conventional forces is not the subject of this chapter. The U.S. monopoly of nuclear forces had some prospect of cancelling out the impact of the conventional imbalance. After 1949, however, it is altogether plausible that the conventional imbalance would alone explain any failure of deterrence.

## POST-1949: "HOW CAN WE DO
## AS MUCH AS CONTAINMENT?"

Before we write off the impact on containment of comparisons of the nuclear stockpiles (that is, once the Soviets had any stockpile at all), we have to address some lingering possibilities of significance for the transitions from U.S. superiority to parity, and from parity to Soviet superiority.

If we were limiting ourselves before 1949 by the containment doctrine, was this because Soviet conventional forces made up for the U.S. nuclear monopoly? Or was it because American timidity, and Soviet resolve, eliminated any impact of this monopoly? If the United States has always tended to be overly frightened by other nations' arsenals and insufficiently confident of its own, then the comparative evolution of the stockpiles might regain some importance subjectively, despite its objective irrelevance. From this perspective, those worried about Western resolve in facing up to communist dictatorships could extrapolate such a conclusion from the mere fact that the United States has not gotten more out of its nuclear monopoly. Once the monopoly was converted into a nuclear duopoly, would the Soviets feel free to move westward, challenging the containment barrier, for some of the very same reasons that the West had felt unable to move eastward as a liberating force? The more the Soviet nuclear arsenal grew, by this interpretation, the more the Soviets would push forward against the barriers of containment. Rather than watching two permanent alliance shields settling in with the nuclear duopoly, we would see the Western shield become ineffective.[17]

Yet this kind of argument for a significant tie between the nuclear arms confrontation and the viability of containment remains difficult to prove. As we survey the years after 1949, the linkage between growing Soviet nuclear power and the undoing of containment will not be as clear and easy to demonstrate.

A very simple and symmetrical picture of mutual deterrence would allow no military invasions of a nuclear power's homeland. And, barring some isolated instances of terrorist outrages, the United States has indeed remained immune. By the same logic of nuclear deterrence, an adversary's assault should not challenge allied territories that the nuclear protector values highly. No conventional military aggressions would be directed against areas for which the protector has plausibly committed himself to nuclear escalation, either by verbal declaration or by deploying "tactical" nuclear weapons into such territories. Again, there have been no invasions of Western Europe.

Similarly, the lines of containment would be more challengeable where the patron could not plausibly attach much value to the territory, where theater nuclear weapons were not deployed, and where nuclear escalation would not be credible. Places like Angola, Zaire, and Grenada, or Afghanistan and Vietnam, are thus open to contention. A portion of the Western failures of containment since 1960 may thus have to be explained not by the Soviet–American nuclear balance, nor even by the comparison of conventional military strengths, but by the emergence of fundamental doubts among many Americans about the appropriateness of resisting communist forces in places like Southeast Asia, Africa, or even Central America. At the same time, in a parallel development (which may also have little to do with nuclear or conventional weaponry, but might interestingly support aspects of Kennan's containment thesis), the political future of Eastern Europe is also now more open to contest than it would have seemed at the end of the 1940s. Perhaps the West here is no longer so much inclined to "limit itself" to containment.

## EXPLAINING CONTAINMENT FAILURES

By reviewing the specific sequence of "failures of containment" since 1949, we will attempt to discern the pattern of any impact that nuclear force levels may have had.

*Fidel Castro's takeover of Cuba* in 1959 must be viewed as a failure of containment, since Cuba was the first country to fall under communist rule after the 1954 partition of Indochina. These were the years when the United States dreaded an imminent "missile gap," a period when Moscow might somehow gain an effective nuclear monopoly in its favor, roughly comparable to what the United States had possessed before 1949. But the linkage to Havana is hardly so direct. Castro did not proclaim himself a Marxist until he had consolidated power, and he had based his guerrilla campaign on a program of ousting the Batista dictatorship and restoring a liberal system of political democracy, garnering a great deal of private American material support in the process.[18]

Castro had thus given out far less advanced warning of a failure of containment than Mao had in China, when only a few venturesome analysts inside the State Department had speculated that the Chinese Communists were "agrarian reformers" who might in the end be largely independent of Moscow. If such uncertainties can account for even part of the slowness of the extension of containment logic to Asia, far greater surprises were probable on the basis of how the confrontation between Castro and Batista had gone. Americans were not the only ones surprised when Castro's regime turned out to be a communist dictatorship modeling itself on and aligning itself with the Soviet Union. Many of Castro's supporters within Cuba were just as rudely surprised. In any event, America's passivity before Castro's accession to power seems to have had little to do with how the United States was counting Soviet nuclear forces in comparison with its own.

The unsuccessful *Bay of Pigs invasion*, launched by the Kennedy administration in an attempt to depose Castro and restore the barrier line of containment, occurred after the Kennedy team had discovered that there was no missile gap. Indeed, since Khrushchev had been bluffing about the production rates of Soviet ICBMs, there was possibly a "missile gap in reverse," and an all-out war would not see many nuclear warheads reaching North America (although Soviet deployments of the shorter range SS-4 and SS-5 missiles could certainly have reached and destroyed much of Western Europe).[19] The total failure of the Bay of Pigs invasion was a more conscious failure of containment than Castro's rise to power, in that everyone was by then aware of Castro's political leanings. It failed predominantly because of the weakness of the anti-Castro forces the United States was backing and the flaws in their conventional military situation.

Much more plausibly tied to the nuclear weapons issue was *the Cuban missile crisis* of October 1962.[20] For reasons that remain obscure, Khrushchev tried to sneak Soviet medium range nuclear missiles into bases in Cuba after having assured Kennedy that no such deployments were being contemplated. The ensuing crisis saw the United States threatening both conventional and nuclear war to force the Soviets to withdraw those weapons.

There are many interesting problems and paradoxes about how to interpret the Cuban missile crisis. First, it was not strictly a round in the contests of containment, since the issue was not the political future of Cuba but rather its use for deployments of nuclear weapons. Khrushchev, afterwards rationalizing his venturesome deployment and ignominious retreat, argued that he had extracted from Kennedy an assurance that Cuba would not again be invaded.[21] This would amount to "containment" of American power, an interpretation by which the Soviet missile deployment was merely intended (like the deployments of American medium range nuclear weapons to West Germany or South Korea) to add credibility to extended nuclear deterrence.

By the time of the Cuban missile crisis, the line dividing the communist and noncommunist worlds had been drawn through Cuba, and nothing happened then or later to shift this particular segment of the Iron Curtain. The missile deployment may have established that Moscow valued Cuba as much as the United States valued South Korea; the relative strengths of both sides' nuclear forces in the crisis were less important than both powers' willingness to risk nuclear war in defense of that containment line.

A failure of Western containment is only at issue here if the Soviet missile deployment is seen as being intended to facilitate the spread of communist regimes beyond Cuba. Perhaps Khrushchev was also trying to humiliate Kennedy and the United States, so as to impress Latin Americans and others with the increase in Soviet comparative power, and hence, to open up new corners of the world to Soviet influence and intimidation. It is also plausible that the Soviet dictator was instead fearful that "the missile gap in reverse" had restored U.S. nuclear power so much that he was trying to convert his SS-4 missiles into the functional equivalent of ICBMs by moving them forward to where they could hit targets in the United States instead of Western Europe. Before the first successful tests of U.S. ICBM and submarine-based SLBM missiles, the Eisenhower administration had similarly moved some intermediate-range nuclear missiles to bases in England, Italy, and Turkey as a "quick-fix" to plug a possible missile gap. In this view of Khrushchev's 1962 deployment, the background of strategic power had hardly slipped from the standpoint of the United States.

The next major failure of containment came with the culmination of the wars that had raged in Indochina since 1945: *the 1975 fall of South Vietnam, Cambodia, and Laos to communist rule*. It is very difficult to explain the American defeat here, any more than the French defeat earlier at Dien Bien Phu, as the result of growth in Soviet nuclear power. The very nature of the terrain and tactics chosen suggests that the Marxists were at all points avoiding the nuclear issue, utilizing the "nickle and dime" "salami tactics" of guerrilla warfare to preclude the West from drawing some line which might bring nuclear escalatory threats into play. Although one sees an occasional Western speculation about applications of nuclear weaponry to reverse the outcome of the wars in Indochina, such speculations fail less because of an awareness that the other side might have retaliated than because there is little reason to feel that nuclear weapons had any utility in the conflict.

The places that have figured most prominently in threats of nuclear escalation since the 1950s — West Germany, Korea since 1952, and Quemoy and Matsu — have not seen failures of containment. The places where containment has failed have been much further removed from nuclear threats, either because they were not worth as much to the two sides or because they did not lend themselves even to ordinary conventional battle.

At the extreme, one wonders what would have happened in Vietnam if the Soviet Union had never acquired nuclear weapons. Would the United States have been able to contain the advance of Marxist rule into South Vietnam if it held a nuclear monopoly, any more than it was able to stop

Mao from taking over all of China? Would it have been willing enough and committed enough to make the necessary sacrifices?

The real breakdown of containment in Vietnam might be traced more to something that had already begun showing itself in the fall of China: A doubt among many Americans about whether we were supporting a better kind of person in Diem (or in Chiang Kai-shek) as opposed to Ho Chi Minh (or Mao), and whether the United States really had something to offer the less developed world. When the comparison is made between Eastern and Western Europe, where the line of containment was originally defined, the moral bases of American self-confidence are reinforced. When the comparison is made in the guerrilla-prone Third World countries, these bases are eroded. It is here that Americans begin speculating that "economic democracy," a fairer division of land, resources, and income, might be more important than "political democracy," with free elections, a free press and individual freedoms.

Whatever sympathies many Americans might have had for Mao were reduced by the Chinese Communist's public affiliation with Moscow, and by the blatant North Korean aggression, surely sanctioned by Moscow, followed by Chinese entry into the Korean War. Yet the political and economic disappointments of the decolonization process around the globe in the following two decades produced further doubts and a weakening of what had once been an American consensus about the goals of foreign policy, and with it came a real weakening of containment.

It is thus no accident that the places where nuclear weapons are brandished the least have been the places where containment has been most under communist attack. In part, this has been the result simply of a sound strategy of the communist central command, intent on avoiding nuclear punishment in any Western escalatory retaliation. In larger part, it is because the places to which we are the least willing to commit our nuclear retaliatory capacities—whether we are in state of superiority, parity, or inferiority (or perhaps even when we had a monopoly)—are the places where we are generally the most confused about American purposes in the world.

In the immediate wake of the collapse in Vietnam, the next two memorable failures of containment came in *Mozambique* and *Angola*. The U.S. Congress seemed determined to forbid any active participation by U.S. forces, even clandestine forces, in resisting the imposition of Marxist regimes in these former Portuguese colonies. Was this determination a result of senators and representatives counting Soviet missile warheads? Or was it because of the count of young American soldiers who had been killed and wounded in Vietnam, and the feeling that we had been backing "the wrong side" for too long in Portuguese efforts to hold on to these colonies?

Another break in the barrier of containment in the same period occurred in *Ethiopia*, where after the fall of Emperor Haile Selassie, a junta of army officers (most of whom had been trained in the United States) declared a Marxist regime and joined in a mutual embrace with the Soviet bloc, which brought the same Soviet military aid and Cuban troops into operation that had turned the tide in Angola. Again the missile rattling was virtually nil. Again the American commitment was minimal, with many Americans seeing the old regime as bad for the Africans involved, and viewing the "socialism" and "economic democracy" of the new regime as preferable to anything that could be extracted from the American model.

Someone seeking a more complete list of failures of containment would of course have earlier listed *Egypt, Syria*, and *Somalia*, along with *Algeria* and *Libya*, each of which was once written off as "in the Soviet camp." For a time, such worries were interestingly rebutted and complicated by a pattern in which the Soviets were first embraced, then later expelled. Thus, while the first signs of a pro-Moscow leaning in a regime like Nasser's would once have brought alarmed visions of a failure of containment, by the middle of the 1960s the general analysis became more optimistically cynical about whether Soviet-style regimes could really be imposed in Africa. "African countries can't be bought, they can only be rented," was the waggish summary, perhaps intended to be a deprecating comment about the ideological fidelity of African leaders, but actually amounting to a compliment on the ability of the region to fend for itself and avoid becoming a pawn of either of the superpowers.

Egypt thus was once viewed as a failure of containment, a judgment largely forgotten today; the same worries were voiced for Algeria. Somalia was written off as a Soviet military base and satellite, until Moscow suddenly switched its allegiances in the seemingly intractable conflict between Ethiopia and Somalia about the future of the Ogaden region. It is possible, of course, that today's Ethiopia (if not Angola and Mozambique) violates the facile generalization that African countries will never become duplicates of Bulgaria or Cuba—that perhaps these countries really are failures of containment. Yet the basic proposition remains: containment did not fail because Americans or Russians (or Ethiopians or Angolans) were regularly comparing the totals of Soviet and U.S. nuclear missile warheads. It failed because the regions involved were geographically as far removed as possible from any direct shadow of nuclear warfare.

The next failure of containment occurs in *Central America*, with the fall of the pro-American Somozas in Nicaragua and the victorious opposition becoming a one-party Marxist regime. Anyone trying to explain the path of events in Nicaragua, and up the domino chain in El Salvador or elsewhere in Central America and the Caribbean, would hardly rely on the comparison of American and Soviet strategic power rather than local applications of conventional and guerrilla forces. If the United States had shifted many of its missiles from land-based silos to additional SLBM submarines in the 1970s as a way of heading off vulnerability of such missiles to Soviet ICBMs, or if the United States had replaced MIRVed missiles with some early version of "Midgetman," could anyone have argued that these actions by themselves would have preserved the chances of political democracy in Nicaragua, El Salvador, or Ethiopia?

The events in *Grenada*, with U.S. military intervention restoring chances for a free-election system, similarly illustrate how containment in either direction may not necessarily depend on the missile balance. The arrival of a Marxist regime on the island could have been seen as a containment failure from the standpoint of the West, and some might argue that it was a result of increases in Soviet strategic power. Yet the American intervention shows how little the augmentation of Soviet missile power can affect events when the territory involved is not plausibly crucial to Moscow, when no means have been found to deploy nuclear weapons to that territory, and when (as a result) nuclear escalation is not plausible. Castro and his Soviet partners failed to contain Western influence in Grenada. It is hardly plausible that in their private discussions, they are lightly shrugging off the precedent of its loss.

One more example of Soviet expansionism, challenging the containment principle, would of course be *Afghanistan*. Yet Afghanistan might instead be seen as a failure of another Kennan formula, developed as an alternative when he became dissatisfied with how the barriers of containment had taken shape across Europe: that of "disengagement."[22] Along with Austria and Yugoslavia, and Sweden and Finland together, Afghanistan might have been a neutral buffer zone between the Soviet bloc and the Western alliance countries.

Yet as Kennan recognized, such a "disengagement" buffer is a success only when it has strength and viability of its own, when it does not instead become a "power vacuum." At various times the West has feared that Yugoslavia might become such a vacuum instead of a buffer. A neutralized, disarmed, unified Germany, as proposed by Kennan, might similarly become such a power vacuum, tempting each side to intervene in order to preempt the other's political and military moves. Afghanistan apparently became such a vacuum in the late 1970s, at least in Moscow's view; and what had been tolerated and left alone, as a noncommunist neighbor of the U.S.S.R., was tolerated no longer.

The important point is that the United States had never made any alliance commitments, conventional or nuclear, to Afghanistan. Such an extension of nuclear deterrence had been proffered at various times to Iran and Pakistan, but not to Afghanistan. The Soviets have intervened militarily in Afghanistan, but not in Iran, despite all the tumult and upheaval since the fall of the shah.

## A FINAL IRONY

With the single slight exception of Grenada, we have listed our breaks in containment entirely by a pessimistic measure for the West. Yet the accounting of whether containment is working or failing may be somewhat more two-sided than this. Offensives have moved across the 1948 demarcation line in both directions, involving different tactics and different sectors of the line, and always related only in very complicated ways to the balance of nuclear arms.

We noted earlier that such Western defeats as Vietnam may have stemmed from American self-doubt about whether we had any good cause to defend in the poorer LDCs, and such self-doubt will now hamper us also in the contests erupting in Central America. There are other corners of the world where Americans will have less self-doubt, where eruptions of political turmoil provide an avenue to commitment to resisting and opposing Moscow.

The clearest cases for commitment emerge in what Kennan's formula had resigned us to leaving under Soviet control: the countries of *Eastern Europe*. Many Americans may now shrug off the harshness of a Marxist regime in Vietnam by stressing economic factors: "the people may not be able to read free newspapers, but at least they are not starving anymore." When the discussion shifts instead to Poland and the restlessness exemplified by Solidarity, however, the common-sense summation comes out quite differently, something more like "the people lost their freedom, and haven't gained anything on the economic side either."

The agitation Americans have felt about violations of the Helsinki accords on human rights, and about repression of the Solidarity movement or dissidents within the Soviet Union itself, suggest that we are hardly content with containment. The Soviet leadership must therefore feel itself as much on the defensive as on the offensive in Eastern Europe and even at home, in fear of Western influences transmitted by blue jeans, movies, and in a hundred other ways, and in fear of signal events like the election of a Polish Pope or the awarding of the Nobel Peace Prize to a dissident. Moscow has to worry that containment will not work any better in its sphere than it has worked to shield American interests in Central America, and that the final Soviet and American missile totals will not make a very great difference.

It is important to note that Western successes in getting around containment might approach the "heart" of Soviet interests. Could the Soviet Union really tolerate the loss of Poland, East Germany, or Hungary to any kind of internal agitation without responding with massive military intervention as in East Berlin in 1953, Hungary in 1956, or Czechoslovakia in 1968, even brandishing its nuclear weapons in the process? Some American government spokesmen are fond of noting how close El Salvador is to the United States geographically, "closer to Texas than Texas is to Washington," but Poland is even closer to the U.S.S.R. geographically, and much more important economically, socially, and politically.

Kennan's containment doctrine was criticized in 1947 by Republican opponents of the Truman administration and by others as too unambitious, resigning Americans to continuing communist control over all of Eastern Europe against the wishes of those countries' peoples. Even in the U.S.S.R. there was no reason to believe that most Russians would have voted communist if they had had a choice of any other political alternative; many of them welcomed Hitler's armies even as invaders in 1941.

Defenders of containment could rebut such criticism by referring to places where Kennan outlines a prediction, not just a hope, that a Marxist regime will be disestablished by containment, kept from realizing and fulfilling its "historical–scientific" mission to spread revolution and communist political arrangements.[23] We are now contemplating some four decades of further evolution of the Soviet role in the world since Kennan's analysis. Has the disillusionment in Moscow that Kennan foresaw actually occurred? Has any amount of such disillusionment caused the grip of the Communist party on the Soviet bloc to slip?

There are indeed widespread signs of malaise and self-doubt in the Soviet system, even if it is not clear that containment has been causing them. From the perspective of many an alarmed Western analyst, Soviet power today is not really contained: the barriers seem to be crumbling as Soviet naval squadrons reach into all the oceans and Soviet influence grows in Africa and Central America. Yet the Soviet Union is hardly viewed from the Third World as the model of an improved life for the future, and it is decidedly not viewed as such in Eastern Europe. The leadership and rank-and-file in the U.S.S.R. are becoming painfully aware of this.

Perhaps Solidarity, together with dissidence within the Soviet Union, is indeed what George Kennan forecast and hoped for as the ultimate results of a negation of Soviet expansionism, his answer on whether we would always have to be content with nothing more than fencing in Marxist totalitarianism. Yet the problem remains as it has been ever since 1949. With Soviet nuclear weapons in existence capable of destroying New York and Washington, how far can we let the challenge to the Soviet empire go before endangering our own interests?

We have thus arrived at the second paradox in Kennan's failure to attach much significance to the prospect of that initial instance of nuclear proliferation, Moscow's acquisition of nuclear weapons. It is not clear how sanguine Kennan or anyone else looking ahead to Soviet atomic bombs could have been about containment's success in debunking the canons of Marxist ideological cant, stripping the Communist party of its confidence in its world role, denuding the Soviet population of whatever faith it had in the Party, and provoking internal ferment analogous to the toppling of the shah in Iran. How would the world react today to riots in the streets of Moscow, comparable to what Solidarity organized in Warsaw? Is it not again an unfortunate but inexorable consequence of the existence of nuclear missiles that we would have to be more worried than cheered by such developments? Just as an army advancing to liberate Moscow might remove the last restraints keeping a Soviet leadership from devastating the world, so might a process of internal revolution or turmoil portending the toppling (and future trial) of the Communist party leadership.

Kennan may thus have been too ambitious in suggesting the possibility of a de-communization of the Soviet Union. In the nuclear duopoly that was barely two years away, such a political change within the Soviet world could have been just as dangerous as a liberation of the Russian people by outside military forces. We may thus have been reading too much into Kennan by arguing that his "settling for containment" reflected an advanced perception that Soviet nuclear forces would soon come into being; his "hopeful" suggestions of another way out of the confrontation might then be faulted for not considering nuclear weapons nearly enough.

The world as yet sees no signs of the equivalent of a Solidarity movement in Moscow. We might think we would welcome such a development as a decisive break in Soviet efforts to "contain" Western liberal influences. Yet when we contemplate the state of the world's nuclear arsenals and the problems of avoiding nuclear war, we have to have some second thoughts.

## NOTES

1. The U.S. commitment to "unconditional surrender" is discussed in Anne Armstrong, *Unconditional Surrender* (New Brunswick, New Jersey: Rutgers University Press, 1961).
2. For a sympathetic analysis of Kennan on these points, see John Gaddis, *Strategies of Containment* (New York: Oxford University Press, 1968), pp. 25–54.
3. George F. Kennan, *Memoirs: 1925–1950* (Boston: Little Brown, 1967), pp. 354–367.
4. For perhaps the most widely read of the interpretations viewing the "X" article as advocating more of a commitment than the traditional balance of power, see Walter Lippmann, *The Cold War: A Study in U.S. Foreign Policy* (New York, 1947). See also Charles Gati, "What Containment Meant," *Foreign Policy* 7 (Summer, 1972): 22–40.
5. George F. Kennan, *Memoirs: 1925–1950*, pp. 296, 311, 437; *Memoirs: 1950–1963* (New York: Pantheon, 1972), pp. 244–246.
6. Kennan, *Memoirs: 1925–1950*, pp. 358–359.
7. The text of NSC-68 can be found in *Naval War College Review* 27 (May–June, 1975): 51–108.
8. "X" [George F. Kennan], "The Sources of Soviet Conduct," *Foreign Affairs* 25 (July, 1947): 574–576.

9. On this Soviet counter-leverage, see the analysis in NSC-68, *Naval War College Review, op. cit.*, p. 81.
10. The rapidity of the U.S. demobilization is recounted in Samuel P. Huntington, *The Common Defense* (New York: Columbia University Press, 1961), pp. 33–38.
11. On the "window of vulnerability," see the Scowcroft Report, *Report of the President's Commission on Strategic Forces* (Washington: April 6, 1983).
12. Maxwell Taylor, *The Uncertain Trumpet* (New York: Harper and Row, 1960), John G. Medaris, *War and Peace in the Space Age* (New York: Harper, 1958), James Gavin, *Countdown for Decision* (New York: Putnam, 1960).
13. Bernard Brodie (ed.), *The Absolute Weapon* (New York: Harcourt Brace, 1946), p. 75.
14. NSC-68, in *Naval War College Review, op. cit.*, pp. 83.
15. William W. Kaufmann (ed.), *Military Policy and National Security* (Princeton, Princeton University Press, 1956), pp. 24–25.
16. Henry A. Kissinger, *Nuclear Weapons and Foreign Policy* (New York: Harper Bros., 1957), pp. 154–155.
17. An argument of this sort is presented by Paul Nitze, *Is SALT II a Fair Deal for the United States?* (Washington: Committee on the Present Danger, 1979).
18. On Castro's rise to power, and the first years of his regime, see Ernst Halperin, *Fidel Castro's Road to Power* (Cambridge, Mass., M.I.T. Center for International Studies, 1970).
19. The assessment of the strategic nuclear confrontation in the first years of the Kennedy administration is discussed in Desmond Ball, *Politics and Force Levels* (Berkeley: University of California Press, 1980).
20. On the Cuban missile crisis, see Elie Abel, *The Missile Crisis* (New York: Lippincott, 1966), Albert and Roberta Wohlstetter, *Containing the Risks in Cuba* (London: I.S.S. Adelphi Paper No. 19, 1965), and Arnold L. Horelick and Myron Rush, *Strategic Power and Soviet Foreign Policy* (Chicago: University of Chicago Press, 1965).
21. Nikita Khrushchev, *Khrushchev Remembers* (Boston, Little Brown, 1970), pp. 500–505.
22. For an overview of various proposals for disengagement, including those of George Kennan's BBC Reith Lectures, see Eugene Hinterhoff, *Disengagement* (London: Stevens and Sons, 1959).
23. Kennan, "Sources of Soviet Conduct," pp. 580–582.

# 6 ALLIANCES FOR CONTAINMENT*

*Terry L. Deibel*

Few informed observers would argue against the proposition that alliances, and security relationships in general, have been a major tool of American foreign policy since World War II. In the 40 years since that conflict ended, the United States has been through at least three major periods of alliance formation, and today it remains committed to literally dozens of nations around the globe. Right now, in fact, the United States is at the crest of a major commitment expansion which began in the middle of the Carter administration and has continued and accelerated under Ronald Reagan.

Nevertheless, it is also quite clear that Americans find something unnatural and even disturbing about alliances. As a nation founded upon principles of *laissez faire* economics, democratic politics, and individualist ethics, the United States tends to approach alliance relationships in an oddly unilateralist mode. Fortunate to have spent most of its national life protected by either its geo-technological isolation or an overwhelming preponderance of power within the international system, the United States has grown accustomed to seeking its security in freedom of action rather than in the restraints and promises of commitment. Whole alliance systems (including SEATO and CENTO) have come and gone since World War II, and even the strongest relationships (like NATO) seem continually prone to tension and crisis.

To raise the issue of alliances as instruments of containment in this context is to pose whole congeries of interesting yet ambiguous questions. Many questions concern what is actually meant by *containment*. If it simply means the goal of preventing direct expansion of the Soviet state, then one could confidently argue for the success of American alliances, since no allied state has ever been attacked by, let alone fallen to, Soviet arms;

---

*Dr. Deibel wrote this essay while on sabbatical from the faculty of the National War College as a Resident Associate at the Carnegie Endowment for International Peace. Its support of this project is gratefully acknowledged.

yet one can prove neither the success of a negative proposition like deterrence nor the causal relationship of alliance ties to that success. If, on the
other hand, containment means preventing the creation of Soviet-allied
and Soviet-armed regimes or the spread of Moscow's influence, then one
has to acknowledge that the Rio Treaty did not stop the emergence of
Castro's Cuba or the Sandinistas' Nicaragua, nor did SEATO preclude
communist control of its protocolary states in Indochina; and contrary-
wise, withdrawal of formal alliance protection from Taiwan in 1980 has
not — at least not yet — led to its absorption by the communist world.
Clearly, the record of alliances as devices for containment is mixed and
incomplete, and the analyst has to be clear about which sort of containment they are to serve.

Then there is the question of what is meant by *alliances*. In its nar-
rowest sense, the term can be taken to mean only those relationships in
which there is a treaty obligation of protection against attack. But to so
limit the definition would leave out virtually all security commitments
formed in recent years. Excluding informal allies would make little sense
in any case, since the language even of American alliance treaties leaves
the United States with a great deal of freedom of action.[1] If alliances are
defined in their broadest sense, however, one would almost need to
include any country with which the United States has a defense relationship, clearly a scope too broad for meaningful evaluation.

This writer hopes to make his way through these analytical thickets in
three stages. The first will be a look at what George F. Kennan meant by
the term and what role the father of containment envisioned for alliances
and security commitments. Second will be a survey of what the United
States has actually done in its commitment policy over the past 40 years,
comparing American policy with the kind of alliances for which Kennan's
or other visions of containment called. And last will be some comments
about alternative commitment policies which might fulfill the purposes of
containment in the years ahead.

## ALLIANCES AND THE THEORY OF CONTAINMENT

Although containment's founder never set forth in one place the full
scope of his strategic vision and may well have altered his views over the
years, scholars who have studied Kennan's writings maintain that his
view of the concept was internally cohesive and has been broadly consistent over time. As reconstructed by John Lewis Gaddis,[2] Kennan's containment had three elements or stages. First (and of greatest importance
by far), Kennan argued for an active U.S. policy to maintain the world
balance of power in the special circumstances following World War II.
That meant preventing the Soviets from acquiring control of centers of

world industrial capacity (other than the Soviet Union and the United States), all of which had been greatly weakened by the war: the industrial heart of Europe, Japan, and the U.K. Second, containment was intended to limit Soviet influence outside the regions Moscow already controlled, which in the late 1940s pointed to a policy aimed at dividing and weakening the world communist movement. Finally, Kennan hoped that over time the Soviet view of international politics could be modified to permit a negotiated settlement with the West and a *modus vivendi* between the superpowers, vastly reducing cold war tensions and establishing a global balance which could endure without constant and intensive American involvement.

What Kennan thought of alliances as a tool to implement his strategic vision is less clear and not so easily explained, since he rarely spoke directly to the issue. His early thought was, however, free of many features which predisposed others to oppose commitments. For example, in a period when isolationism was still a strong current of American thought, Kennan was urging his countrymen to take the kind of active role in world politics that formation and maintainance of alliance systems would require. At a time when great hopes were placed in the United Nations as an alternative to alliances, Kennan had grave doubts about an organization which he thought was based on the illusion that a universal legal scheme could do away with power realities.[3] And if others might oppose American ties to unsavory regimes which fell short of American standards of good government, Kennan was realist enough to argue that the United States should not make the domestic systems of other states a determinant of its foreign relations.[4]

In fact, far from precluding security commitments, there were aspects of Kennan's views on U.S. foreign policy in the late 1940s which would almost seem to have required a role for alliances. Always concerned that the United States would overextend itself, the founder of containment said on more than one occasion that America needed allies to share the burden of free world leadership; he also argued that a strong American defense posture was necessary to maintain allied confidence.[5] In a September 1946 lecture to the first National War College class, he explicitly included alliances among "Measures Short of War" that the new U.S. policy would need.[6] Perhaps most significant, the classic mechanism for executing containment, as stated in the famous "X" article, was "the adroit and vigilant application of counterforce at a series of constantly shifting geographical and political points," a task that would seem to have demanded a rather extensive network of allies and bases.[7]

In the end, though, the major thrust of containment à la Kennan was against alliances as a primary tool of American national security policy. On one level, this was due to Kennan's own character and philosophical cast of mind. As his refusal to write out a comprehensive statement of containment indicates, Kennan preferred a "particularist" rather than a "universalist" approach to foreign policy;[8] he was extremely doubtful of "the ability of men to define hypothetically in any useful way, by means of general and legal phraseology, future situations which no one could really imagine or envisage."

> I had little confidence in the value of written treaties of alliance generally. I had seen too many instances in which they had been forgotten, or disregarded, or found to be irrelevant, or distorted for ulterior purposes when the chips were down.[9]

Then, too, the author of containment was a thoroughgoing elitist who imputed as little moral as political value to areas outside the five major centers of industrial power.[10] Kennan worried that, if the United States started creating a structure of anti-Russian alliances, there would be "no logical stopping point until that system has circled the globe and has embraced all the non-communist countries of Europe, Asia, and Africa."[11] Alliances, in other words, would wind up associating America with the *hoi polloi* of the world, areas and peoples that Kennan really did not believe counted.[12]

But there were more substantive reasons why Kennan was unenthusiastic about security commitments as instruments of containment. At its core, Kennan's reasoning put a great premium on flexibility; the United States, he believed, had to be able to shift its counterpressure to any region where the Soviet Union might need to be contained. He argued therefore for small mobile American military forces which, despite their need for basing at various points around the world, should remain free to strike wherever needed.[13] Added to this was Kennan's affinity for a "strong-point" rather than a "perimeter" defense.[14] Increasingly impressed over his lifetime with the scarcity of American resources, Kennan argued that the United States must at all costs avoid spreading itself too thinly around the world and remain able to concentrate its defensive power on certain key points that were essential to protecting its vital interests. An extensive system of alliances might "lock in" the United States and deprive it of the maneuverability needed to meet the Soviet challenge wherever it occurred.

But Kennan also opposed alliances because he deplored their emphasis on a single *means* of containment. Never believing that the threat from the U.S.S.R. was primarily one of armed force,[15] he feared that the use of alliances would militarize U.S. relationships with much of the world, thereby diverting allies' energies from the tasks of political and economic reconstruction so necessary for resistance to the *real* threats of ideological subversion and political infiltration. Having a strong proprietary interest in the Marshall Plan (whose implementation was the reason for his being asked to create and head the State Department's Policy Planning Council), Kennan feared that an emphasis on military means would absorb U.S. resources that should be used to back economic and political reconstruction.

Finally, Kennan tended to downplay the role of alliances in a successful containment strategy because of his concern about how the existence of an extensive network of American security commitments might shape the future of the international system and the American role in it. For Kennan, the whole point of American postwar policy was to restore those areas important to the balance of power to conditions of economic, social, and political health that would enable them to resist Soviet pressure on their own; his vision for the future was of a world of independent power centers, a pluralistic world rather than one divided between the superpowers. In alliances, by contrast, Kennan saw a formula for keeping great nations in tutelage under the United States.[16] Ultimately, he feared that a militarized policy would derail the third stage of containment, that holding American military power "tightly at every point to the borders of the Soviet orbit" would make impossible the negotiations that might lead away from confrontation and into a *modus vivendi* with a mellowed Soviet leadership.

> I . . . wanted to hold the door open to permit the eventual emergence of large areas . . . that would be in the military sense uncommitted, as between the two worlds. In each case, I was prepared to see us withdraw our military forces if Soviet power would be equivalently withdrawn and if we could look forward to the rise, in the areas thus thrown open, of political authority independent of Soviet domination.[17]

## ALLIANCES AND THE PRACTICE OF CONTAINMENT

Reasoning on the basis of his overall approach to world affairs and American foreign relations, then, one is left with the ironic conclusion that the author of containment disapproved of one of the primary instruments used to implement his policy. Interestingly, Kennan's difficulties with alliances grew out of fundamental differences of vision similar to those in today's debate over containment and its future. On the one side of this debate are those who see the Soviet Union as a uniquely expansionist state, driven by ideology to conquer the world for communism, a nation that understands only force and with which no settlement will ever be possible; on the other are those who consider the Soviet leadership to be motivated by traditional security concerns, cautious and defensive in nature, and willing to respond to positive and negative inducements in ways that permit traditional diplomacy to operate. As Table 6.1 indi-

Table 6.1. Two Schools of Containment

| | | |
|---|---|---|
| 1. *What drives Soviet expansion?* | | |
| | Ideology | Historical insecurity, conspiratorial internal rule |
| 2. *What is to be contained?* | | |
| | International communism | Soviet state power |
| 3. *What should be the condition of the balance of power?* | | |
| | U.S. superiority is necessary | Parity is acceptable |
| 4. *What areas are vital to the balance?* | | |
| | All areas of world | Industrial areas only |
| 5. *Is a differentiated policy possible?* | | |
| | Self-confidence and psychological credibility demand the United States resist even marginal changes in balance of power | Since its resources are limited, the United States must differentiate between peripheral and vital interests |
| 6. *What is the primary means of containment?* | | |
| | Military | Political/economic |
| 7. *How persistent is Soviet expansionist behavior?* | | |
| | Hitlerian, total | Abnormal, but limited |
| 8. *Does USSR have significant weaknesses, and how should they affect U.S. policy?* | | |
| | Definitely; should be exploited to weaken and destabilize the Soviet regime | Probably; can be used through negotiations policy to benefit stability |
| 9. *To what kind of Soviet behavior should U.S. policy be linked?* | | |
| | To internal liberalization | To external policies |
| 10. *Is a settlement possible?* | | |
| | Doubtful; negotiations are a trap for the United States | Negotiations can work if properly prepared |

cates,[18] people in one school tend to see military force as the pre-eminent means of containment and argue that virtually all areas of the world are vital to the balance of power, whereas those in the other school of thought favor economic and political means of containment and contend that the United States must differentiate between peripheral and vital interests, lest it overextend itself in a useless effort to stop the spread of communism everywhere. Finally, where the first school of thought would link American policy to internal liberalization in the U.S.S.R. and would exploit any indication of Soviet weakness to destabilize the Kremlin, the latter dismisses such policies as futile and dangerous, arguing instead that Soviet weaknesses provide opportunities for meaningful, if limited, negotiations which can be exploited by linking U.S. policy to Soviet international behavior.

George Kennan, of course, was and remains very much of the second school and has participated in the public debate on containment during the past 40 years from that perspective. He would argue, however, that containment's implementation has often been (as it is today) in the hands of officials of the first school, who have transformed alliances from temporary expedients into fixed elements in the diplomatic firmament: ". . . what was conceived as an instrument became, little by little, an end in itself."[19] In that judgment, Kennan is broadly accurate, but alliances are actually an adaptable instrument of policy that can be used to support either view of containment. In fact, one can identify at least three major periods of alliance creation in American diplomacy since World War II, distinguishing each according to the motives which impelled policymakers at the time, the kinds of nations involved, and the characteristics of the resulting relationships. Although Kennan opposed each group of alliances more strenuously than the last, it is worth examining these alliances in some detail to see which concept of containment they were intended to further and what can be said of their success.

## THE TRUMAN/ACHESON ALLIANCES

Most of the first postwar system of American alliances should have had some chance of receiving Kennan's approval.[20] He had always maintained that to be effective, alliances must reflect a certain "solidarity with other like-minded nations" based on a "real community of interest and outlook."[21] These conditions were certainly fulfilled by the North Atlantic Treaty of 1949 and the Japan and ANZUS treaties of 1951. Moreover, the Truman/Acheson alliances were specifically designed to achieve Kennan's first stage of containment: the protection of non-communist centers of world industrial capacity. They were, in fact, the considered and deliberate products of the broader shifts in American foreign policy that were taking place as the nation came to grips with Soviet hostility and adjusted its occupation policies in Germany and Japan accordingly.

The North Atlantic Treaty, for example, resulted from a European effort to involve the United States in the containment of a rehabilitated Germany when it became clear that that nation would have to be rebuilt quickly if Europe was to resist Soviet pressures.[22] In 1949, officials of the

Truman administration were willing to give an American guarantee of European security, not primarily because they considered it necessary for deterrent purposes, but because of its psychological value in maintaining the self-confidence Europe needed to continue with its economic and political rehabilitation. Kennan grudgingly agreed with this rationale but still could not bring himself to approve the treaty, in spite of his belief that the Europeans were America's "real and natural allies."[23] His main objections were the familiar ones that the alliance would militarize the relationship with Europe, diverting local resources from economic reconstruction, and that it would freeze East–West divisions, preventing the kind of Soviet–American settlement he hoped for. In fact, Kennan argued that the European community should be strictly continental in scope, so that the admission of Eastern European states would be easier, and that Greece and Turkey should be kept out of NATO, so that the U.S.S.R. would not feel encircled by the alliance. The only compact he favored the United States joining was a "world-trading, maritime bloc" including the Canadians, the British and certain Commonwealth, Iberian and Scandinavian countries, based on a single currency and destined for eventual federation.[24] This association apparently would have had no military character at all.

In the end, of course, Kennan's fears of NATO's long-term development turned out to be reasonably accurate. When, in 1950, North Korea's attack on South Korea seemed to demonstrate that the Soviets really might begin a third world war, NATO was transformed from a political, confidence-building measure into an alliance-in-being with substantial numbers of U.S. troops and an organization headed by an American military commander. Kennan believed there was no need for NATO as a military deterrent; he remained certain that the Russians "had no idea of using regular military strength against us."[25] And when, in 1954, the European Defense Community failed and Britain moved to rearm West Germany as a member of NATO, Kennan strongly objected for the same reasons.[26]

In the Far East, the alliances with Japan, the Philippines, Australia and New Zealand were the results of similar megatrends in American policy. Prior to the Korean conflict, the United States was moving deliberately towards a Japanese peace treaty that would (as in the case of Germany) bring that nation into the Western camp. But the Truman administration, oriented to a Europe-first strategy and convinced that European commitments were all it could afford to support, was not interested in a NATO-like pact for the Pacific until the North Korean attack seemed to demonstrate the urgency of security guarantees.[27] In early 1951 when John Foster Dulles canvassed opinion in the region on an early and lenient Japanese peace treaty, he found that the Philippines, Australia and

New Zealand demanded U.S. commitments as protection against a re-armed Japan.[28] Indeed, those nations refused to enter into a multilateral pact with their recent enemy, with the result that the three treaties still in force were signed separately in mid-1951.[29]

In 1948, George Kennan had written that Japan and the Philippines were essential "cornerstones of a Pacific security system,"[30] but by 1951 he had found reasons to dissent from all three Pacific treaties. In his book *Memoirs: 1950–1963*, Kennan argues that the evident determination of the United States to keep its military forces in Japan and bring that nation into the Western alliance system was "among the various considerations that might have impelled Stalin to authorize" the North Korean attack.[31] Before the war in Korea, he had hoped that the United States "would eventually be able to arrive at some general understanding with the Russians, relating to the security of the northwestern Pacific area," which would have made permanent stationing of U.S. troops in Japan "unnecessary."[32] Once the Korean War was underway, Kennan urged the United States to offer the Russians demilitarization and neutralization of both Japan and Korea as *quid pro quo* for a peace settlement. He felt that it would be "unnatural" for the United States to hold the line permanently in Korea, and that mutual demilitarization of Northeast Asia could be enforced by the kind of distant striking power he advocated for the American military.[33]

Those on the opposite side of today's containment debate, it can be safely assumed, would have considered Kennan's hopes for reconciliation unrealistic and his dismissal of the military threat naive and dangerous. Doubtless, they would have applauded both the formation of the Atlantic and Pacific alliances and the transformation of NATO into a deterrent force-in-being, regretting only that the Alliance never in subsequent years armed itself sufficiently. And in fact, by the mid-1970s, Kennan himself apparently came to support both the NATO and the Japanese alliances. Although he did not endorse them explicitly, he wrote positively of the two relationships in *The Cloud of Danger*, a book otherwise filled with what his opponents in the debate would consider calls for American retreat. The book's section on Europe, for example, endorses an increase in American conventional capacity in Europe and concludes with the statement that the American stake in European security is "one of the very few really vital interests this country possesses; . . . [I] would rather see us concentrate our efforts [there] . . . than waste them on a thousand peripheral efforts in other parts of the world."[34] In the same book Kennan recommends continued close American ties with the Japanese on the slightly different grounds that Japan's great industrial power is "so tremendous a factor in world affairs" that the United States dare not risk its alienation. "Left to themselves," he warns, "the Japanese . . . would have to give a wholly different value to their relations with their great mainland neighbors; and we could never be sure where these new relationships would find their ending."[35] While these reconsiderations may simply be the result of 20/20 hindsight or the recognition that wrecking established alliances would have quite different effects than not creating them in the first place, they also reflect his original concerns regarding the essential balance of power and a community of interests, thereby suggesting that his original opposition to the NATO and Pacific treaties was more tactical than substantive.

Indeed, after some 35 years' experience with this first group of American alliances, it is difficult not to appreciate their contribution to either vision of containment. Even those who believe that there is no serious Soviet military threat to deter can do little more than dismiss these arrangements as wasteful on the margins; Kennan was wrong in fearing that they would spur military buildups that would impede economic recovery in Europe, Japan, or the ANZUS. Nor have they made it impossible to negotiate with the Russians, for example, about European security. Indeed, one could argue that the strength of NATO during the 1950s and 1960s made possible the 1971 Berlin settlements and the CSCE/Helsinki negotiations, which eventually brought an end to successive cold war crises in Europe — ironically by legitimizing rather than transcending the East–West division of the continent.

At the same time, the positive services of these alliances have not been insignificant. They have provided the framework for defense relationships among the world's leading free countries, helping (as Kennan eventually acknowledged) to protect these major weights in the world balance of power. For those to the right of the debate who believe that the military threat from the East is real, these alliances may well seem to have provided just the aggregation of military force necessary to deter attack. Those who contend that controversies within these alliances (such as the various NATO crises over nuclear forces or the current U.S. rift with New Zealand over port visits) serve only to demonstrate collective weakness are making an argument akin to that of a patient who rejects all medication on the grounds that nothing can provide a total cure. Even less convincing is the argument that disputes on matters other than defense (such as that with Japan over trade) should cause us to act in ways that would jeopardize the security benefits these alliances provide. In short, although one cannot predict with certainty what would have happened had the Truman/Acheson system of alliances not been created, it would seem hard for those on either side of the contemporary debate not to judge them as successful instruments of containment and worth sustaining for the future.

## THE EISENHOWER/DULLES ALLIANCES

It is doubtful that similar statements could be made about the second group of U.S. postwar alliances, those negotiated by Secretary of State Dulles during the Eisenhower years (including the Taiwan and South Korean alliances, SEATO, and CENTO). Though these also were treaty alliances with superficial resemblances to NATO, they joined the United States to countries with whom it hardly shared a great complementarity of interests. Nor were these relatively weak, developing states intrinsically important to the world balance of power as Kennan defined it, although in the perfervid logic of the high cold war, they were made to seem so. Perhaps most important, the Dulles alliances were anything but deliberate manifestations of an overall strategy. For Dulles, some would argue, tactics all but replaced strategy as a guide to policy.[36]

In a sense, of course, one could see the Dulles alliance system as perfecting the containment of the U.S.S.R. at its perimeters that began in the Truman years, an idea quite different than the "strongpoint" defense preferred by Kennan. Through these alliances, Dulles connected NATO with the Pacific defenses he had earlier negotiated, *politically* by tying the developed European and Pacific powers into SEATO and CENTO, and *geographically* by completing the arc of allies from South Korea, Taiwan, and the four Indochinese nations through Pakistan to Iran, Iraq, and Turkey. But Dulles' core strategy was not global alliances, but massive retaliation, the effort to get "more bang for the buck" by substituting central nuclear power for dispersed conventional forces. And the alliances he created appear to have been tactical responses to the shortcomings of that strategy, last-minute, crisis-driven efforts to make credible a deterrent threat that otherwise could hardly be believed.

A Southeast Asian alliance, for example, was first conceived as a prerequisite for U.S. military intervention to save the French position at Dien Bien Phu. Months later, SEATO came to fruition as an American scheme to hold the line against further communist gains in Indochina after the collapse of the entire French effort and the negotiated partition of Vietnam at the 1954 Geneva Conference (the latter an outcome Dulles considered tantamount to appeasement and which he had worked frantically, if unsuccessfully, to forestall).[37] The bilateral alliance with Taiwan was signed during the first Formosa Strait crisis of 1954–1955, which began with a bombardment of Quemoy just a few days before the United States and its allies met in Manila to sign the SEATO pact. Although the Eisenhower administration was deliberately vague as to precisely which of the offshore islands it intended to defend, the treaty's purpose was to dissuade the People's Republic of China from going too far in pressing its military case against the Chiang regime.[38] The alliance with Korea had been signed a year before in a somewhat similar effort to reinsure the precarious armistice which had just ended the Korean war, by making it clear (in a way the Truman administration had conspicuously failed to make clear its position before June 1950) that the United States would come to Korea's defense in case of a second armed attack. And the Baghdad Pact, engineered by the British in 1955 as a way of maintaining their military presence and political influence in the Middle East as Nasser pushed them out of Egypt, was transformed by the United States into CENTO after a 1958 coup in Iraq appeared to create a gaping hole in the "northern tier," allowing Soviet penetration of the region.[39]

Collectively, then, the Dulles alliances represented a codification and re-emphasis of deterrence, draping American protection around Third World states who could hardly be of material help (except perhaps with manpower) should a war actually come.[40] It appears that from time to time the secretary of state harbored rather grandiose thoughts about a macro-alliance, linking all his pacts into a global structure which could maintain an inclusive perimeter defense against Soviet expansion. In Dulles' book, *War or Peace* (1950), he expressed admiration for the idea of a General Protocol under Article 51 of the U.N. Charter, a total insurance policy without territorial limit; and during the debate on the Eisenhower Doctrine he told the Senate Foreign Relations Committee that the United States might "end up with a . . . universal doctrine reflected by multilateral treaties or multilateral [sic] worldwide authority from the Congress."[41] As this last remark indicates, Dulles wanted to enhance the deterrent effect of his system with general congressional authorizations (as he had done with the Formosa Resolution and Eisenhower Doctrine), authority which would also offer escape from the constitutional restrictions which had prevented U.S. military intervention at Dien Bien Phu. But by 1959 the Congress was already becoming wary of such schemes, and in any event, the idea of a single worldwide alliance seems for Dulles to have been more rationalization after the event than a conscious strategy from the beginning.

It is far from difficult, given what we have seen thus far of Kennan's views, to imagine what he thought about the Dulles alliances. They had none of the characteristics that eventually recommended the Truman/Acheson pacts to him; and in the "incurable conflict between the ideal military posture and the goal of winning the political war"[42] against the U.S.S.R., the Dulles pacts had radically exacerbated the pro-military imbalance which he so deplored in Acheson's policy. Kennan spelled out the specifics of his disgust at what he called "the madness of universal involvement" in *The Cloud of Danger*. In the whole region east of Iran (including the Indian subcontinent, Southeast Asia, and the Southeastern Pacific through the Philippines) Kennan could see "no vital interests of the United States anywhere," a condition he thought should preclude U.S. "political involvement, military aid, [and] association as members of regional pacts. . . ."[43] In particular, the United States should renounce its military relationship with Pakistan ("a matter which concerns intimately our relationship with the Soviet Union"), terminate its bases in the Philippines ("the original justification . . . has now been extensively undermined"), reduce U.S. representation on Taiwan to *de facto* status and cancel the defense treaty ("shabby . . . but . . . a step that will surely have to be taken at some point" in the developing relationship with China), and "extract ourselves, as gently and prudently as we can, from our military involvement" in Korea ("one of the two most explosive and dangerous spots" in the world).[44] As he put it in 1976 when he confessed to being "in a sense" an isolationist,

> I do not advocate that we should suddenly rat on NATO and abandon our West European allies. I don't even mean that we should do anything abruptly to curtail our commitments anywhere. To do so would be a new offence [sic] in its own right. But I do feel that we should not accept new commitments, that we should gradually reduce our existing commitments to a minimum even in the Middle East, and get back to a policy of leaving other people alone and expect to be largely left alone by them. We greatly exaggerate the hazards of doing so.[45]

It may well be unfair to impute too much to these views of 1976; they were not too far, after all, from the center of American opinion in those post-Vietnam years, and many of them found resonance in the policies of the new Carter administration. The moderate left of the containment debate today probably would refuse to follow Kennan on Korea after the experience of the Carter troop withdrawal plan of May 1977, would feel that the Clark and Subic bases retain their importance for a minimal American military presence in the Pacific, and would argue that the American relationship to Pakistan must be considered in a new light after the Soviet invasion of Afghanistan. What is clear, however, is the predictive power of Kennan's original criteria for effective alliances. The Truman/Acheson relationships, reflecting a community of interests among like-minded states and supporting key elements of the balance of power, remain and endure. But most of the Dulles alliances are gone, overturned by world events beyond the control of American power or will, or intrinsically unable to demonstrate their cost-effectiveness to the great bulk of the American people.[46]

Can one say, nevertheless, that these alliances were effective instruments of containment while they lasted? Is it possible that the very process of forming them provided some temporary deterrence, or that the local confidence they induced or the framework they provided for American aid made a difference in economic growth and political stability? Here the pattern seems mixed. Korea and Taiwan are obvious economic success stories, and some would argue that even the ill-fated Vietnam conflict provided critical time for the development of reasonably stable and prosperous regimes in places like Thailand, Malaysia and Indonesia. But in the Philippines or Korea, the American relationship may well have simply created the conditions for political stagnation, sowing the seeds of its own destruction. And in Iran, the American embrace was obviously a long-term liability, whatever its short-term contribution to stability. Equal, if yet unconfirmed, doubts can be raised about Pakistan.

## THE CARTER/REAGAN ALLIANCES

Of course, those on the right of the containment debate would undoubtedly argue not only that the Dulles alliances were successful in their time, but also that their demise was a result of the political impact in the United States of views very much like those Kennan espoused, not a result of any unsoundness of conception or lack of American power. The third system of postwar American security commitments was negotiated in large part under the Reagan administration by those of this mindset. Interestingly, these new commitments are not at all mirror images of the kind of commitments Dulles negotiated 30 years ago; if they are creations of the right in the containment debate, they also reflect the vast changes that have taken place in world politics and American power since the 1950s. They are creatures, in other words, not just of Iran, Nicaragua, and Afghanistan, but also of Vietnam, OPEC, and Watergate.

Geographically, like the Dulles pacts, the Carter/Reagan alliances center on the Third World, but in a much more diffuse and far-ranging pattern. After all, the possibility of perimeter defense has long been foreclosed by the reach of Soviet power-projection forces and the Kremlin's success in penetrating the Dulles salient with proxies (like Cuba and the Vietnamese empire), allies (such as Ethiopia, Syria and South Yemen), and even its own forces (in Afghanistan). Thus, the new pattern of U.S. commitments includes some refurbished allies like Thailand, Pakistan, Saudi Arabia, Honduras, and Morocco, as well as new converts like Egypt, Oman, and Somalia. Central America and the Caribbean have a much higher priority now (given Soviet/Cuban penetration), and the Far East enjoys a somewhat lower visibility after the debacle of Vietnam, while the Middle East seems to remain equally critical even in an era of oil glut. Broad congressional authority does not buttress these alliances; although there is a plethora of U.S. statements of support for individual countries, only the Carter Doctrine reminds one of the repealed Formosa and Eisenhower resolutions. Nor are grand multilateral alliances in prospect for rationalizing this "system," which seems every bit as *ad hoc* and crisis-driven in origin as its predecessor. The only remembrances of Dulles' schemes are pale, proxy alliances like ASEAN, the Gulf Cooperation Council, or the Organization of Eastern Caribbean States, which enjoy only U.S. support, not direct American commitment.

Functionally, these new commitments are also very different than those of 30 years ago. In most cases bilateral rather than multilateral, these ties are underpinned by no formal organizational apparatus. Lacking treaties, the new commitments are based more often on arms transfers and military training, economic aid, *ad hoc* diplomatic contact, and facilities construction and/or use. These commitments have to be highly discreet, both on the American side (given public and congressional skittishness about new commitments) and on the foreign side (since visible ties to the United States often seem to have destabilizing effects on Third World regimes). American physical presences in-country are austere, so the military power needed to back these new pledges must often be over-the-horizon or even held back home in the form of mobile conventional forces. In fact, when all these characteristics are added up, one can hardly call these new security partners "allies" in the traditional sense of the term; they are only associates or "coalites," and American freedom of action with regard to them remains at a very high level. They are, in short, far weaker commitments than either of their predecessor systems.

If the Carter/Reagan alliances do not directly protect Kennan's major industrialized centers of the world balance of power, and if one rules out as impractical any perimeter containment of the Soviet Union, then it may be worth a moment to ask what function these commitments do fulfill. Although for most of these coalites direct attack is unlikely, the weaker Carter/Reagan ties might well perform a rudimentary deterrent function, given the superpowers' extreme reluctance to tread on each other's toes. Yet to value them for that function would require a very "un-Kennanesque" and intensely bipolar outlook which Dulles would have recognized as his own: a belief that the balance of power is so finely poised that the United States cannot tolerate the extension of Soviet influence to any of these areas. Even so, there remain the tools of infiltration, subversion, and proxy assault, to which alliances have never been a very good counterweight, particularly in countries as unstable as most of those in this new group of security partners.

Perhaps, however, there are other purposes for these new associations. Two uses suggest themselves. First, the quest for the facilities and access rights ("basing" is out of the question) that would be required by U.S. forces in the event of their deployment to places of vital interest has been a major determinant of American alliance policy since the days of Zbigniew Brzezinski's "security framework" for the "Arc of Crisis."[47] The result has been a series of what might be called "secondary" commitments, offered as *quid pro quo* for basing access, to states that (even less

than Dulles' allies) share Kennan's solidarity of interest and outlook with
the United States. The reason, ostensibly, is so that the United States would
be really able to defend those states of primary interest — a process Barton
Gellman called "the unhappy tendency of our strategic interests to have
interests of their own."[48] The other motivation, while apparent in outline for some time, has only recently become obvious. It is the need,
under the so-called Reagan Doctrine, for relationships solid enough to
provide platforms for the supply of America's own proxy warfare,
whether conducted from Honduras by the contras against Nicaragua,
from Thailand by the Cambodian resistance against Vietnam, or from
Pakistan by the Afghan rebels against the Soviets directly.

Kennan, needless to say, would have deplored all this. He has never
believed in destabilization, except perhaps by the subtle example of the
West measuring up to its own best traditions, a possibility of which he has
long since despaired. And as to the impact of bases, he has argued that
"no great country . . . could sit by and witness with indifference the progressive studding of its own frontiers with the military installations of a
great-power competitor." Yet, as he wrote of American policy,

> Year after year nothing would be omitted to move American air bases and
> missile sites as close as possible to Soviet frontiers. . . . Time after time, as
> in Pakistan or Okinawa, the maintenance and development of military or
> air bases would be stubbornly pursued with no evidence of any effort to
> balance this against the obvious political costs.[49]

Even before the massive Reagan base-agreement "buys" in the Philippines, Spain, Portugal, Greece, and Turkey, Kennan was outraged at the
"tribute" exacted from the United States for such facilities, arguing that
his country should never put itself in the position of paying "huge annual
bribes as a form of hush money" to keep foreign leaders quiet while the
United States retained installations they did not want on their territory.[50]
For both these reasons, Kennan has urged American abandonment of
facilities in Greece and Turkey, as well as those in the Philippines.[51]

## ALLIANCES AND THE FUTURE OF CONTAINMENT

Although Kennan's criticisms may not be surprising, it is remarkable
how little contemporary controversy the Carter/Reagan commitments
seem to have stirred. Perhaps, because they have not come before Congress as formal treaties, there has been no occasion for a great debate like
those over NATO or the Dulles pacts. Or perhaps this set of agreements
has been spared serious questioning because it seems a logical part of the
widely accepted effort to restore American military power. Possibly the
American people are not even aware that extensive commitments have

been made. What criticism there has been seems almost monochromatic, with isolationists on the right joining liberals on the left to deplore the drain such relationships pose for American resources, to doubt these allies' ability to contribute to the common defense, and to worry about the long-run effect on American solvency.[52] Their solution is similar to or even more radical than Kennan's "pruning of unnecessary or marginal involvements and . . . paring down of America's commitments," with only a few on the right arguing for more security ties in the form of an "all-oceans alliance" or standing proxy armies overseas.[53] As there is little questioning of whether alliances of this tentative kind can be effective as instruments of containment, there is still less discussion of what kinds of relationships might be best adapted to the security environment of the future.

Although thorough analysis of such far-reaching questions must await another occasion, it is obvious that few easy answers present themselves. On the one hand, one is tempted to say that the Carter/Reagan alliances are the best one can do, given the world of the 1980s; that the commitments they embody are an unavoidable concomitant of security dealings with the Third World, however marginal their deterrent effect may be; and that their drain on American resources is simply the price one pays to execute the Nixon Doctrine in the hope that one day new coalites will become real additions to the West's deterrent power.[54] On the other hand, there is the nagging sense that so much instability lies between now and then, that surely such a policy will put some facilities and weapons in hostile hands (like Iran's F-14s or Vietnam's Cam Ranh Bay), and that in the meantime (as Walter Lippman once suggested) the effort to contain the Soviets everywhere is forcing the United States into "dubious and unnatural" alliances which impose great strains on the United States' relations with its natural allies of the Truman/Acheson years.[55] Who can believe that the Carter/Reagan alliances will last even as long as the Dulles ones? In fact, it may be that world conditions are proving Kennan right the first time, that until the developing world arrives at a greater degree of economic and political maturity, fixed commitments will have little further utility as instruments of containment. Such, at least, are the dilemmas which history suggests attend the conduct of American alliance policy in a revolutionary era.

## NOTES

1. Terry Deibel, *Commitment in American Foreign Policy* (Washington, D.C.: National Defense University Monograph Series 80-4, 1980).
2. John Lewis Gaddis, *Strategies of Containment* (New York: Oxford University Press, 1982), pp. 36-51.
3. *Ibid.*, p. 26, 29.

4. Barton Gellman, *Contending with Kennan* (New York: Praeger, 1984), p. 78.
5. George F. Kennan, *Memoirs 1925-1950*, Vol. I (Boston: Atlantic Little Brown, 1967), p. 378; Gaddis, *Strategies*, p. 39.
6. Gellman, p. 125.
7. "X" [George F. Kennan], "The Sources of Soviet Conduct," *Foreign Affairs* 25 (July 1947), p. 576.
8. Gaddis, *Strategies*, pp. 27-28.
9. Kennan, *Memoirs* I, p. 408.
10. Kennan's colors in this regard showed clearly during his first trip to Latin America, where he found Mexico City "violent [and] explosive," was "appalled" by Caracas, found Rio "repulsive" and São Paulo "still worse," and on Lima commented only that its dirt was "untouched" since the last rain 29 years earlier! *Ibid.*, pp. 476-479.
11. Gaddis, *Strategies*, p. 72.
12. Gellman, *Contending with Kennan*, p. 54.
13. *Ibid.*, p. 120.
14. Gaddis, *Strategies*, pp. 58-65.
15. See Gellman, *Contending with Kennan*, p. 136.
16. Kennan, *Memoirs* I, p. 464.
17. *Ibid.*, p. 463.
18. Many of the perspectives indicated on the chart are revealed by the authors of the essays in Aaron Wildavsky, ed., *Beyond Containment: Alternative American Policies Towards the Soviet Union* (San Francisco: Institute for Contemporary Studies, 1983).
19. Kennan, *Memoirs* I, p. 428.
20. I have left the Rio Treaty out of consideration here because of its very different origins and purposes and because many of its characteristics belong more to the Dulles system than the Truman one.
21. Gellman, *Contending with Kennan*, pp. 125, 34.
22. See Alan K. Henrikson, "The Creation of the North Atlantic Alliance, 1948-1952," *Naval War College Review* 32 (May-June 1980): 4-39.
23. Kennan, *Memoirs* I, p. 350.
24. Kennan, *Memoirs* I, p. 454, 411, 458. Kennan has certain personal ties with Scandinavia, where he regularly spends his summers in Norway.
25. Kennan, *Memoirs* I, pp. 407-408.
26. *Ibid.*, p. 446.
27. Townsend Hoopes, *The Devil and John Foster Dulles* (London: Andre Deutsch, 1974), p. 94. The administration refused to actively support Chiang Kai-shek's efforts in that direction, and the new NATO Council rejected the idea of a NATO-like Pacific pact in September 1949.
28. See David Lange, "New Zealand's Security Policy," *Foreign Affairs* 63 (Summer 1985): 1009.
29. The three being the Japanese, Philippines, and ANZUS pacts. Hoopes, *Devil and Dulles*, pp. 105-109.
30. Kennan, *Memoirs* I, p. 381.
31. George F. Kennan, *Memoirs 1950-1963*, Vol. II (New York: Pantheon, 1972), p. 39.
32. Kennan, *Memoirs* I, p. 393.
33. Kennan, *Memoirs* II, pp. 45-52.
34. George F. Kennan, *The Cloud of Danger* (Boston: Little, Brown & Co., 1977), p. 127.

35. *Ibid.*, p. 108.
36. Hoopes characterizes Dulles as a "man who went from the specific to the specific, without any enduring ideas to offer, and so susceptible to immersion in the twists and turns of his tactical ingenuity that he chronically lost his sense of proprotion and not infrequently his sense of reality." *Devil and Dulles*, p. 358.
37. See account of SEATO's formation in Leszek Buszcynski, *SEATO: The Failure of an Alliance Strategy* (Kent Ridge: Singapore University Press, 1983), pp. 1–42; also Hoopes, pp. 202–244.
38. There is some possibility that Chiang's campaign for such a treaty, under way since the Korean pact and encouraged by the American military, may have provoked the crisis in the first place; and it is clear that Eisenhower used the treaty to restrain Chiang as he had earlier used the Korean pact to leash Syngman Rhee. See Hoopes, pp. 263–272.
39. While Dulles at first hung back from full membership in the pact because of his concern about its effect on moderate Arabs, the United States later eased into membership, beginning as an observer, joining the Military Planning Committee in 1957, and becoming in effect a full participant — indeed, stepping in to save the organization — during the 1958 crisis. Guy Hadley, *CENTO: The Forgotten Alliance* (Sussex, UK: Institute for the Study of International Organization Monograph No. 4, University of Sussex, 1971), pp. 1–9.
40. Gaddis, *Strategies of Containment*, pp. 152–153. Gaddis points out that Dulles' alliances actually extended U.S. formal commitments to only four nations not already covered. Still, it seems puzzling that an administration so concerned with the limitations on U.S. resources would have involved the country in the support of nations which could only be a drain on the limited dollars available for defense.
41. Hoopes, *Devil and Dulles*, pp. 241, 408. Indeed, after the SEATO conference the United States seems to have intended to make the alliance part of a grand Pacific defense arrangement including Japan, South Korea, Taiwan and the ANZUS in a NATO-type alliance; see Buszcynski, *SEATO*, p. 42.
42. Kennan, *Memoirs* II, p. 141.
43. Kennan, *Cloud*, pp. 92–93.
44. *Ibid.*, pp. 93, 97–98, 104, 231, 111.
45. Interview with George Urban, September 1976, reprinted in Martin F. Hertz, ed., *Decline of the West? George Kennan and his Critics* (Washington, D.C.: Georgetown University Ethics and Public Policy Center, 1978), p. 13.
46. CENTO is gone; all that is left of SEATO is the commitment to Thailand; of the bilateral pacts only that with South Korea remains, hostage to Kennan's primary interest in Japan.
47. Brzezinski, *Power and Principles: Memoirs of the National Security Advisor, 1977–1981* (New York: Farrar, Straus, Giroux, 1983), pp. 443–454.
48. Gellman, *Contending with Kennan*, p. 41.
49. Kennan, *Memoirs* II, pp. 141, 143.
50. Kennan, *Cloud*, p. 98.
51. *Ibid.*, pp. 116–117.
52. See, for example, Earl Ravenal, "The Case for Withdrawal of Our Forces," *New York Times Magazine* (March 6, 1983); 58–61, 75; Irving Kristol, "Does NATO Exist?", *Washington Quarterly* 2 (Autumn 1979): 45–53; Alan Ned

Sabrosky, "Allies, Clients, and Encumbrances," *International Security Review* 5 (Summer 1980): 117–149; James Chace, *Solvency* (New York: Random House, 1981).

53. Kennan, *Cloud*, p. 122; Ray S. Cline, "All-Oceans Alliance," *World Power Trends and U.S. Foreign Policy for the 1980's* (Boulder, Colorado: Westview Press, 1980), pp. 181–203; Charles Wolf, Jr., "Beyond Containment: Redesigning American Policies," *Washington Quarterly* (Winter 1982): 107–117.

54. Indeed, perhaps the economic growth of American-allied NICs in the Pacific has already obviated Kennan's dictum that only five industrial centers can really make a difference in world power.

55. Lippman, *The Cold War* (New York: Harper, 1947), pp. 29–30.

# 7 CONTAINMENT AND THE SHAPE OF WORLD POLITICS

*Richard H. Ullman*

Containment — as an explicit, self-conscious strategy — was very much a product of the international environment of the early postwar era, when the United States enjoyed both unrivaled power and unrivaled standing in "the opinions of mankind." It was therefore hardly surprising that Americans like George Kennan who gave such thought to the shape of the international system should see in this fortunate circumstance a way of containing the outward expansion of the only other member of the system capable of posing both a military and an ideological challenge.

Today, with military capabilities more diffused and pretensions to ideological ascendency more subject to skeptical questioning, the goal of containing Soviet power within a given geographic sphere is more difficult to achieve. Nevertheless, containment survives as a strategy and, indeed, as the organizing concept against which both U.S. administrations and their critics measure quite disparate strands of foreign policy. Yet — as Kennan never tires of saying — precisely because the state system has proved to be so much more resilient than it seemed in the 1940s, American policymakers can well afford to be more relaxed as they assess the ebbs and flows of Moscow's influence.

## KENNAN AND THE SHAPE OF EUROPE

Kennan's famous "X" article of 1947 gave little explicit attention to the shape of world politics, either as the international system existed at the time or as it might evolve over the coming decades. That lack of attention is not surprising: Kennan's focus then was on "The Sources of Soviet Conduct," and on his reckoning that conduct was driven primarily by domestic imperatives. Soviet conduct could certainly be affected at the margin, however. Indeed, the margin — literally, the geographic borders between the Soviet empire and the non-Soviet world — was where Kennan would bring to bear "a policy of firm containment, designed to confront the Russians with unalterable counter-force at every point where they show signs of encroaching upon the interests of a peaceful and stable world."[1] For Kennan, the Soviet Union in 1947 was "by far the weaker party" compared to "the Western world in general." However, he worried that the United States might prove itself incapable of exercising sufficient moral leadership to hold the West together until the time when the amply apparent strains within Soviet society would "eventually find their outlet in either the break-up or the gradual mellowing of Soviet power."

An astute commentator has observed that, so far as he could discover, never once in a long career had Kennan "brought himself to pen the word 'superpower'." That might be, Barton Gellman suggests, because Kennan has always disliked the notion of bipolarity, and has instead sought a return to a multipolar balance of power such as the one prevailing before World War I.[2] Indeed, for him a central purpose of American foreign policy after World War II was the restoration of a balance of power in Europe and Asia. The basis for that balance had been shaken, if not shattered, by the war and the vacuum of power created by the defeat of Germany and Japan. To restore a balance, therefore, it would be necessary for the United States to assist actively in these nations' economic and psychological revival, together with that of the industrial democracies that had fought them, so that none of those centers of strength should fall under the domination of a power hostile to the United States — meaning the Soviet Union.

The purpose of containment, therefore, was to provide a shield behind which the societies of Western Europe and Japan could gather the physical and mental resilience necessary to resist communism. In 1947 and later on, Kennan clearly regarded the Soviet threat as more political and psychological than it was military. He had no doubt that the United States was militarily superior to the U.S.S.R. The United States was not ravaged by war; its economy was vastly more productive and its people more energetic. What concerned him, he said in the "X" article and in many other forums, was whether Americans had the political and psychological maturity for a task that was both so demanding and at the same time so quotidian as the calm "exertion of steady pressure over a period of years."[3]

The decade that followed saw not only the restoration of these key industrial centers to economic and political health, but also their organization — largely but not entirely under U.S. auspices — into an alliance aimed at containing Soviet power. Judged by any reasonable standards, the effort was quite successful — much more so, indeed, than many critics expressed at the time. Eastern Europe was "lost"; so, apparently, was China. But these geopolitical outcomes were very much the products of strategic choices made during the war; nothing within the power of U.S. policymakers in the postwar years could have changed them.

As Kennan has reminded us ever since, however, the United States might have prevented the division of Germany. But the Truman and Eisenhower administrations chose not to seriously explore Moscow's proposals regarding the possibility of trading Germany's unification for its demilitarization and neutralization. Rather than run the risk that the unified, neutralized German state might fall under Soviet influence and, eventually, Soviet control, they preferred instead to settle for the certain half-loaf of the Federal Republic of Germany firmly embedded in the Western military alliance and economic community. This decision (in fact, a series of incremental decisions), more than any other that the West had it in its power to make, froze the postwar international system into the geopolitical shape that has endured until today. Once Germany was divided between communist and non-communist states that were themselves not only the principal forward bastions for Soviet and American armed forces, but also potent (if compliant) military powers in their own right, the division of Europe into two relatively rigid blocs was a foregone conclusion.

That division, in turn, has been one of the two dominant features of international politics since the late 1940s. Although the U.S.–Soviet competition has been global and, especially over the last two decades, has seemed to be most intense in the various theaters of the Third World, it is Europe that has always been the ultimate prize. The line between East and West in Europe has been the focus of the two most powerful permanently stationed aggregations of military force ever assembled. Hypothetical European contingencies have shaped the military doctrines of the two superpowers and have been the major factors driving both the procurement and the deployment of weapons themselves. And while the spark that ignites armed conflict between Washington and Moscow may originate elsewhere, it will only find the forcing winds and the tinder that can fan it into World War III if it reaches Europe.

## THE IMPACT OF NUCLEAR WEAPONS

The other dominant feature of the international political landscape has been the existence of nuclear weapons, the potential source of the most fearsome flames of war. Although not used in anger since 1945, nuclear weapons pose a menace that has been integral to the division of Europe and, indeed, to the rigidity of international politics. The division of Germany took place while the United States enjoyed a nuclear monopoly; although Soviet forces east of the Elbe River considerably outnumbered American, British, and French forces in the Western occupation zones, one reason they demurred from offering armed opposition to Western measures and programs was certainly the U.S. possession of an atomic trump.

There is an important sense, it should be noted, in which nuclear weapons and the division of Europe are antithetic. Bloc formation is part of a classical pattern of collective security in which states join alliances in order to magnify their military power. Yet nuclear weapons make such blocs irrelevant. As nuclear superpowers, the United States and the Soviet Union do not need allies to safeguard the physical security of their homelands. Indeed, it is now generally accepted that because Washington and Moscow need to extend security guarantees to their allies, the European alliances raise rather than reduce the risks for the superpowers. On the Western side, that problem is the essence of what has come to be called "NATO's nuclear dilemma" — how the United States can make its commitment to retaliate credible, with nuclear weapons if necessary, either for a nuclear or a massive conventional attack upon its European allies, when honoring such a commitment would likely bring down nuclear weapons on its own territory. For the Soviets, geographical proximity to their allies may make the dilemma less pointed, but it is nonetheless real.

NATO (and perhaps also the Warsaw Pact) has thus been rent by two contradictory impulses. One, coming especially from the United States, has been to raise the nuclear threshold so that the awful decision to use nuclear weapons might never have to be faced. That has meant struggling to find the economic resources and political will to field conventional forces capable of delaying a nuclear response to the outbreak of war long enough to reach a diplomatic resolution of the conflict. The second impulse, arising mainly from the Europeans, has been to question the worth of large expenditures on additional conventional forces, since any war in Europe is likely to be nuclear from the outset. This second position seems credible when one considers that (a) NATO could match Warsaw Pact conventional forces only with an enormous effort, (b) nuclear weapons will remain the real deterrent to war in any case, and (c) many Europeans would rather risk the low probability of nuclear war than do anything that might make it more likely that a war of any kind (even conventional) would be fought on their territory.

Thus, while nuclear weapons have obviously reinforced the dominant roles the United States and the Soviet Union have played within their alliances, they have also increasingly been a solvent that has unstuck the glue in once-tight relationships. Washington's allies ask themselves whether they are really more safe with U.S. nuclear weapons on their territory or adjacent waters. (New Zealand is the most recent, but not the first, to answer that question in the negative. It is, however, the first to be threatened with ostracism by Washington.[4]) Moscow's allies are more mannerly than to voice objections to Soviet nuclear policy in public. It is known, however, that Czechoslovakia and East Germany, and no doubt Hungary and (though not directly affected) Rumania, were unhappy with the Kremlin's decision to respond to NATO's 1983 deployment of intermediate-range nuclear forces (INF) in Western Europe with corresponding deployments in Eastern Europe.

China, of course, is the *cause célèbre* that exemplifies the corrosive effect of nuclear weapons on the Kremlin's alliances. The initial rift between Moscow and Beijing was caused by Soviet refusal to supply nuclear weapons technology at a time when the People's Republic felt threatened with a U.S. nuclear attack and wanted its own retaliatory capability instead of uncertain guarantees from an uneasy ally. Unlike Moscow's Eastern European allies, China could break away because of its sheer size and because no Soviet troops were stationed on its territory. It could therefore present the Soviets with a *fait accompli*.[5]

## KEEPING SCORE IN THE THIRD WORLD

During the early 1970s, when Richard Nixon and Henry Kissinger were shaping the agenda for American foreign policy, analysts were preoccupied with the question of whether the international system should still be regarded as bipolar. *Emergent* multipolarity was the term favored in the White House. We now know, however, that even with the qualifying adjective, the term was premature. During the intervening years, the other potential centers of power — Western Europe, Japan, and China — had not gained in relative strength by comparison with the superpowers. Yet neither do we today have bipolarity of the kind that prevailed during the 1950s, when the United States and the U.S.S.R. not only wielded predominant military power but also presided over much more unified blocs of allies. (Lack of unity may today seem more characteristic of Washington's alliances than Moscow's. But recall that analysts once routinely referred to the "Sino-Soviet bloc.") What we now have is an international system in which the two superpowers still possess pre-eminent military capabilities but do not control events to the extent they did a generation ago. And each — especially the United States, but also the Soviet Union — has considerably less ability to induce its allies to march to its drum, particularly when the route of the march leads "out of area," beyond the European theater in which each alliance prepares to confront the other.

Yet despite these changes in the structure of international politics, there has been strikingly little diminution in the pervasiveness of the "scorekeeper" mentality that has characterized both superpowers over the entire period since 1945. Each consistently behaves as if the defection of any state with which it has been aligned would be a blow to its security. That is obviously true, and for good political and military reasons, in the case of what might be called the core allies—NATO and Japan for the United States, and the Warsaw Pact and (once) China for the Soviet Union. But the superpowers have also behaved as if this were true for states whose political alignment should matter much less—for example, in recent years, Afghanistan and Central American states. In these instances, the military forces of the states involved count for little. Afghan forces can contribute nothing of significance to Soviet security, nor could they seriously threaten it. The same is true for U.S. security and the combined military forces (not to mention those of any one state) of Central America. In fact, it is arguable that even as bases for the rival superpower, these territories are overrated. In peacetime they would be costly to supply and maintain; in the event of war they could easily be neutralized; and the communications and surveillance activities that might be conducted from them are being carried on adequately from existing facilities nearby.

It is, however, the political consequences of possible defections in these peripheral states, more than their practical effects, that actually seem to worry Moscow and Washington. The Soviets have never stated the motivations for their invasion of Afghanistan, but high among them apparently was the fear that if a fundamentalist Islamic regime ever came to power in Kabul it would exercise a potentially destabilizing attraction on Soviet Moslems across the border. That is, in fact, not an unreasonable supposition. Certainly it seems more reasonable than the assumptions that evidently underlie the Reagan administration's policy in Central America—that Marxist–Leninist regimes among the small, fragile states in the isthmus would exert a falling-domino effect upon other Latin American states, or that their coming to power would release a horde of refugees to beset our borders.

The scorekeeper mentality has far more pernicious effects on the United States than it does on the Soviet Union. That is because ascribed wins and losses abroad—"Who lost Patagonia?" as William Bundy once put it[6]— become issues in our competitive politics at home. And in order to gain popular and congressional support for measures designed to prevent new "losses," presidents explicitly make implementation of those measures a test of the credibility and reliability of the United States as an ally. It is not surprising that foreigners—and foreign leaders—sometimes appear to take our presidents at their word. Thus when President Reagan asserts, as he so often does, "what happens in Latin America and the Caribbean will not only affect our nation but also will shape America's image throughout the world. If we cannot act decisively so close to home, who will believe us anywhere?" his message is played back, as it was in April 1985 in a message to the U.S. Congress from a group of well-known European conservatives: "If you fail in Nicaragua, we must ask, where will you fail

next? If freedom and democracy are not worth defending in your own
hemisphere, where are they worth defending?"[7]

This process is pernicious *not* because foreign friends and adversaries
are likely to believe that a U.S. administration's failure to draw a line in
the sand of some Third World country means that it or its successors will
fail to stand by a core ally under attack. Such perceptions do not seem
widespread. For example, there is no evidence that U.S. allies in Europe
and Asia viewed Washington's "abandonment" of South Vietnam in 1975
as the start of a process of unraveling, and began to trim their own sails
accordingly. Rather, they saw it as the end, at last, to a wasteful diversion
of strength and effort away from other interests — assuming that U.S. presidents once did see South Vietnam as a "vital interest" — that were "more
vital" still. What *is* pernicious, however, is that American administrations
and publics begin to believe their own rhetoric. Then the process of attempting to forestall revolutionary change in the name of containment
becomes an undifferentiated goal that appears applicable everywhere,
and by which Americans measure their own foreign policy performance.
Stanley Hoffmann once observed that the appropriate metaphor for much
of contemporary international relations was the labor of Sisyphus, whose
endless effort to roll a gigantic rock uphill had long since ceased to have
any meaning outside itself. The image seems especially appropriate for
American foreign policy in the Third World.[8]

Moreover, the metaphor fits despite what is often cited as the greatest
structural change in international power relationships since the basic
shape of the postwar world order was set — the achievement by the Soviet
Union over the last 25 years of a capability to project conventional military force rapidly over long distances. That capability is still not equal to
that of the United States, but it is respectable. More important, it developed from virtually nothing. Yet it is striking how little difference to the
course of events Moscow's new capability seems actually to have made.
The standard list of Soviet interventionary successes includes Angola,
where Soviet-supported Cuban troops installed a Marxist regime, and
Ethiopia, where they saved one. Yet each involved a highly special set of
circumstances — a situation approaching stateless anarchy in the first and
a state repulsing an old-fashioned cross-border invasion in the second. In
neither case did it seem remotely likely that the United States or its allies
would introduce military forces of their own.

Except for these instances (indeed, even *in* these instances), Moscow has
behaved with caution. Its apparent threat to send airborne troops to rescue the beleaguered Egyptian Third Army Corps near the Suez Canal in
1973 evaporated when the Nixon administration placed U.S. forces on
worldwide alert. On perhaps three occasions it has provided clients with
air defenses manned by Soviet personnel, but only when there was no

likelihood that attacking aircraft would be American.[9] And although it has supplied a variety of clients on a variety of continents with weapons and military training, such efforts long predated and certainly have not been dependent upon the enhancement of Moscow's own interventionary capabilities. As an arms supplier, also, Moscow has acted cautiously — refusing, for example, to send some clients weapons so advanced as to alter a regional balance or (as in the case of Nicaragua) to furnish Washington an excuse for attacking its client. Aside from the communist regimes of Eastern Europe whose political existence was always guaranteed by the threat of direct Soviet military intervention, the only other Soviet clients who may feel reasonably certain that Soviet forces will be at their side in substantial numbers if they are endangered are the regimes in Afghanistan and Vietnam — the former by virtue of physical proximity, the latter because it is threatened by China, not the United States. Even the Cubans, who have carried more than their share of Moscow's mail, know they will almost certainly have to fight alone if they get into a shooting war with Washington.

If American political leaders could only adopt a time horizon longer than four (or two!) years, they might find that they have every reason to take a more relaxed view of the Soviet threat to U.S. interests in the Third World. In particular, they would not feel compelled to make every instance of Soviet involvement an explicit test of the credibility and reliability of the United States. To urge such a longer view is not to counsel complacence; it is to recognize that many of the Third World regimes targeted by revolutionaries enjoying a greater or lesser degree of Soviet support have been so thoroughly weakened by their own previous domestic failures as to be able to remain in power only by means of massive repression, massive U.S. assistance, or both. And it is to suggest that even revolutionaries who come to power with (or because of) Soviet support are unlikely to wish to be dependent upon Moscow afterward. America's experience with the People's Republic of China should demonstrate that a supposed satellite beyond the Kremlin's direct reach is not likely to remain a satellite unless immediate enemies — and especially the United States — threaten it so directly that its leaders see no alternative to the Soviet connection. Cuba under Fidel Castro would surely not have evolved into a liberal democracy, but its orientation might have been very different had U.S. policy not made it dependent upon Moscow for economic survival.

## CONTAINMENT IN THE THIRD WORLD

It is in the realm of U.S. policy toward Third World revolutionary regimes that containment still presents questions rather than answers. In

Europe and Northeast Asia, the lines have been clearly drawn ever since George Kennan's time. What is at issue in these geographic zones are the methods that should be used by the United States, in conjunction with its allies, to respond to "traditional" overt border-crossing aggression. That is far from a trivial issue, involving very difficult questions about the kinds of military forces America's allies should buy, doctrines and strategies for conventional defense, the role of nuclear weapons, and so forth. But there is virtually no debate over what might constitute aggression or how responsibility for aggression might be determined; nor is there any need for such a debate.

In the Third World, however, these are highly debatable questions, and the answers will not come easily. Indeed, the term *aggression* — either through conventional military means or, as is much more likely, through the entire spectrum of activities that constitute unconventional warfare — may well define the range of impermissible behavior too narrowly. Certainly it seems too narrow for the Reagan administration, which has on occasion expressed the view that even if revolutionary regimes like the Sandinistas "let their neighbors alone" they might nevertheless, merely by existing in their present form, still destabilize their regions. And if questions such as these are unresolved, so also are ones regarding the means by which containment should be pursued.

In dealing with such matters, the United States now finds itself quite often alone. That is one result of a far-reaching structural change in the international system: the coming to independence since 1960 of the great majority of the states that were once colonies of the European powers. Rich and powerful among the poor and weak, the United States has increasingly been on the losing end of lopsided votes in international forums. However, in questions involving political change in the Third World, the United States often finds itself estranged not only from the Third World majority, but also from its principal allies.[10]

This is a profound departure from what might be called orthodox containment. Far from being able to orchestrate coherent counter-pressure to what it assesses as Soviet expansionism, the United States often has great difficulty in persuading its allies that in a given instance, there is a need for action. Differences in analysis began with the Vietnam war, when successive administrations in Washington were unable to convince the allies to accept their diagnoses of the nature of the conflict, of the stakes involved for the West, or of the appropriate Western responses. It was then that anti-Americanism — augmented because of the way in which the United States chose to fight the war — spread beyond fringe-left parties in Europe and Japan.

Such differences in assessment have extended since the late 1960s to the Middle East as well. Publics and governments in Europe and Japan do not share the American commitment to Israel, and have been generally skeptical of the claim, put forward by several presidents, that the Arab–Israeli conflict should be viewed as part of the larger East–West conflict. And the years since 1973 have seen the slightly bizarre spectacle of the United States appearing much more concerned about the possibility of Soviet disruption of Persian Gulf oil supplies than the governments of Western Europe and Japan, whose societies are vitally dependent on those supplies.

Differences in assessment between Washington and its allies extend, of course, to Latin America, and particularly to Central America. But in one important respect, Central America has been dissimilar. The Reagan administration has made no more than token efforts to convince its partners that they should share its concern regarding the consequences for U.S. national security (and, by extrapolation, the security of the Western alliance) of an insurgent victory in El Salvador or of the survival of the Sandinistas in Nicaragua. That many observers do not share the administration's concern has been amply demonstrated. Indeed, some NATO allies have continued to send aid to the Sandinistas at the same time the United States has been trying forcibly to overthrow them.

These divergences of view have outraged many Americans—in and out of government, and in Congress in particular—but they are scarcely surprising. Indeed, it would be surprising if divergent views did not exist. States view one another through the prisms of their own domestic politics. And at the center of political controversy in virtually every state are assessments of risk, estimates of the potential harm that other states might cause, and choices among the range of measures that should be taken to forestall that harm. But assessments of risk are also related to capability. When a state no longer has the power to defend what it once defined as an interest, it will begin to define its interests differently. Some interests that were once thought to require active military protection may seem no longer to need it; others may cease to be regarded as interests at all. Risks a polity knows it cannot forestall will often seem less dangerous than those it thinks it can.[11] Alone among the Western allies, the United States defines its interests—and threats to those interests—in global terms because it alone has the ability to project military power throughout the globe.

## CAUSES FOR CONTAINMENT

What, then, is left of containment nearly 40 years after the "X" article? The observations thus far are not intended to suggest that containment of the Soviet Union is no longer a valid objective for U.S. foreign policy, but we should be clear what it is that we are trying to contain. There is no dispute over the contention that "classic" aggression with conventional military forces should be resisted if it cannot be deterred. Here the record is good. The security system represented by the core alliances organized by the United States has clearly been successful. We will probably never know if, over the course of four decades, Soviet leaders have ever seriously contemplated attacking westward from the Elbe or eastward across the Straits of Japan, but we know that they have not done so.

Indeed, in this restricted but scarcely unimportant sphere of what might be called orthodox military containment, the few apparent failures do not support a conclusion that the policy itself has failed. Forces allied to Moscow moved into South Korea in 1950 and into Cambodia in 1979, but only after South Korea (not a U.S. ally at the time) had explicitly been defined as outside the United States defense perimeter, and after the regime that ruled Cambodia had become a universally loathed pariah. In the first instance, the United States learned (but also taught) a costly lesson. In the second, it seems clear that in invading Cambodia, Vietnam was pursuing purposes that were historically very much its own, not Moscow's; for a number of reasons, Washington properly drew the line at the border of its regional ally, Thailand. A murkier instance was Angola in 1975. There, as we have already noted, the Soviets supported one faction in a civil war, taking advantage of unique circumstances — the combination of the absence of any recognized authority and the previous invasion of the country by South African forces.

Finally, there was Afghanistan. The forces that invaded in December 1979 were Moscow's own, not proxies. However, no matter how literally one might take the notion of "confront[ing] the Russians with unalterable counter-force at every point where they show signs of encroaching upon the interests of a peaceful and stable world," the facts of geography made any immediate Western military response out of the question. Yet those same facts make Afghanistan, in the most literal sense of the word, peripheral. The most the West could do — and has done fairly effectively since 1979 — was to arm the Afghan resistance. Military containment will not stand or fall on the record of that very special situation.

It may be argued, however, that "orthodox" military containment makes for easy cases. Much more difficult — and prevalent — are those instances in which there has been no border-crossing movement of regular military forces, but rather, a pattern of Soviet-supported subversion, infiltration, and insurgency. North Vietnam's long campaign against South Vietnam was such an example; only at the end did it become an "orthodox" war. Another example is the current effort by insurgent forces to overthrow the government of El Salvador. There have been many more. In some, the Soviet role has been minimal, no more than that of a minor supplier of weapons and training to one or more insurgent factions.[12] In other instances Soviet support may have been decisive, though it is obviously difficult to say for certain.

These cases of "unorthodox" war are the instances in which, if the United States chooses to intervene, it is likely to find itself doing so either alone or, as occurred in Vietnam, with only token assistance from allies.[13] Then, ironically enough, George Kennan's 1947 emphasis on the American domestic political landscape once again becomes the primary factor. If the United States is going to make any but a brief, Grenada-style military effort abroad, the danger must be clear and present and the stakes must be apparent. Otherwise, as Secretary of Defense Caspar W. Weinberger implied when he defined the conditions under which he would recommend the use of American military force, the political consensus necessary to sustain an operation involving even small numbers of fighting men would not be forthcoming.[14] This is a limitation that no administration is likely to overcome through "public education."

## CONTAINMENT AND ITS ALTERNATIVES

Weinberger's strictures contrast sharply in practice, if not in theory, with the appeal for an assertive "nationalist-unilateralist" foreign policy — "activist" rather than "reactive" — made recently by Irving Kristol in the name of a "self-consciously ideological . . . new conservatism." Kristol and his neo-conservative friends want to take the gloves off in the conflict with the Soviet Union. Among the gloves are "all those 'foreign entanglements' our State Department has so assiduously contrived over the past 40 years," including NATO, the Organization of American States, and even the United Nations. They are, Kristol says, "ineffectual barriers against 'aggression' . . . but very effective hindrances to American action."[15]

In proclaiming the end of the era of "liberal internationalism," Kristol foresees no return to "old-fashioned, nationalist isolationism." Yet surely that would be the likely result of the unilateralism he proposes. Freed of the emotional and even cultural linkages inherent in the structure of post-1945 international institutions, Americans might well decide that the only value worth much exertion is the physical security of the United States (and just perhaps, of Israel), and that in an era of seemingly ever more versatile nuclear weapons, little can happen beyond the nation's borders that will really jeopardize that security. The "support of the American people and their elected representatives" that Weinberger regards as crucial would not be forthcoming for the politically forceful (and militarily force-wielding) policies required by Kristol's vision of an ideologically assertive United States.

There is irony here. The contemporary international system finds the United States at the center of a web of entanglements that arguably provides it with no additional security and which, indeed, adds vastly to the burdens American taxpayers are asked to bear. (The commitment to NATO, especially, powerfully shapes the U.S. military force structure and makes it more costly.) To critics like Kristol, these entanglements mandate compromises that open doors for the expansion of Soviet influence and, potentially, control. Effective containment therefore requires that we free ourselves from paying attention to the hopes and fears of others, and march to our own drums. Yet there is every likelihood that an increasingly self-centered United States might conclude that very little of the rest of the world really "matters." In such a political climate, containment would come to seem less and less relevant as a goal for American foreign policy.

Like Sisyphus with his rock, the United States seems stuck with the present structure of world politics. Changing the ground rules that underlie that structure (as would have to be done to rid us of our entanglements) would not be likely to result in a nation more capable of shrinking the domains of the world's evil empires; sustaining the requisite domestic political support for doing so would be an impossible task. We are therefore stuck as well with a version of containment that has also become part of the system's ground rules. That version offers us and our partners ample insurance against some of the risks that we perceive. Before we attempt fundamentally to alter the quality of that insurance, we should carefully examine the quality of our perceptions.

There are, to be sure, many facets of the present U.S.–Soviet relationship that lie beyond what we have come to think of as containment. One is the realm of negotiations. "Orthodox" containment, as it was articulated during the first decade or so following World War II, placed very little emphasis on negotiations between Washington and Moscow. The U.S.S.R. was considered to be virtually impermeable; the purpose of containment was to erect a barrier (what an earlier generation called a *cordon sanitaire*) behind which the Soviet state might evolve in more benign directions. Yet over the past two decades, by seeking explicit agreements, American administrations have attempted to shape not only Soviet external behavior but also Soviet society itself. These efforts have, as a matter of course, included negotiations on limiting arms, on military intervention (e.g., in the Middle East), and on relations with Third World clients (e.g., arms sales). But they have also extended to human rights (e.g., Jewish emigration) and to important dimensions of the Soviet internal economy (e.g., grain imports).

Thus far, U.S.–Soviet negotiations have given rise only to fairly modest results. Yet that poor record is due in considerable measure to the way negotiations have been conducted on the American side. All too frequently, bureaucratic infighting and congressional pressures have led U.S. negotiators to lack clear objectives or to be unable to make real concessions. In the realm of arms control, especially, they have often had little to put on the table: The military services and the nuclear weapons laboratories have been tenacious at making sure that future options are not closed off and that weapons already in the inventory are not bargained away. That has also been true of efforts to constrain the military roles of the two superpowers in the Third World—for example, negotiations during the Carter administration on limiting transfers of conventional arms or demilitarizing the Indian Ocean.[16] During Ronald Reagan's first presidential term, the idea of any negotiations at all with the "evil empire" was virtually anathema; the administration was anxious not to offend its militant right-wing supporters, including Kristol and other neoconservatives. And although Reagan in his second term appears to be less motivated by such domestic political considerations, he nevertheless has firmly rejected offers of potentially far-reaching concessions from Moscow when they seemed likely to interfere with his administration's plans for new defensive and offensive nuclear weapons.[17]

Indeed, the record of U.S.–Soviet negotiations points up a fundamental change in the structure of international relations over the last four decades. Containment is now a two-way street. In order to restrict Soviet options (for that is what containment means), American policymakers must now accept limitations on their own. That applies to nearly every strand of Soviet behavior that Washington would like to change, from deploying new missiles in Europe to supporting insurgent movements in the Third World to easing restrictions on Soviet citizens seeking to emigrate. Reciprocity does not mean that limitations must be identical, however. The road to human rights concessions runs not through matching concessions by Washington (there are none to make, nor are Soviet leaders concerned about "human rights" in the United States) but, as Gerald Ford's administration learned, through guarantees on trade and credits.

There are those who would say that the very need for reciprocity points up the ultimate bankruptcy of containment as practiced by every American administration since Franklin Roosevelt's. Rather than containment, they say, the preferred approach should have been to destroy Soviet power before it could grow: containment has only served to preserve (or even to nurture) the Soviet state rather than to alter it.[18] The observation may be valid; it is also irrelevant. So drastic an enterprise, no matter how accomplished, would have required an American nation and leaders radically different in character from what we knew in 1947 and have known since.

As George Kennan himself has often pointed out, the United States has been far from adept at "employing force for rational and restricted purposes;" wars once begun have tended to become crusades, as did the two

world wars.[19] But preventive war against a major adversary (as distinguished from, say, the war against Spain of 1898, or the invasion of
Grenada in 1983) has never been part of the American repertoire. It is
impossible to imagine a president ordering one—or the political system
complying. Containment is indeed the antithesis of preventive war. And
the critics of containment have yet to suggest an alternative strategy that
is within the capability of the American political system, or is even
remotely as well-suited for enabling the United States to cope with the
world as it was in 1947—or as it is today.

## NOTES

1. "X" [George F. Kennan], "The Sources of Soviet Conduct," *Foreign Affairs*
   25 (July 1947):581.
2. Barton Gellman, *Contending with Kennan: Toward a Philosophy of American Power* (New York: Praeger, 1984), p. 43.
3. From a draft lecture prepared by Kennan for delivery on February 20, 1947,
   quoted in *ibid.*, p. 133.
4. From the outset of the NATO alliance, Denmark and Norway have both
   refused to allow nuclear weapons on their territory in peacetime, and the
   United States honors this preference while at the same time adhering to a
   longstanding policy of not discussing the location of U.S. nuclear weapons.
   Denmark and Norway do, however, allow visits of nuclear-powered or nu-
   clear-armed vessels to their ports.
5. It is worth noting, also, that China's separation came by stages. The initial
   phase of the dispute was closely followed (indeed, was overlapped) by the
   Cultural Revolution, which surely seemed so unpromising to Western interests that the U.S.S.R. did not feel directly threatened. By the time China had
   unambiguously turned to the West, its independence from Moscow was so
   well established that no Soviet "rescue" was remotely possible.
6. William P. Bundy, "Who Lost Patagonia? Foreign Policy in the 1980 Campaign," *Foreign Affairs* (Fall 1979):1–27.
7. This particular Reagan quotation (there have been many like it) was from an
   address to a group of Cuban exiles, May 20, 1983; the *New York Times*, May
   21, 1983, p. A4. The 88 Europeans (and an Australian, former Prime Minister Malcolm Fraser) took a full-page advertisment in *ibid.*, April 18, 1985,
   p. B28.
8. Stanley H. Hoffmann, *The State of War* (New York: Praeger, 1965), p. 49.
9. The first instance was the so-called Egyptian–Israeli "War of Attrition," in
   1970, when the U.S.S.R. shored up Egyptian air defenses with Soviet pilots
   flying MIG-21 interceptors and ground crews manning surface-to-air missiles
   (SAMs). The second occurred following Israel's total destruction of Syrian
   SAMs in Lebanon in 1982; Moscow is said to have set up several batteries of
   long-range SAM-5s in Syria wholly manned by Soviet crews. The third
   instance is present-day Angola, where the Soviets are said in mid-1985 to
   have set up defenses against South African air attacks.
10. On this theme, see Sanford J. Ungar (ed.), *Estrangement: America and the
    World* (New York: Oxford University Press, 1985), *passim*.
11. For a discussion of differences of assessment as an issue in Anglo–American

relations, see Richard H. Ullman, "America, Britain, and the Soviet Threat in Historical and Present Perspective," in W. Roger Louis and Hedley Bull (eds.), *The 'Special Relationship': Anglo-American Relations since 1945* (London: Oxford University Press, 1986), pp. 105–108.

12. That was the case, for example, in the guerrilla war against Ian Smith's white minority regime in Rhodesia. Moscow supported Joshua Nkomo's ZAPU forces. In the end, they lost to Robert Mugabe's ZANU, which had China's support, but even had they won it is unlikely that Moscow would have had any significant influence in the Zimbabwe that emerged from the war.

13. Australia, New Zealand, and South Korea — perhaps only the last with any enthusiasm — sent contingents to assist the United States in Vietnam, a marked contrast from the Korean War, in which the "United Nations Command" included many American allies.

14. Secretary Weinberger's speech, to the National Press Club on November 28, 1984, was excerpted in the *New York Times* the following day and printed in full, with minor modifications, in the form of an article, "The Use of Force and the National Will," in the *Baltimore Sun*, December 3, 1984.

15. Irving Kristol, "Foreign Policy in an Age of Ideology," *The National Interest* 1 (Fall 1985):6–15.

16. See, for example, Strobe Talbott, *Endgame: The Inside Story of Salt II* (New York: Harper and Row, 1979), pp. 164–80; and Raymond L. Garthoff, *Détente and Confrontation: American–Soviet Relations from Nixon to Reagan* (Washington, D.C.: The Brookings Institution, 1985), pp. 755–763.

17. Thus, at summit meetings with Soviet Party Chairman Mikhail S. Gorbachev at Vienna in November 1985 and at Reykjavik in October 1986, Reagan summarily rejected Soviet proposals that, in exchange for limits on U.S. plans to develop new anti-missile defenses, Moscow would agree to 50% reductions in strategic offensive forces. And following the Geneva summit, the administration, asserting that Soviet assurances could not be trusted, bluntly rejected a Soviet proposal for a comprehensive ban on nuclear weapons testing that seemed to depart substantially from Moscow's previous unwillingness to allow intrusive on-site inspections. Such a ban would have curbed the development of new offensive warheads. (See the *New York Times*, November 22, 1985, p. A12, and December 20, 1985, p. A13.)

18. For an extreme version of this argument, see "Containment: A View from the Kremlin," an address by Senator Malcolm Wallop to the symposium, "Containment and the Future," November 7, 1985, National Defense University, Washington, D.C., reprinted in *The Congressional Record*, Senate, 20 Nov. 1985, pp. S16050-53.

19. See, for example, Kennan's *American Diplomacy 1900-1950* (Chicago: University of Chicago Press, 1951), chapters IV and V (the quotation is on p. 84).

# PART 2

# CONTAINMENT FOR THE FUTURE

# 8 THE "X" ARTICLE AND CONTEMPORARY SOURCES OF SOVIET CONDUCT

*Jerry F. Hough*

Even with the hindsight of almost 40 years, George Kennan's "X" article remains a remarkable document.[1] It was, of course, first of all a political statement and one with a message far more complex than many remember. On the one hand, it offered a powerful argument against the naive assumptions associated with Henry Wallace. Kennan cautioned that we "must continue to expect that Soviet policies will reflect no abstract love of peace and stability." Soviet "political action," he warned, "is a fluid stream which moves constantly, wherever it is permitted to move, toward a given goal. Its main concern is to make sure that it has filled every nook and cranny available to it in the basin of world power." The answer that he proposed was "a policy of firm containment, designed to confront the Russians with unalterable counterforce at every point where they show signs of encroaching upon the interests of a peaceful and stable world."

Yet, on the other hand (and given Kennan's subsequent positions, one wonders if this were not a more fundamental purpose of the article than is sometimes assumed), it repeatedly attempted to calm fears that the Soviet Union was "like Napoleon and Hitler," or that it was seeking immediate victory. The "fluid stream" that he warned against was of "political action." Nowhere did Kennan refer to a military threat; instead, he constantly highlighted Soviet weakness. The Kremlin that Kennan described was "basically flexible in its reaction to political reality [and] . . . by no means unamenable to considerations of prestige." Kennan counselled patience and painted a rather hopeful picture of the future if only "the western world finds the strength and resourcefulness to contain Soviet power over a period of 10 to 15 years."

In Kennan's discussion of the subject emphasized in the article's title — "The Sources of Soviet Conduct" — it is striking how little attention a man identified with the realist school of international relations paid to such

139

factors as the interests of the Russian state. Indeed, the concept of national interest is totally absent from the piece, as is any discussion of a
desire for security as a driving force in Soviet policy. Instead, Kennan
found the sources of Soviet conduct in other spheres: first, in communist
ideology; second, in the imperatives of maintaining power at home.

On the first point, Kennan emphasized most what he called "the Soviet
structure of thought . . . the mental world of the Soviet leaders." He
referred to communism as a "mystical, Messianic movement," to the communists' "particular brand of fanaticism," to their assumptions about an
"innate antagonism between capitalism and socialism" and about the
"infallibility of the Kremlin [as] the sole repository of truth." With this
way of looking at the world, he said, "there can never be on Moscow's
side any sincere assumption of a community of aims between the Soviet
Union and powers which are regarded as capitalists. . . . There can be
no appeal to common purposes, there can be no appeal to common mental approaches."

On the second issue, Kennan explicitly asserted "that the stress laid in
Moscow on the menace confronting Soviet society from the world outside
its borders is founded not in the realities of foreign antagonism but in the
necessity of explaining away the maintenance of dictatorial authority at
home." He placed great emphasis upon "the concept of Russia as in a
state of siege" as virtually the sole legitimating mechanism for the dictatorship. "The millions of human beings who form that part of the structure of power must defend at all costs this concept of Russia's position, for
without it they are themselves superfluous."

Kennan's view of the future was somewhat ambivalent. Certainly, he
gave great attention to the possibility of change in the Soviet Union, if
only the communist movement were contained. Through most of the article, he wrote as if he had cataclysmic change in mind. His analysis of the
narrowness of support for the Soviet rulers led in this direction. He argued
that "the excesses of the police apparatus have fanned the political opposition to the regime into something far greater and more dangerous than it
could have been before the excesses began," and he discussed at length the
possibility that the succession might lead to an unravelling of the structure of power. "The possibility remains (and in the opinion of this writer
it is a strong one) that Soviet power, like the capitalist world of its conception, bears within it the seeds of its own decay, and that the sprouting
of these seeds is well advanced."

Yet, in his conclusion, Kennan raised the possibility of a far more moderate kind of change:

> The United States has it in its power to increase enormously the strains
> under which Soviet policy must operate, to force upon the Kremlin a far
> greater degree of moderation and circumspection than it has had to observe

in recent years, and in this way to promote tendencies which must eventually find their outlet in either the break-up or the gradual mellowing of Soviet power. For no mystical, Messianic movement — and particularly not that of the Kremlin — can face frustration indefinitely without eventually adjusting itself in one way or another to the logic of that state of affairs.

## KENNAN AND SOVIET THOUGHT IN THE 1940s

The Kennan article was written more than 40 years ago. How does it stand up as an analysis of the Soviet Union of its time and as a prediction of the future? How relevant is the analysis for understanding the contemporary Soviet Union?

In the long debate about the origins of the cold war, widely differing views have been expressed about Soviet intentions and thinking in the late 1940s. A variety of evidence, including the contemporary statements of Maxim Litvinov about which Professor Mastny has written,[2] suggests that Kennan was basically right in his description of the way that Stalin thought. Stalin did seem to fear that a more open posture toward the West would strengthen liberal tendencies at home. Ideology did increase Stalin's suspicions of the West and his hostility toward it.

In retrospect, the "X" article stands up less well in its tendency to overgeneralize about communist thinking, even at that time. In talking about "the powerful hands of Russian history and tradition" sustaining the Soviet leaders in the belief that "the outside world was hostile and that it was their duty eventually to overthrow the political forces beyond their borders," Kennan glossed over the fact that the Great Russian members of Lenin's Politburo — Bukharin, Rykov, and Tomsky — became the core of the Right Opposition, which seemed to have a more relaxed attitude toward markets and the West.

Even in 1947, there is evidence of a debate at the highest levels of the Politburo. There is one curious aspect of the "X" article that is almost never noted. It was published in the same issue of *Foreign Affairs* that carried an article on Anglo-American competition by Eugene Varga, the director of the main Soviet scholarly institute concerned with the outside world and a man who provided a weekly package of analysis and advice for Stalin on the subject.[3] Paradoxically, as the person chosen to present a Soviet view of the West, Varga had a way of thinking about the subject that was extremely different from Kennan's generalizations about Soviet thinking.

While concluding that Britain and the United States were united in the chief aims of their foreign policy, Varga asserted that "England is trying to pursue a foreign policy of her own." Treating differences between the domestic policies of the British Labor Party and the Truman administration as quite significant, as well as differences in foreign policy between

Truman and Roosevelt and between Bevin and the left wing of the Labor Party, Varga implies that Western governments had some independence from their ruling classes.[4]

In the Soviet media, Varga was even more explicit. He denied that governments were subordinated to "the monopolies," and scornfully dismissed the idea that "now in 1947 the working class and the Labor Party has no influence on the policy of England, that the financial oligarchy makes all the policy."[5] He suggested that the influence of the masses on the bourgeois state could become so great that it could serve as the vehicle for the transformation of capitalism into the peaceful transition to socialism, and he spoke of British nationalization as something serious.

> Today, thirty years after the victory of the Great October Revolution, the struggle in Europe is becoming in its historical development more and more a struggle for the tempos and forms of the transition from capitalism to socialism. Although the Russian path, the Soviet system, is undoubtedly the best and fastest path of transition from capitalism to socialism, historical development as Lenin had theoretically predicted, shows that other paths are also available for the achievement of this goal.[6]

Varga differed from policy not only on the possibility of different paths to socialism, but also on the question of East–West relations. In his book he had suggested that "the democratic forces in all countries" were so strong and had such a strong potential impact on governmental policy that "the relationship of the capitalist countries to the Soviet Union will not be the same as it was in the prewar period."[7] He argued that Lenin's theory of the inevitability of war between capitalist countries was no longer valid, and that political independence for countries such as India could have real meaning in terms of their foreign policy.

Of course, Varga's institute was closed, and he himself, while not arrested, published little for the rest of the Stalin period. But while the "X" article was basically accurate in its description of the pattern of Stalin's thoughts and the thoughts of some other members of the Politburo such as Molotov, it remains a fact that Varga's views could still be published through the fall of 1947. It is difficult to believe that he, too, did not have support in the Politburo. By all indications, one of these supporters was Georgii Malenkov, chairman of the foreign policy subcommittee of the Politburo and the number two figure in the political system after 1949.

I have raised the question of Varga and Malenkov not because I want to engage in revisionism on the origin of the cold war. I think that Stalin had an impregnable position and a set of views that was not conducive to any very different foreign policy outcome. I emphasize the point, rather, as a reminder that not all Marxist–Leninists thought alike, even in the Stalin period.

## RECENT CHANGES IN SOVIET THINKING

Varga's thought pattern also is important to emphasize because much of it became orthodoxy in the post-Stalin period, and virtually all of it became highly respectable. In fact, on the questions of the inevitability of war, of peaceful paths to socialism, and of the possibility of an independent foreign policy by Third World countries, Varga's position became unchallengeable doctrine in 1956. His denunciation of the proposition that Western governments are subordinated to the "monopolies" of Wall Street has been incorporated in innumerable party documents and, though challengeable, is accepted by virtually everyone in the Soviet foreign policy establishment. The degree of the impact of the masses on Western foreign policy is the subject of continual debate, but the Varga position is adopted by all the pro-détente forces.

It is now possible to present an image of international relations in the Soviet press that is at the polar opposite from the two-camp image. Thus, the head of the International Organizations Department of the Ministry of Foreign Affairs, V. Petrovsky, has warned against "turning [the concept of] global conflict into an absolute. . . . The concept of international conflict as an eternal, root category or even essence of international relations . . . in whatever phraseology it is clothed, in practice, ignores the objective fact of the constantly widening collaboration in politics, economics, and science and technology of states of different systems."[8]

The framework in which this point is most frequently raised is in discussions of global problems, general human problems, global interdependence, and the like. Discussions of these problems usually center on such questions as pollution, food supply, the energy crisis, oceanic issues, and so forth. One such article, written by an official of the Central Committee apparatus, contained a three-page section on "the discontinuation of the arms race as the necessary condition for solving economic problems."[9] On Moscow television in 1982, Georgii Arbatov pointed to yet another common interest when he said that "everybody is dependent on the stability of the international economic system and the international monetary system."[10]

Sometimes this image is simply implied in the use of phraseology far from that of irreconcilable class conflict or "two camps." One scholar writes of the "human association";[11] a foreign ministry official asserts that "mankind continues to exist as a united whole";[12] a Central Committee official speaks on Soviet television of "we Europeans," linking Russians together with West Europeans;[13] two other scholars refer to "the two lines in world politics—between the proponents of an aggressive policy and the advocates of the preservation and deepening of détente," without suggesting that these two lines coincided with the division between classes or even between the two systems.[14]

The Soviet media also contain views on revolutionary prospects abroad that are far from those of the Stalin era. For example, a number of leading Soviet Latin Americanists have been insisting that the major countries of that region are closer to southern Europe in their socioeconomic development than to most of Asia and Africa, and that their political development is likely to follow the path from military dictatorship to constitutional democracy as seen in southern Europe in the mid-1970s. These scholars draw the logical conclusions so far as the proper tactics of the communist parties are concerned. One of the most outspoken, Boris Koval, the deputy director of the Institute of the International Workers' Movement, has contended that "in a whole group of countries, the toilers, in practice, have to select not between capitalism and socialism, but between bourgeois democracy and fascism." Indeed, he went so far as to suggest that the struggle for democracy (in a presocialist system) would be the determining feature of Latin American politics for many years and perhaps decades.[15]

Koval made his opinion clear regarding the position of local communists in this struggle. While maintaining their independence, they should be willing to cooperate with the moderates where there was a coincidence of interests — and the preservation of representative democracy was certainly one such case. In 1982, Koval specifically cautioned against an underestimation of the revolutions in Peru from 1968–1975, and Zimbabwe in 1980. Although these revolutions did not produce socialism, they did lead to a change in political system, and in his opinion this was not insignificant. He wrote with near contempt of "petty-bourgeois revolutionism" based on peasants and white collar forces,[16] and while he did not say so, it was difficult to forget that the Central American guerrilla movements were, first of all, based on intellectuals and peasants.

Similar views are expressed about revolution in Asia and Africa, although everyone recognizes the possibility of radical victories in the most backward countries. Virtually all Russian scholars openly assert in print that the Soviet model, based on internal mobilization of resources and complete suppression of the private sector, is undesirable in the Third World. They believe that outside resources are necessary and that the socialist countries are too poor to provide them in all but a few cases. Hence, Western investment is inevitable and even desirable, and most see political dependence on the West flowing from economic dependence. Privately, many of the major scholars simply stated that "the United States has won in the Third World." Many of the scholars of the Institute of Oriental Studies, in particular, have this view.

These statements bespeak a pattern of thought totally different from that depicted in the "X" article. I do not want to imply that all Soviet citizens think in this way. In the debates in Soviet journals and on television talk shows, other persons continue to insist on the importance of the class factor, on the implacable hostility and expansionism of the United States, and on the possibility of successful revolution in the Third World. Many treat Soviet–American relations as far more a zero-sum game than a realm for possible cooperation.

Yet, at a minimum, the persons on the unorthodox side are not eccentric outsiders. Arbatov is a Central Committee member, and the deputy directors of the Institutes of the International Workers' Movement and of Oriental Studies have posts in the *nomenklatura* of the Central Committee. Koval, in particular, is very closely associated with Vadim Zagladin, the first deputy head of the international department and a man whose own writings come very close to a revisionistic position. In 1982, a reliable Soviet source said that Zagladin was the one man in the foreign policy establishment with whom Chernenko was consulting during the last year of Brezhnev's life.

## KENNAN'S PREDICTIONS OF THE FUTURE

What, then, are the implications of the opening up of the debate and the spread of the Varga viewpoint through large parts of the Soviet foreign policy establishment? The first implication is that we must be extremely careful before we begin to infer the sources of Soviet behavior from the assumptions of Marxism–Leninism as they were perceived by Stalin 30 years ago; we should be extremely careful, and I could make the point more strongly. It simply is illegitimate to say that if we read the "X" article, if we study and understand the Soviet Union of the 1940s and the 1950s, we can confidently say that we understand the contemporary motivation and pattern of thought of the Soviet leaders at the present or in the future. The fact that men like Gromyko, Ustinov, and Ponomarev already held important posts at that time and have been at high levels for 40 years does of course imply considerable continuity—although Gromyko and Ponomarev used to be closer in their thinking to Varga than to Stalin—but now that they have lost control of Soviet foreign policy, we may be dealing with people who think very differently.

It is, of course, one thing to say how *not* to understand the sources of Soviet foreign policy; it is something else to say what those sources actually are. In understanding the sources of Soviet conduct today, it is not only fair but worthwhile to consider how "X" viewed our own time, that is, Kennan's 1947 projections of the future.

In fact, Kennan's predictions were in many respects quite accurate. He was right that if events stubbornly kept disconfirming the ideological predictions, messianic communism would begin to mellow. It is fascinating to read the debates of the 1960s and 1970s and watch the impact on Soviet thinking of events from the Cuban revolution to the internationalization of world production to the Islamic revolution — events which changed the direction of the debate.[17]

Kennan's predictions were also right about the connection between domestic and foreign policy. A more relaxed attitude toward the outside world and a more relaxed attitude toward unorthodox views *have* gone together in the Soviet Union, most spectacularly during the de-Stalinization of the mid-1950s. The same is true of the relationship between declining support of the Soviet economic model abroad and the deepening belief of Soviet intellectuals that the model needs modification at home.

Kennan's predictions were even right about the instability of the Soviet political system, if one defines that system as the totalitarian model did: an overpowering dictatorship, an absolutely rigid and dogmatic ideology, an irrational terror that arrested totally innocent people as well as those who broke the rules of the system, the sending of millions of people to camps on various political criteria, a xenophobic reaction to anything Western, and a sheer craziness like that shown in the rejection of great Russian scientific discoveries like the Mendelian theory of genetics. Although some remnants remain, that political system has essentially disappeared. The problem in the Soviet Union in the last decade has not been an overpowering dictator who lashes out at the elite and society on the basis of his dogmatic ideology, but leaders who will not take strong action on any basis, who do not know what they want to do or are afraid to act, who say as Andropov did on economic reform, "I have no recipes."

And yet, one rereads Kennan's predictions with frustration. He correctly stated, as already quoted, that irrational police action was undercutting support more than helping it; but he did not draw the conclusion that the curbing of the police (the transformation of the Soviet Union from a totalitarian dictatorship into an authoritarian dictatorship, to use the definitions of the 1950s) would produce a regime that has proved very stable for 30 years. He underestimated the sources of support for the basic communist system in the Soviet Union and paid too much attention to the possibility of its collapse in contrast to its evolution.

Similarly, in foreign policy, Kennan was right about a mellowing of ideology and about a modification of foreign policy in a more cooperative direction. But whatever he may have thought privately (and Kennan has been a rather pessimistic man about human nature and governments), his article did not prepare the reader for the kind of challenges that a mellower Soviet Union would continue to pose, or for the continuities in many kinds of behavior.

## FACTORS INFLUENCING SOVIET FOREIGN POLICY

The basic problem, it seems, is that the sources of Soviet foreign policy in 1947 were limited neither to rigid ideological suspicion and hostility nor to Stalin's desire to consolidate his power. A series of other factors were also at work in shaping Soviet policy at the time, which came more into focus when the factors that Kennan emphasized began to fade.

First, ideology is not simply a dogmatic guide to action. It also provides the definition of values on which the legitimacy of a system rests. Two superpowers with competing ideologies would inevitably come into conflict on this basis alone. For example, the United States in all meaningful senses has accepted Soviet control of Eastern Europe. Yet, for reasons of internal legitimacy and human rights, there was no way that the United States could fail to provide moral (and some concrete) support to Solidarity when it arose in Poland. This produced a strong reaction in much of the Soviet elite.

Similarly, the Soviet Union in all meaningful senses has written off Central America. The Soviets would not react if the United States sent troops to El Salvador or invaded Nicaragua, and they have been unwilling to bankroll Nicaragua economically, thereby virtually guaranteeing that the Sandinistas or their successors eventually will have to move toward the right. Yet, the basic Soviet value structure and the dynamics of competition with the United States makes it inevitable that the Soviet Union provide moral support and small-scale aid to the Salvadoran rebels. This has produced a strong reaction in the United States.

Second, the momentum of events and past commitments needs to be emphasized. A "winter Olympics" image of international relations might be useful here, for once a nation "pushes off down the ski jump," frequently without fully thinking through what it is doing, it picks up speed rapidly and finds it difficult to change course. This, too, is an aspect of Soviet behavior that we ignore at our own peril. When a radical revolution occurs, it is difficult for the Soviet Union not to become committed at some low level. When the United States challenges Soviet allies frontally, it is difficult for the Soviet Union not to increase its support to them. Similar mechanisms operate on the American side.

Third, any analysis of the factors shaping Soviet foreign policy that does not prominently include a drive for basic national security and the promotion of a series of innate national interests seems deeply flawed. Even if Russia became democratic or America became communist, the relationship between the two superpowers would likely remain one of conflict at least until sometime in the twenty-first or twenty-second century when countries such as China, India, and Brazil become superpowers, leading to new alignments.

Indeed, this point, often ignored by hawk and dove alike, is the place where any serious analysis of Soviet goals and intentions must begin. Hans Morgenthau, the leading realist international relations theorist of the 1950s, was correct in insisting that international relations always involve a struggle for power, that all countries are engaged in an attempt to expand their power and influence. In that sense, all countries, including even Denmark, are expansionist within their means. Similarly, all countries are looking for opportunities to make gains and are, in that sense, opportunistic. And of course, all are attempting to preserve what they already have, and in that sense they are all defensive. To argue whether the Soviet Union is expansionist or defensive misses the point. It is both. So to suggest that better understanding can produce an era of total good feeling is to show naivete. But it is just as naive to suggest that we refuse to cooperate with the Soviet Union on any issue until it accepts a definition of détente that requires it to stop promoting its interests, thus preventing cooperation where we have common enemies (such as Islamic fundamentalism) or common causes (such as the containment of the Iran–Iraq war).

The crucial questions in international relations are not those of ultimate goals. They center on the *risks* a leader is willing to take to achieve these goals. (All Argentine governments have wanted the Falklands, but none of the others took the risks of the last military government.) They center on *means* chosen to achieve goals. (The Japanese are still trying to dominate Southeast Asia, but use economic means instead of military.) They center on the *priority* assigned to various conflicting foreign policy goals. (The balance the United States makes between the commitment to Israeli policy and the commitment to the peace process in the Middle East is always an excruciating choice.) And, above all, these questions center on leaders' changing *perceptions* of cost–benefit ratios for different foreign policy options.

It is through such a prism that Soviet foreign policy needs to be viewed. Soviet policy of the Brezhnev era, especially during its last years, was marked by much less willingness to take risks than that displayed under either Stalin (in Berlin and Korea) or Khrushchev (in the Third World or the Cuban missile crisis). It was marked by a growing pessimism about the possibility of achieving revolutionary goals in the Third World, but even more by an unwillingness or inability to make hard decisions on priorities. The Soviet Union continually pursued a number of contradictory goals, and would not choose between them in a way that would have permitted any of them to be achieved. It courted American allies, but did so through peace-campaign techniques that had long proven ineffective rather than through the making of meaningful concessions. Similarly, Soviet leaders could not bring themselves to make reductions in secrecy that would have been necessary for real arms control.

## DOMESTIC IMPERATIVES IN THE GORBACHEV ERA

One looking toward the foreign policy of the Gorbachev era would be wrong to see any basic change in the Soviet drive to pursue its interests.

However, a real change is possible in the way that the Soviet Union defines its interests or priorities, and in its willingness to make hard choices between alternatives.

At the end of his *Time* interview, Gorbachev added that "few words that are important in understanding what we have been talking about all along." He asserted that "foreign policy is a continuation of domestic policy," and then asked his Soviet and foreign readers "to ponder one thing. If we in the Soviet Union are setting ourselves such truly grandiose plans in the domestic sphere, then what are the external conditions that we need to be able to fulfill those domestic plans?"[18]

Gorbachev ended the interview enigmatically ("I leave the answer to that question to you"), but his emphasis on the point was significant. The connection between domestic and foreign policy *has* been a close one in Soviet history. Kennan was right in saying that Stalin was thinking about (and afraid of) the domestic consequences of good relations with the United States. One of the major factors behind the continuation of the bipolar policy throughout the Brezhnev period was his preference for the present Soviet economic system. As long as the Soviet leaders want strict central planning and foreign economic relations limited to centralized bilateral trade (and want the same for Eastern Europe), there are few advantages in this age of unlikely foreign attack to a real multipolar foreign policy.

So to understand the changes in Gorbachev's foreign policy, we must understand the nature of his domestic imperatives. Gorbachev has indicated that his goal is to raise Soviet technology to world levels. He has stated (and he is right) that superpower status in the twenty-first century depends on it. The Soviet Union faces an enormous window of military vulnerability at the end of the century. If the Western armies and weapons become fully computerized, if contemporary weapons such as tanks become obsolete, if SDI were to work (or simply have important spin-offs for conventional weapons), if China with its billion-plus population were to begin to modernize seriously, if Japan were to have a change of government and return to the foreign policy of the 1930s, an unmodernized Soviet Union could be in enormous danger. With 40% of the Soviet army in the twenty-first century made up of Central Asians, the Soviet Union can have a computerized army only if all its population has been brought into the twenty-first century.

Raising Soviet technology to world levels is incredibly difficult. Many Westerners would say that it is impossible, but this is wishful thinking. John Foster Dulles said in 1955 that Japan could never challenge the United States in high technology markets. We should not make similar mistakes with the Soviet Union. Nevertheless, the difficulty remains. Brezhnev demonstrated that the importation of Western technology is no panacea, and something radically different must be tried.

The experience of Japan, Taiwan, and South Korea suggests that one secret for solving the problem of technological backwardness is a policy of exporting manufactured goods. Those countries began to export not when they reached world levels of technology, but when they were quite backward. They did so because only such a strategy could subject their manufacturers to foreign competition, forcing them to improve the quality of their exports to world levels. Soviet manufacturers enjoy a level of protectionism unknown in the outside world, and an attack on this protectionism is absolutely vital if the Soviet economy is to be modernized.

## IMPLICATIONS FOR FOREIGN POLICY

If the need to raise the quality of Soviet technology is to be the driving force behind Soviet foreign policy, a number of implications follow.

First, radical revolution in the Third World has been unsuccessful in all but pre-industrial societies such as Afghanistan, South Yemen, Ethiopia, and Nicaragua, and the politics of industrializing Third World countries are moving to the center and the right. The number of pre-industrial countries is declining; these countries are by definition not significant economic and military powers, and even radical pre-industrial societies such as China and Mozambique are showing a tendency to moderate their policy. A Soviet foreign policy that focuses on promoting revolution in countries like Nicaragua (with $2\frac{1}{2}$ million people) while neglecting countries such as Mexico (with 79 million) is following a losing strategy.

That strategy becomes even more counterproductive if one considers economic factors. An export strategy will be difficult to pursue in the industrial world because a country with inferior goods must compete by lowering prices, a practice which inevitably runs into protectionist pressures and charges of dumping. The Third World is the natural place for Soviet leaders to begin competing with Western manufacturers, and only moderate regimes there have the necessary purchasing power.

In many respects, a move toward courtship of moderate Third World countries is already under way. The crucial case is the Philippines. The Soviet Union is not only not supporting the communist revolution materially, but the Soviets gave a medal to former President Marcos for past service as ambassador to the Soviet Union, and the U.S.S.R. was the only country to send congratulations to him on his fraudulent victory in the February 1986 presidential election. Similar tendencies are seen in the establishment of diplomatic relations with Oman, sports diplomacy with Saudi Arabia, and diplomatic flirtation with Israel.

Second, in the military realm, the logic of Gorbachev's domestic policy is to shift the emphasis from short- to long-range defense needs. Current spending levels on procurement, readiness, and manpower are unnecessary, especially with China reducing its army by a million people. Similarly, with a slow deployment of the mobile SS-25 being the least expensive answer to American development of first-strike weapons, the Soviet Union can reduce its strategic expenditures regardless of any arms control agreement with the United States. By contrast, the Soviet Union has a great military problem in long-term perspective. To meet this problem, the Soviet Union needs to pour money into research and development, especially in areas (such as computerization) that will be necessary for the military technology of the twenty-first century and for civilian technology as well. SDI and Chinese modernization are the perfect threats for Soviet leaders to emphasize because they post no short-term danger at all but symbolize the long-term danger.

Third, the short-term logic of Gorbachev's domestic needs is to deemphasize relations with the United States and even to stress anti-Americanism while focusing on relations with Western Europe and Japan. Paradoxically, doves such as Marshall Shulman and hawks such as Richard Perle have been united in a different view of the requirements of Soviet liberalization and modernization. Both assume that such a program requires arms control agreements with the United States. The doves have argued for détente to promote such a development; the hawks have argued for a hard-line policy either to prevent it or to obtain major concessions from the Soviet Union in the process.

This position seems fundamentally wrong, because no Soviet leader can afford to give the U.S.S.R.'s main enemy a veto power over its domestic evolution. In fact, modernization, though it requires an economic opening to the West, is much easier to sell domestically in the name of anti-Americanism than in the context of agreements with the United States. If a Soviet leader says that a more relaxed information policy and opening to the West is possible because the United States can be trusted, Soviet conservatives will think him deeply naive. But if a Soviet leader says this is necessary as the only way to have the computerization that is needed to thwart the American danger, or if he can say that the United States is trying to force the Soviet Union into an arms race to bankrupt the Soviet economy, he can put the conservatives on the defensive. And if he says that the opening to the West can be accomplished through concessions to Japan and Europe, then he is in a position to defend it as a measure that undercuts American alliances. All the evidence suggests that this is precisely the strategy Gorbachev is following.

For these reasons, Gorbachev is likely to present the United States a challenge it has not seen for years. We have grown used to a Soviet Union that only uses ineffective peace campaigns, that concentrates on (with the exception of India) small, pre-industrial countries in the Third World, and that has allowed its economic system to lose all its attractiveness. As

Gorbachev moves to correct these mistakes, the United States, too, will have to develop a new approach. The mellowed Soviet Union that Kennan correctly predicted will be far more worthy an opponent than one hidebound by ideology and the imperatives of conspiratorial rule.

## NOTES

1. "X" [George F. Kennan], "The Sources of Soviet Conduct," *Foreign Affairs* 25 (July 1947):566–582.
2. Vojtech Mastny, *Russia's Road to the Cold War* (New York: Columbia University Press, 1979).
3. Varga was a Hungarian by birth, but he had lived in the Soviet Union for over 25 years and was at the heart of the foreign policy establishment. What he was saying in print was that the basic two-camp image of the world was wrong, that Lenin erred in his argument with Bernstein about the possibility of evolution to socialism under the bourgeois state, and that his own native Hungary should not be subjected to the Soviet model of socialism. (At the time, Varga was supporting Hungarian leader Imre Nagy in his fight against collectivization of Hungarian agriculture.)
4. E. Varga, "Anglo-American Rivalry and Partnership: A Marxist View," *Foreign Affairs* 25 (July 1947): 594–595.
5. "Diskussiia po knige E. Varga 'Izmeneniia v ekonomike kapitalizma v itoge vtoroi mirovoi voiny,' 2, 14, 21 maia 1947 g., Stenograficheskii otchet," *Mirovoe khoziaistvo i mirovaia politika*, no. 11 (November) 1947, Supplement, p. 61.
6. E. Varga, "Sotsializm i kapitalizm za tridtsat' let," *ibid*, no. 10, 1947, pp. 4–5.
7. *Izmeneniia v ekonomike kapitalizma v itoge vtoroi mirovoi voiny* (Moscow: Gospolitizdat, 1946), p. 319.
8. V. Petrovsky, "Dogmy konfrontatsii (Ob amerikanskikh kontseptsiiakh 'global'nogo konklikta')," *Mirovaia ekonomika i mezhdunarodnye otnosheniia*, no. 2, 1980, pp. 21, 22.
9. S. M. Menshikov, "Global'nye problemy i budushche mirovoi ekonomiki," *Voprosy filosofii*, no. 4, 1983, pp. 113–115.
10. Studio 9, May 1982. Translated in FBIS, *Daily Report–Soviet Union*, June 1, 1982, pp. CC6.
11. V. N. Shevchenko, "K kharakteristike dialektiki sovremennoi epokhi (chast' parvaia)," *Filosofskie nauki*, no. 5, 1981, p. 23.
12. V. Petrovsky, "Kontseptsiia vzaimozavisimosti v strategii SShA," *Mirovaia ekonomika i mezhdunarodnye otnosheniia*, no. 9, 1977, p. 71.
13. Vitalii Kobysh, on Studio 9, December 24, 1983. Translated in FBIS, *Daily Report–Soviet Union*, December 27, 1983, p. CC10.
14. D. Tomashevsky and V. Lukov, "Radi zhizni na zemli," *Mirovaia ekonomia i mezhdunarodnye otnosheniia*, no. 2, 1983, p. 10.
15. B. I. Koval' and S. I. Semenov, "Latinskaia Amerika i mezhdunarodnaia sotsial-demokratiia," *Rabochii klass i sovremennyi mir*, no. 4 (July–August) 1978, pp. 115–130. B. I. Koval', in "Mezhdunarodnaia sotsial-demokratiia v Latinskoi Amerike," *Latinskaia Amerika*, no. 4, 1978, p. 103.

16. See "Revoliutsionnoe dvizhenie v Peru: uroki, problemy, perspektivy," *Latinskaia Amerika*, no. 1 (1984), pp. 162–163; and "Rabochii klass i revoliutsionnost' narodnykh mass: opyt 70kh godov," *Rabochii klass i sovremenny mir*, no. 2 (1983), pp. 8–9, 13.
17. The evolution of the debates on the Third World from the 1950s into the 1960s and 1970s is described in Jerry F. Hough, *The Struggle for the Third World: Soviet Debates and American Options* (Washington: Brookings Institution, 1986).
18. "An Interview with Gorbachev," *Time*, September 9, 1985, p. 29.

# 9 SOCIO-CULTURAL IMPERATIVES TO A NEW CONTAINMENT POLICY

*James H. Billington*

Almost every serious observer says that the United States needs a steady, rational policy toward the U.S.S.R. in order both to avoid miscalculation on the Soviets' part and to sustain unity among our allies. Yet the oscillations in U.S. policy toward the U.S.S.R. have continued and perhaps increased in the two decades since the fall of Khrushchev. Whereas the Soviet Union has consistently had a foreign policy far more effective than its basic system, just the opposite is true of America. As a society, America has experienced continuing growth and remarkable dynamism without, however, finding an effective foreign policy.

Although each of the three most recent chief American policymakers has displayed certain strengths in dealing with the Soviets, each has also encountered difficulties. Nixon developed both a new relationship with China as a check against Soviet power and a framework for negotiating directly with Soviet leaders. Yet détente may have encouraged the American public to expect too much, and it failed either to provide real incentives for Soviet restraint or to project higher ideals to the post-Stalinist generation.[1] Carter's human rights emphasis projected such an ideal; but his contradictory signals interrupted the continuity of the negotiating process with the Soviet leaders, and the SALT treaty he *did* negotiate could not be sold domestically after the invasion of Afghanistan.

If the net effect of the Nixon–Ford era was to heighten the Soviet elite's sense of condominial self-importance, the net effect of the Carter policies was to make the Soviet leaders angrier at (though not more afraid of or deterred by) their American adversary. Reagan, by institutionalizing the increased defense effort of the late Carter years and adding the Strategic Defense Initiative (SDI), has introduced an element of genuine fear into the Soviet leadership while sustaining the human rights emphasis. He may have made long-range gains by indirectly encouraging forces for change within the rising generation of Soviets, but the initial stridency of his challenge created short-term problems for American policy by stimulating nationalistic sentiments that tend to support militaristic policies.

## THE SOVIET–AMERICAN RELATIONSHIP

To determine how best to undertake the difficult task of developing constructive new initiatives, we need to examine afresh the basics of how the U.S.S.R. relates to the United States. Neither the Russian empire nor the U.S.S.R. has ever been at war with the United States. Relations in the eighteenth and nineteenth centuries were distant, but generally amicable. Even today the U.S.S.R. does not pose to the United States a direct geopolitical threat of the classic kind — a threat of conquest or direct intimidation from a contiguous power. The U.S.S.R. poses, rather, a special, complex threat deriving from its capacity to:

1. Destroy the United States directly in minutes or hours with missiles and nuclear weapons;
2. Reduce the United States to vassalage in a matter of months or years by establishing geopolitical dominance of Eurasia through conventional attack and imperial politics; or
3. Bleed the United States to death and eventually reduce it to vassalage over the next few decades by becoming an increasingly dominant force in the Third World.

With such awesome capabilities, the classic question of Soviet perceptions and intentions becomes even more important. The new political generation in the U.S.S.R. will have difficulty scaling back the heightened political expectations its predecessor has built up along with its military arsenal during the last two decades; and the risk of reaching a point of no return on the way to war is aggravated by the radically different ways in which Soviet and American leaders perceive reality.

This perceptual gap is not, I believe, greatest in the area most immediately menacing to both the U.S.S.R. and the United States: the nuclear missile face-off. Both sides have a rational grasp of the basic nuclear facts and dangers, which can be perceived in both statistical and visceral ways that transcend cultural or ideological blinders. The perceptual gap is almost certainly much greater in the area of potential geopolitical dangers to our Eurasian allies. There is a tendency, rooted deep in Russian history, for Soviet leaders genuinely to perceive as defensive the kinds of aggressive action or preemptive threat that seem clearly offensive to us and our allies.

But the area in which the perceptual gap may be widest (and the risk of real war greatest) is in the unallied and turbulent two thirds of the globe we call the Third World. There is a radically different perception not just of the facts at issue in the Third World, but also of the forces at work and the basic legitimacy of outside involvements. Ironically (but perhaps mercifully), the danger of war is almost certainly greatest in that area of threat in which there is the least direct and immediate danger to the two superpowers, and the greatest chance of avoiding their automatic involvement. But, for precisely these seemingly reassuring reasons, we may continue to neglect this crucial area of danger — and the perceptual gap may continue to widen, even as Soviet involvement deepens and the number of proxies and potentially uncontrollable independent actors increases.

An important, if elusive, factor in Soviet–American relations is the peculiarity of national psychology on both sides. Particularly important are the very different ways in which each of these multiethnic, continent-wide civilizations on the periphery of Europe feels itself to be different from traditional European powers and, in fact, unique in the world. To oversimplify, Russians tend to feel uniquely persecuted and they long to be respected; Americans tend to feel uniquely favored and wish to be loved. The Puritan Anglo-Saxon base of America infused its public culture with a sense of respect for the individual based on law, but left the culture with an awkwardness about public manifestations of love; the Orthodox Russian base of Soviet culture provided communal love in almost embarrassing excess, but was weak in conferring individual self-respect in the public realm.

As their global reputations slipped in the course of the 1970s, each country turned to a new leader who spoke to these special needs. With Andropov, the U.S.S.R. produced a specialist in persecuting its internal opposition from an institution, the KGB, that commanded awesome respect; with Reagan, America produced a specialist in communicating its sense of national favor using the techniques of an institution, the cinema, that inspires confidence based on affection. Revived nationalism in each superpower added in turn to the difficulty each experienced in communicating with the other, while generating a certain restiveness in Eastern as well as Western Europe among allies who find it difficult to understand their respective dominant powers.

Soviet attitudes toward the United States derive in important ways from the historic attitudes of Russian leaders toward the West. Those attitudes include tendencies to see the West as a unitary enemy dedicated to exploiting Russia, but one which is morally weak and politically divisible. At the same time, there is the well-known sense of Russian inferiority, combined with a certain love–hate dependence on the U.S.S.R.'s principal Western adversary. Many of these attitudes result from the fact that Russia does not have a secure sense of its own cultural identity, has repeatedly been attacked from both East and West, and has for much of its history lacked clear external boundaries or well-defined internal civil procedures. The United States has replaced the Germany of the late nineteenth and early twentieth centuries (and the France of the late eighteenth and early nineteenth centuries) as the essential "West" that Russians must both publicly confront and privately learn from.

There are, then, very deep cultural difficulties in U.S.-U.S.S.R. communication, differences reinforced by the Reagan administration's focus on redressing the strategic military balance. Such U.S. action may be necessary to check the Soviet leaders' inertial belief that they could continue to make foreign policy gains free of cost. But projecting power in missiles and space programs risks revalidating to the Russian people precisely the image of a hostile West seeking material predominance they so love to hate.

## OPPORTUNITIES FOR A MORE SOPHISTICATED APPROACH

Although we have little real experience with Mikhail Gorbachev, it is at least clear that the new generation of leadership in the U.S.S.R. is committed to far-reaching economic changes. These, in turn, could lead (albeit unintentionally) to dramatic changes in the Soviet political system. The objective need for systemic economic reform legitimizes demands for change within the political oligarchy; and the cumulative effect of massive deferred maintenance at a time of domestic economic stagnation will make it increasingly clear that projected economic targets cannot be met without systemic change.

Sociologically, there is an almost unimaginable contrast in basic formative influence between Soviet leaders of the past 20 years and those of the next 20 years. The generation of Brezhnev–Andropov–Chernenko was formed in the Stalin era of massive purges, violent social upheaval, and world war, whereas that of Gorbachev grew up in the postwar, post-Stalinist era of unprecedented peace and (by Soviet standards) rising prosperity and educational levels.

Finally, this volatile socioeconomic context is politically energized by the intensity and depth of the striving (begun during the 1960s and 1970s within the nonpolitical educated population) to continue the artificially arrested process of de-Stalinizing the U.S.S.R. in order to satisfy the thirst both for more efficiency and for a non-Stalinist Russian national identity. Although the dissident tip of the iceberg has been virtually eliminated since the repression began in 1979, there is a far larger, presently submerged mass of sentiment for serious reform within the establishment. A thirst for basic restructuring is evident in writings on a host of intellectual and social questions, and occasionally in direct reform proposals leaked to the press (such as the Novosibirsk documents). Indeed, the extremely protective way in which the geriatric Stalinist elite so long resisted bringing post-Stalinist leaders into top-level positions reflects (at least partly) the classical reactionary oligarchy's instinctive fear that, when both policy and personnel changes have been so long delayed, they are likely to be far-reaching.[2]

Given the continued militance of Soviet leaders on foreign policy, America faces the difficult task of speaking simultaneously both to outer power and to inner searching. Although the latter is largely concentrated among (though not confined to) the better-educated professional leaders, that group includes many of those exercising major line responsibility in the government and economy within the Gorbachev generation. This reality requires a much more clearly defined and differentiated dialogue with the U.S.S.R. than we have yet had. We need a dialogue that is tough and specific with the older, outer forces of power, but broad, exploratory, and even generous with the younger forces that are pushing for innovation and change.[3]

Such a differentiated approach is not an easy order for a democratic society that always wants a simple, monolithic line of policy, preferably with a chronologically guaranteed outcome. But such a distinction is essential for a sustainable policy that will avoid either of two oversimplified but persistent American delusions about the U.S.S.R. The first is that liberalization is somehow built into the process of national development and should be helped along by more accommodating attitudes toward the present leaders. The second is that the Soviets' continuing hostility somehow reflects built-in historical characteristics of immutable Russian (or Bolshevik) attitudes, for which there is no remedy except continuous confrontation by external force. We must, in my view, clearly reject the implied determinism of either of these views while accepting the element of instinctive insight in each.

In fact, Soviet leaders are hostile to us not primarily because of Russian history or even communist ideology, but because they are the political beneficiaries of one of the greatest state-committed atrocities of this century: Stalin's demonic purges of his own people in general, and of the most talented political and intellectual leaders, in particular. The Brezhnev–Chernenko generation compounded the crime by stopping Khrushchev's process of de-Stalinization, which might have opened up possibilities for modification of orthodoxy and creative innovation. The Gorbachev generation may not need to bear the guilt or perpetuate the paranoia of those whose careers were built on the genocidal policies of the 1930s, but their legacy will be difficult to shake.

The main hope of the surviving Stalinists for a full-blown transmission of their repressive form of rule to the next generation currently lies in their efforts to convince their subjects that now, as in the 1930s, there is a growing external danger so great as to justify a partial return to Stalinism. Particularly since the harshly repressive turn of 1979, Soviet leaders have increasingly been using the high Stalinist tactic of fanning domestic fears that "the West" threatens the identity — perhaps even the existence — of Russia itself. The recent blossoming of pictures of Stalin on Soviet automobiles indicates that the popular appeal of this seemingly repellent tactic may be greater than we like to think. As a result, there is at present both a need (because the old guard is actively fueling a growing chauvinist mystique in the U.S.S.R.) and an opportunity (because of the possibility of a different outlook among the successor generation) for important fresh American initiatives.

## PRIORITIES IN POLICY OBJECTIVES

To move the U.S.S.R. effectively in a direction less threatening to the United States, any such initiatives must satisfy a daunting list of substantive and formalistic requirements:

1. Substantively, the United States must check the Soviet external power thrust without providing material for the internal legitimation of the Stalinist oligarchs.
2. At the same time, we must provide a message of rational hope for those interested in more basic structural reforms who may be positioned to push them forward.
3. The content of U.S. proposals must be dramatic and substantive enough to be widely perceived as serious even in the U.S.S.R.
4. The form these proposals take must be sufficiently comprehensible within Russian culture and universal enough in tone that they will not be perceived as the prepackaged ultimatums of a rival culture.

This extremely difficult task has yet even to be attempted by American leaders. Many of the requirements are in obvious tension with each other. President Nixon had an instinctive feel for items 3 and 4 in the list above, but not for items 1 and 2; Carter at various times stressed items 1 and 2, but not items 3 and 4. Reagan's concentration on item 1 has raised the stakes, increasing both the danger and the opportunity for the United States. Can we (and, if so, how do we) further a strategic policy toward the U.S.S.R. that is intrinsically constructive, presumptively sustainable in our own political system, and perceived as stable and "serious" by friend and foe alike?

A clear sense of what we really want of the U.S.S.R. has always been missing from American foreign policy. The simple objective of containing Soviet external expansion is modest and inherently appealing. But it is, in the last analysis, a cop-out when dealing with a country whose external behavior results so largely from its ideology. Moreover, responsible American leadership has the right and obligation to try to help any nation capable of destroying us to develop moral and structural restraints against doing so. The Helsinki Final Act makes important parts of Soviet internal policy matters of formal international commitment by the Soviet government, and these human rights questions are an important part of the moral consciousness of the coming generation in the U.S.S.R.

Should we, then, act on the assumption that the U.S.S.R. will not be capable of moderating its external behavior until the Soviet empire either transforms into something like a liberal democracy or disintegrates into a number of independent national entities? Such an assumption (which would have to be made explicit in our kind of society) would present the Soviet leadership (never more Great Russian than now) with what has historically been most difficult for Russians to accept: the external imposition of a foreign ideal. The more we presume to prescribe and proclaim our blueprint for their future, the more we encourage their reactionary xenophobia. It is necessary that American policy focus primarily on modifying Soviet policies toward the outside world. But important changes in foreign policy are likely only if there is also evolution within the U.S.S.R. Changes must be defined by Russians for Russians, not thought of by us as somehow representing imperfect approximations of ourselves.

There are, I think, three preliminary steps we must take in order to reach higher ground. They constitute both a logical sequence and a moral ordering of priorities. Each step depends on the preceding one for its effectiveness; each demands that we overcome currently fashionable illusions. We must find the courage to accept the full measure of responsibility we bear for preventing thermonuclear war, reducing the risks of any violent confrontation, and beginning to develop a new global agenda.

*Preventing thermonuclear war* is too serious a matter to be dealt with either by continuing business as usual or by simply proliferating token approaches. In view of the unprecedented nature of our accumulating destructive possibilities, bold pacifist gestures or unilateral moves toward disarming probably deserve more serious consideration than they usually get. It is not enough simply to answer "better red than dead" with "better neither than either." The deeper point is that becoming red is in fact more likely to lead to becoming dead. No wars have been more violent, no conflicts more bitter in the postwar era than those among communists (witness the Cambodian holocaust); and this reality is the logical fruit of a system that, as we noted previously, produced the largest genocide that any political oligarchy has directed against its own people in modern history. In the welter of social science research on war, one fact is clear: democracies rarely fight democracies.

In preventing nuclear war there has, of course, been some record of success. Deterrence has kept thermonuclear peace for almost 40 years. The greatest danger of nuclear war in the short term almost certainly comes from the possession of these weapons by an insecure Soviet oligarchy free of all accountability to its own people. The priority task for preventing nuclear war at the present time thus still may be to make sure that the Soviet leaders believe in the reality of our deterrent power and will.

But if this task is necessary, it is emphatically not sufficient, not just for the familiar reasons that accumulated weapons tend ultimately to be used, or that new delivery technologies may be destabilizing, or even that greater complexity and numbers of weapons means a heightened probability of accidents and breakdowns in command and control. The real danger is the growing tendency to make weapons the measure of everything else in international relations. Paradoxically, even those who focus on reducing, freezing, or otherwise creatively restructuring the arsenal may involuntarily complicate the problem. Even if adopted, such measures may amount only to technological carvings on the totem pole, symbolic actions that do not go to the heart of the main problem: the growing risk that other kinds of violent confrontation could involuntarily lead to nuclear war. Unless the unifying ideals for our own people transcend the ultimately materialistic ones of prosperity measured in productivity and security measured in weapons, our kind of civilization may subtly become ever more fixated on the thermonuclear totem in a garrison state. America as we have known it will be in its terminal travails, the only real question being whether we end with a bang or a whimper — burning in space or freezing in place.

*Reducing the risks of violent confrontation* may well be the area of U.S.–Soviet relations in which creative new initiatives can most immediately be taken. Sophisticated American churchmen are increasingly saying that vast nuclear arsenals can only be justified if the time during which war is deterred is used creatively to build the structure of a peace sustainable without them. This task can be advanced in at least four ways, each step moving ahead by building on the one before:

1. Strategic arms talks with the U.S.S.R. should focus increasingly directly on the final objective of eliminating *all* thermonuclear, chemical, and biological weapons. This objective cannot, of course, be immediately accomplished, but neither can the lesser objectives of most recent arms

reduction talks. In this television age, a dramatic concentration on the ultimate objective would begin to suggest a ritual of shared renunciation rather than of rival totem worship.

2. Our own conventional military forces should be built up in conjunction with our allies so that the subnuclear geopolitical threat in Eurasia is minimized and a greater deterrent is created against the Soviet Union's use of its conventional military strength for conquest or intimidation. This need argues for, among other things, conscription — perhaps as part of a broader national service commitment for young Americans.

3. Soviet authorities should be engaged in an institutionalized process to create "rules of the game" in the Third World that will lessen the risk of confrontation through proxy activities, arms shipments, or terrorism. The existence of such a process could subtly undermine that part of the Soviet bureaucracy that services a variety of subversive undertakings inherited from either Imperial Russia or the Communist International, and could help deter new Soviet "venture capital" investments in overseas movements that disrupt peaceful evolution or that directly threaten us.

4. In the commercial and educational spheres, the United States should initiate a major new set of overtures to the emerging post-Stalinist generation. These programs should be aimed just below the high political level and structured so as to reach a broad cross-section of the emerging professional elites while avoiding the custody of the Moscow *apparatchiks* who now so dominate contacts with this country.

A final way to break the hypnotic fascination of the arms race (and the xenophobic conservatism it helps foster in the U.S.S.R.) is to *begin to develop a new global agenda,* opening a multinational dialogue about what kind of world we want to see by the year 2000. Such a dialogue should be not just another intra-Western intellectual exercise in "globaloney," but an effort to involve the Soviets with Western leaders in a serious forum sufficiently remote from immediate policy issues to permit the Soviets to begin climbing off their outmoded ideology without asking them directly to reject it. A dialogue of this kind has the great advantage of being limitable to younger people who will themselves live in the twenty-first century.

We are in one of those rare periods when the U.S.S.R. is facing long-deferred policy choices that could determine the Soviet course for the rest of this century. To hold their system together and give it fresh dynamism, they must infuse it either with new fear through repressive chauvinism or new hope with scope for incentives. Our policy must be to do all we can to further the latter possibility. Because the Soviets have difficulty taking initiatives in times of transition, we must take some. It is surely in our interest — as leaders of the free world who must provide vision and example to our friends—to do so boldly and comprehensively rather than reluctantly and piecemeal.

## GLOBAL VALUES AND THE SOVIET SYSTEM

We can do more to help set a new agenda if we speak to the Soviets in terms that do not so much tout *our* particular institutions as affirm more universal values, values that could point to a variety of Russian futures less dominated by external threats. Freedom, for example, is a universal ideal in our time, but parliamentary democracy and private property may not be. The emergence in the U.S.S.R. of a relatively autocratic system that nevertheless widens civic participation, human rights, and local control over productive forces would be conducive to greater concentration on domestic development rather than on the projection of global power. Changes of this kind would enable a new generation of Soviet leaders to follow the old Byzantine pattern of changing the *content* of their policy without changing the *form*, and thus avoid undergoing the cultural indignity of acknowledging a foreign model.

For the immediate future, we will need to remain tough and specific in our negotiations with the U.S.S.R., conveying continuing firmness to them while sustaining unity with our allies. But we may have more reason for hope about long-range change in the U.S.S.R. now than in the immediate postwar period, not just for reasons of internal development, but also because of some surprising external ideological currents that may not leave even a relatively isolated Soviet society unaffected. I would mention only four, each of which suggests that history in the late twentieth century may move in new and unpredictable directions which are basically more compatible with the American than with the Soviet model. The latter has lost all its subjective appeal to anyone outside the Soviet Union who is free to make a choice, and these currents may make the Soviet model seem objectively inadequate even within the U.S.S.R. itself by the end of the century.

The first of these four rather neglected currents of our time is *replacement of revolution by evolution* as the pattern of social change and source of political legitimation. It has always been a sloppy cliche, and may now be an anachronism, to say that we live in an age of revolution. The inventory of Leninist victories does not seem very impressive given the length of the postwar era, the extent of its disruptive change, and the size of the Soviet investment in subversion. This observation holds despite some successes in extremely authoritarian societies like Cuba, Ethiopia, and Nicaragua, and in the transition from the French colonialism in Southeast Asia and from the Portuguese in southern Africa.

The real dynamism in social, economic, and political development during recent years has lain in constructive evolution toward democracy rather than in destructive revolution leading to dictatorships. In Western Europe and Japan, South Asia, southern Europe, and South America, democratic evolution rather than totalitarian revolution has increasingly been the means of bringing dramatic change and fresh legitimation to stagnant societies. As the revolutionary fire burns itself out on peripheral killing fields, the Parisian establishment which first lit and long tended the flame has decisively turned away from it in one of the most dramatic of recent intellectual developments. As historians inventory the horrors perpetrated in the name of rival revolutionary ideologies, humanity seems increasingly inclined to look to evolution rather than revolution for fresh beginnings.

The most profound and perhaps prophetic challenge to a Soviet-type regime in Eastern Europe has come, not from any revolutionary (or counterrevolutionary) elite driven by ideology, but from a spontaneous popular movement in Poland calling not for power but for radical *evolutionary* change. The more likely model for radical evolutionary change in the Soviet Union is the Hungarian model — probably as adapted by the Chinese, who, of course, turned to evolution as a specific alternative to, and repudiation of, the revolutionary spasm of the Cultural Revolution. Because of the Russian fascination with large-scale foes, China (like America) may have more potential as a hidden model than might otherwise seem logical.

A second powerful force in the world that is operating now in a way it was not operating in the immediate postwar period is the *rising importance of education and communication* within a far more sophisticated populace. The increase in the educated population of the world may be a more portentous development than the global population explosion itself. Although deliverance via education is not automatic (as Nazi Germany reminds us), the spreading taste for unrestricted pursuit of truth powerfully challenges systems like the Soviets' that claim to encapsulate truth in state policy or a state newspaper.

A third force at work in the world that may seem almost the opposite of the preceding one is the *return of the sacred*, which seems strangely to advance alongside the thirst for secular learning. Far from becoming irrelevant in our time of rapid modernization, religion has in many parts of the world become a resurgent part of that change. The most original and most unforeseen new developments of the last decade in the Third World and the communist world — respectively, the rise of Khomeini in Iran and Solidarity in Poland — were both examples of political movements deeply rooted in a prophetic monotheistic faith. Much of that which is genuinely innovative in the conservative politics of North America and the radical politics of Latin America can similarly be traced to religious sources. Once again, this may be a force that the Soviets can at times manipulate to their political advantage abroad, but not over the long term at home. The force of religion could provide a positive element within the otherwise ominous nationalist revival currently taking place in the U.S.S.R., with the 1988 millennium of Russia's conversion to Christianity possibly serving as a quiet catalyst.

A fourth force at work in the world is the widespread desire among peoples to assert their own *cultural and ethnic uniqueness and identity*, even at a time of increased technological interdependence. This development poses, of course, grave problems for the multinational Soviet imperium, but it also opens up new possibilities for productivity if the Soviet leaders can bring themselves genuinely to decentralize and to increase local autonomy.

In summary, then, if America can maintain Western unity and provide tough but not provocative leadership in the difficult times ahead, the Soviets might at last genuinely transform their system. George Kennan's 40-year-old prophecy might thus be fulfilled—somewhat later and in a different way than originally anticipated—by a radical evolution drawing both on older Russian traditions and on recent outside experiences. Encouraging change will require a combination of toughness and imagination on our part, and a willingness for short-term sacrifice in the free world. Something might come of it that is presently unforeseen by either us or the Soviets, but which would draw them back from the dangerous international politics of the recent past. It would be ironic if, in the next century, those who have known what it was like to live without liberty would come to value that old ideal more than those who simply took it for granted in this century.

## NOTES

1. There is a certain nostalgia now for the policies of the Nixon–Ford era, fueled by Nixon's articulate return to public discourse and by the enduring popularity of Ford and Kissinger. It is also to some extent a vehicle for expressing dissatisfaction with the policies of both Carter and Reagan. But, however one ultimately judges the Nixon–Ford policies, there does seem to have been an underlying illusion of condominium with the U.S.S.R. that was bound to fall apart, both because it was based on nineteenth-century models not sustainable in this age and because the relative power of both superpowers vis-à-vis other rising forces in the world is steadily declining.
2. I described at length my reasons for believing in the strength and vitality (though not yet the political "clout") of this process of ferment within the U.S.S.R. in an article in the *Washington Post*, November 14, 1982.
3. I argued for this distinction in another article in the *Washington Post*, November 20, 1983.

# 10 INCHING BEYOND CONTAINMENT: DÉTENTE, ENTENTE, CONDOMINIUM AND "ORCHESTRAINT"

*Alton Frye*

Though long in doubt, the success of détente cannot be questioned. The former adversaries have broken through their suspicions and misunderstandings to a level of communication and good feeling that would have been undreamed of a few short years ago. Students and tourists, businessmen and officials, flock eagerly — and by the thousands — between the two countries. Commerce has begun to flourish and, although early expectations for economic relations were too high, the communist state's astonishing shift toward policies which incorporate greater latitude for individual initiative and material incentives has won the admiration of most Americans. Even in the sensitive areas of nuclear technology and military hardware, there are the beginnings of cooperation.

Politically, where once the two governments eyed each other with unrelieved skepticism predisposed to hostility, their leaders now receive each other with unfeigned warmth and cordiality. Where each side not long ago read the other's every gesture as a calculated maneuver for advantage, each now lavishes the benefit of every doubt on the other. Frictions which used to justify martial preparation and ominous rhetoric are now managed as minor irritants which cannot be allowed to impede the steady course of amity. So intent are the two nations on forging a durable friendship that even the truly serious disputes between them are shunted aside for the time being. It is, after all, a measure of sturdy relations that lingering time bombs may be described forthrightly so long as they are tied to slow-burning fuses of indefinite length.

*Mirabile dictu!* Détente is indeed alive and well between China and America. As the wag puts it, from the era of "ping-pong diplomacy" to that of "Deng Xiaoping-pong" diplomacy, the ball has been bouncing right in Chinese–American relations. There could scarcely be a greater contrast with the faltering, on-again off-again attempts to achieve similar results between the United States and the Soviet Union. What accounts for the difference?

Culture? It is not clear that Americans are better equipped to cope with Oriental authoritarians than with Eurasian ones; the *hauteur* bred by centuries of Chinese civilization is as difficult to handle as the insecurity chronically displayed by the Soviets. The absence of significant bilateral disputes? On the contrary, the festering disagreement over Taiwan is closer to a territorial *casus belli* than any issue between Washington and Moscow. A history of friendly association? America's missionary impulse did run to China and not to Russia, but that link evoked no affection in the heart of Mao Tse-tung's followers — while millions of Soviet and American citizens recall with satisfaction their wartime alliance against Hitler. Russia remains an enigma, but, unlike the People's Republic of China, it has never drawn American blood as an enemy of the United States.

The search for a new path which Washington and Moscow might follow together leads one to examine a central puzzle of modern history. How do enemies among nations become friends, or at least tolerable acquaintances? Answers to that question fit together in strange and contradictory fashion. Not only Chinese–American, but also German–American, Japanese–American, and Italian–American relations offer suggestive cases. Within the span of a few years, nations striving to annihilate each other came to see their very survival as dependent on intimate collaboration. In several instances, however, improved relations followed total military defeat of one state, and in the European cases, powerful ethnic and cultural ties worked to reinforce the desire for better relations. A cynic would be tempted to say that the lesson of history is, "war cures enmity." But we know the other half of that truth — it also breeds it, and no one could propose to relieve the recurrent strains in Soviet–American relations by active combat.

In some degree, the explanation for wholesome U.S. relations with those former enemies is the Soviet Union itself. The fears and animosities generated by Soviet policy in the last four decades have formed a critical bond in the ties of other nations. Their shared anxiety about the Soviet Union has brought them into much closer association than might otherwise have been likely. "The enemy of my enemy is my friend" has proven to be a cardinal principle of contemporary world politics. If hot war is no acceptable alternative to cold war, a more refined option could be to find surrogate enemies to share, common threats to overcome, dangers that can be met only through mutual action.

This may seem an excessively negative approach to relations between nations. Americans are prone to accentuate the positive, looking for opportunities; the presidential optimism of our day captures this national trait in high degree. Yet a focus on risk and hazard is a realistic reflection of the downbeat and wary tone that has marked most of the diplomatic experience between the United States and the Soviet Union. At a still more elementary level, that focus builds upon a central finding of psychological research, namely, the Maslow hypothesis that the most powerful motivations in human behavior flow from a sense of values threatened.[1] Governments and nations are not individuals, but the task of reconciling differences among them can usefully begin with concern for the psychological qualities of the individuals who lead them. The premise here is, if one can define threats to shared values in ways to which both Soviet and American leaders can respond, there will be opportunities to resolve some of them by cooperative action.

There are familiar explanations for the perpetual difficulties between Moscow and Washington. They are the only true superpowers, able to compete on a global scale. They alone pose threats of ultimate destruction to one another. As the pre-eminent states of the capitalist and communist worlds, their obligations to lead their respective ideological camps bring them into continuing controversy with each other. These factors have continuing force. They both complicate and make more urgent the effort to dampen conflict between Soviets and Americans. The two countries' status and relations are unique in ways which create special impediments to the kind of transformation wrought in other bilateral relationships.

Each superpower serves as the devil in the other's efforts to rally the faithful. At the same time it is worth remembering that, however coercive Soviet policy toward satellite states may be, some independent governments value ties to Moscow for the same reason others turn to the United States: namely, to have a powerful friend against nearby enemies. The dynamic that opened circuits from Washington to Beijing by way of Islamabad also did so between New Delhi and Moscow. Syria has leaned toward the Soviet Union not because of ideological affinity but because of straightforward reasons of state. Time and again states with grievances against the United States (or, more often, against friends of the United States) have discerned advantage in a Soviet connection, whether or not they wished to be part of any bloc.

The critical question for Soviet and American statesmen is whether they serve their own nations best by emphasizing an open-ended contest for secondary allies in the complex balance of power, or by forging direct accommodations with the primary party, the other superpower. For decades the two governments have oscillated between these options, but the relentless quest for favor among lesser states has easily overpowered explorations of ways to tone down the cold war. Yet a balanced assessment of previous efforts in that direction is prerequisite to considering current possibilities for new departures in superpower relations.

# THE RECORD OF DÉTENTE

Simon Serfaty has aptly characterized the duality of America's efforts to apply containment while probing for the possibilities of détente: " . . . neither policy has ever existed without the other . . . neither is truthfully remembered; both are conveniently imagined."[2] For some analysts, the record reads "détente is a fraud" and "balance of power politics is the only option." In fact, the record is too complex to support such sharp conclusions. It points toward several, more shaded judgments. The first is that a stable balance of power is the necessary starting point for attempts at détente. The second is that preserving a stable balance is a principal function of any détente. Properly construed, détente will be an instrument for both Soviets and Americans to maintain their position in the balance of power. Otherwise, accommodation would be tantamount to surrender.

A third judgment is that détente works better in some areas than in others, and that it sometimes benefits third parties more than the superpowers. This thought is captured by the remark that "Europeans expected less from détente and got more, while Americans expected more and got less." Frankly put, a number of governments have at times feared improved relations between the superpowers, reflecting the fact that other states have in some respects been the beneficiaries of superpower rivalry. The bidding contest between Moscow and Washington has enabled some states to extract concessions from both superpowers even while stressing loyalty to one. Yet intervals of reduced tension have opened different opportunities for such states. It is probably accurate to say that most allies on both sides have come to prefer détente to its alternatives. Moods and attitudes vary over time, but for some years now the basic disposition among American allies in Europe has been toward reviving and extending the détente experiments of the Nixon years.

Is the problem then mainly one of unrealistic expectations among Americans? The widespread perception that détente was oversold in the 1970s undoubtedly conveys a public view that for a combination of domestic political considerations, policymakers deliberately inflated expectations about the likely fruits of improved relations with Moscow. But, judged in the longer sweep of history, if Americans expected more from détente than was reasonable, they gained more than they realized. A legislator once admonished a witness that he was making progress more difficult by refusing to recognize its achievement. The observation applies to many critiques of détente.

Though a term of the 1970s, détente loosely describes a phenomenon of every administration since Franklin Roosevelt's. From the Eisenhower years onward, the search for normal relations with Moscow has ebbed and flowed, but consistently returned with heightened intensity. The litany of failures in the process—from Hungary (1956) and Czechoslovakia (1968) to Angola (1976) and Afghanistan (1979), from the abortive Paris summit of 1960 to the stalemate over SALT II in 1980—is well known and frequently recited. Too often neglected, however, are entries on the other side of the ledger.

The Austrian State Treaty of 1955 was a signal achievement of superpower diplomacy. Responding to President Eisenhower's initiative, and going against the grain of prior Soviet practice and international legal doctrine, the two sides managed to craft a *de facto* open skies regime which, through space-based observation systems, enhanced strategic stability immeasurably. The difficult passage through the Cuban missile crisis was followed by the 1963 Limited Nuclear Test Ban Treaty and significant steps to open scientific and cultural exchanges. Even in the depths of the Vietnam conflict, the two governments found a basis for cooperation in the Nuclear Non-Proliferation Treaty of 1968, and in other pacts which shored up mutual restraint in outer space and Antarctica.

The Nixon years brought extraordinary political progress. The 4-power Berlin accord muted one chronic source of friction. The superpowers began the continuing process of strategic arms negotiation, achieving low limits on strategic defense set by the Anti-Ballistic Missile (ABM) Treaty of 1972 and raising the prospect of far-reaching restraints on offensive forces. An important gain was the agreement designed to prevent incidents at sea between the two sides' naval forces. The Threshhold Test Ban Treaty and the Peaceful Nuclear Explosions Agreement of 1974 nudged verification procedures toward cooperative measures and useful exchanges of data, procedures further extended in the inconclusive negotiations for a Comprehensive Nuclear Test Ban in the later 1970s. The Ford–Brezhnev agreement at Vladivostok and the Helsinki Final Act pointed toward further progress in containing the growth of strategic weaponry and in lowering tensions in Europe. The SALT II agreement of the Carter period advanced toward actual reductions in the number of strategic launchers and toward qualitative restraints, capping the number of warheads permitted on individual missiles and limiting the total number of MIRVed systems (those with multiple independently targetable reentry vehicles). The Soviets joined the London Suppliers Club to explore ways to regulate civilian trade in nuclear materials and systems in order to contain the spread of weapons capabilities.

Many interpret these episodes as examples of wishful thinking, naive American gestures exploited by clever Soviet leaders to steal a march on the West by creating the impression that "peace had broken out." They stress commitments not fulfilled in the Helsinki process, provisions bent or broken in arms control agreements, and obligations for restraint in other areas honored mainly in the breach. They give little credit for agreements whose major terms have been applied in good faith, ignoring the problems which would have grown worse in the absence of efforts at mutual restraint.

To assess the prospects for success in the late 1980s, one needs to ask both why superpower efforts to address mutual problems have so often faltered and whether the burdens imposed by past failures provide new incentives to resolve them now. On the first question, conventional wisdom veers toward the conclusion that the détente of the 1970s did not bite deeply because the two governments saw it as a cover for continued pursuit of their geopolitical ambitions. Weighed against those ambitions, the profits of détente seemed too skimpy to warrant greater self-restraint in other areas of competition.

That view is plausible, but it takes too little account of the particular sequence in which the Nixon–Brezhnev efforts began to unravel. As Raymond Garthoff has documented, mutual disappointments and suspicions mounted so rapidly that the thrust of détente was almost immediately weakened.[3] An important issue is whether the Soviet behavior which Americans found so objectionable would have occurred if the hoped-for trade benefits with the United States had materialized; if the Jackson–Vanik amendment had not undermined quiet diplomacy to facilitate Jewish emigration; if the United States had not pursued its own anti-Soviet campaigns in the Persian Gulf region, the Far East and elsewhere; if American leadership had not been so dislocated by Watergate and Vietnam. Had détente become a growing tree instead of a shriveled twig, would Moscow have found dabbling in Africa such a temptation, infringements of Helsinki worth the political cost, or superfluous military expenditures justifiable?

Similarly, Moscow needs to consider its responsibility for the stunted form détente assumed. What advantage did it find in purchasing heightened tension with the United States by adventurous diplomacy in Somalia and Ethiopia; by gratuitous support in Angola of those Cuban surrogates bound to inflame American opinion; by virulent anti-American propaganda beamed to Iran during the protracted U.S. ordeal there; by playing so close to the edges of arms control agreements that it placed its own good faith under a cloud? Would not the Soviet Union be more secure today if its attempt at intimidating NATO's European allies had not provoked deployment of Pershing II and cruise missiles; if its large-scale strategic and conventional deployments had not undermined support in the United States for the SALT II Treaty; if its bullying tactics in Poland had not once more highlighted the oppression of Eastern Europe; if its bloody intervention in Afghanistan had not outraged the world?

Obviously, perceptions about such matters differ greatly within and between the superpowers. Both governments need to reflect upon them critically—and self-critically. A careful evaluation of the abortive experiment of the Nixon–Ford–Carter/Brezhnev period can go far toward making possible more substantial success in the Reagan/Gorbachev phase now unfolding.

The purpose here is not to replace skepticism with naivete. It is to ask whether these efforts to change central features of Soviet–American relations were fundamentally misdirected or well-conceived policies which were overwhelmed by other factors—extraneous political crises, inopportune shifts in leadership, technological developments out-of-phase with political initiatives, impatience for immediate and comprehensive success in a process that required years to bear full fruit. Most importantly, do these and similar initiatives of past decades constitute building blocks for future policy, or must any attempt to construct more wholesome relations discard them and begin anew?

## PRELUDE TO A NEW DÉTENTE

The view here is that there is much on which to build. The danger in damning prior measures of détente as wholesale failures is that it will contaminate arrangements and policies that are vital to larger innovations. Change has occurred within and between the two superpowers, and one must recognize its significance if further change is to be steered in mutually beneficial directions. It is a far different world when Soviet leaders have abandoned the doctrine that war between socialist and capitalist states is inevitable. It is a far different world when a Republican president explicitly renounces the goal of "military superiority" embraced by his own party platform. It is a far different world when the men who guide both governments testify that "nuclear war can never be won and must never be fought." For in those altered professions lies the acknowledgment that "victory" is not an option, that neither superpower can prevail over the other. The two sides have barely begun to act on the implications of that finding: perpetual cold war is futile, its attendant risks unjustifiable, and the search for viable political and strategic understandings between Moscow and Washington an inescapable duty of statecraft.

A chain of logic descends from these theses. Both governments are in fact animated by a common dread of nuclear war.

- Avoiding nuclear war requires a stable strategic balance, which in turn dictates mutual restraint in the development, deployment and use of nuclear weapons. Because the risk of escalation to nuclear war arises in any military conflict between the superpowers, avoiding conventional war is a vital interest of the two parties.
- The risk of conventional war is in turn regulated by a massive balance

of forces deployed on the central front in Europe, but it is less well-controlled in numerous Third World settings where Soviet and American political interests may draw the superpowers into direct conflict.

•   Other risks to the superpowers arise from the possible spread of nuclear weapons capabilities to additional states; neither has confidence that the acquisition of nuclear weapons by others will induce sufficient responsibility to guarantee that they will not be used in regional conflicts, perhaps increasing the danger that the superpowers will be drawn into war.

These are core values shared by the two powers. All of them could, in principle, be served best by explicit arrangements between Moscow and Washington, together with other states where appropriate. Despite complaints about the superpowers' excessive preoccupation with arms control, it is not surprising that they find their vision of other possible common interests obscured by the paralyzing hazards accompanying the nuclear competition.

In important respects these core values provide a surrogate for the "common enemy" that has helped forge positive shifts in other relationships between adversaries. But the operational question is how far the common dread of nuclear war can be exploited to move the United States and the Soviet Union toward collaboration. To what extent will other interests lead the superpowers to risk these shared values? Specifically, can the two governments be persuaded to subordinate their broader political competition to the requirements of central strategic stability?

One difficulty we face is language. The very term *détente* carries a certain opprobrium in some quarters. It was ruled out of legitimate political discourse in the United States by a moderate president defending himself against charges of softness on the Soviets. Because of what happened in Soviet–American relations during the 1970s, it carries an aura of overblown rhetoric and undersatisfied expectations. Its long-standing service as a slogan in Soviet propaganda makes it heavy baggage for Americans to bear in trying to formulate a policy readily identifiable with U.S. national interests. Even the phrase, *hard-headed détente*, sensible though it sounds, labors under the unhelpful handicap of trying to salvage a controversial noun by dressing it up with a presumably more palatable adjective. *Containment without isolation* appeals to some, but is rather bulky in English and condescending in Russian. We need to free consideration of Soviet–American relations from rusty rhetoric and dilapidated symbols.

Let us then restate the objectives one might propose for an altered relationship between the superpowers and give it a different name. The goal recommended here is a relationship in which the superpowers acknowledge that their own interest requires them (a) to give priority to the

Soviet–American relationship, (b) to orchestrate their behavior in key respects, and (c) to exercise sufficient restraint bilaterally and otherwise to protect that central relationship against disruption. Until we contrive a more felicitous term, one may call such a relationship *orchestraint*.

A minimalist view would hold that little can be expected beyond a measure of self-control on both sides directed at avoiding strategic war, whether by inadvertence, escalation, or miscalculation. A maximalist goal would be to shape a form of condominium in which, in the interest of suppressing danger to themselves, the superpowers would bargain directly — not only on bilateral issues but also on arrangements to be imposed on other states whose disputes threaten to ignite wider war.

## MEASURES OF ORCHESTRAINT

In some respects the two countries are already well beyond the minimalist standard. They have not managed to elaborate and enforce general codes of conduct, but they have created some standards for strategic behavior and have ratified important *de facto* developments, notably the prevailing use of national technical means to keep an eye on each other. Their acceptance of such means has produced interesting byproducts, for instance in the Soviet Union's alert of the United States regarding possible preparations for a nuclear test in South Africa. They have curbed the long-standing games of "chicken" between their navies and moved to modernize the "hot line" set up in the 1960s.

The fact that some arms control provisions have not been fully or faithfully implemented should not blind one to the fact that many have been. Since 1972, the two sides have dismantled hundreds of strategic launchers to remain within aggregate limits. Not all of those weapons were obsolete, a fact confirmed by the continued service of retired missiles as boosters for space launches. Many would have remained on station, if for no better reasons than bureaucratic inertia and determination not to yield something for nothing. The superpowers have not violated the fractionation rule by multiplying warheads on individual missiles beyond levels set in the SALT II Treaty, even though the agreement was not ratified. Evidence suggests reasonable compliance with the 150-kiloton ceiling on underground detonations set by the Threshhold Test Ban Treaty — again despite its non-ratified status. The record is mixed, but it is not barren.

At the other end of the spectrum, no leader on either side has even proposed anything remotely resembling a superpower condominium. As a general proposition, the improbability of condominium is apparent. Neither Moscow nor Washington is likely to trade known, trustworthy relations with friends for a reckless embrace of its principal adversary. Perhaps the closest thing to a step in that direction was the 1969 Soviet probe for U.S. acquiescence in the event of a possible attempt to destroy the embryonic Chinese nuclear capability. The hint was quickly rebuffed by American negotiators, but it raised the question of whether the two sides might agree to deny other states entry into the nuclear weapons club. That would have amounted to a kind of "functional condominium" to cope with a specific problem, as distinct from the kind of shared power over territory normally conjured up by the term.

Far different is another concept designed to universalize nuclear deterrence as a means of discouraging the spread of nuclear weapons to other countries. It contemplates joint superpower action to deter proliferation by offering to make available to any victim of nuclear attack the means for proportionate reprisal. Without having to build a nuclear arsenal of its own, a potential victim could in theory be shielded against nuclear threat or attack by the deterrent value of promised access to the superpowers' arsenal. A Soviet–American commitment to respond in this way to additional proliferation could be a far more potent anti-proliferation policy than the negative and positive security assurances they have tendered in various forms to non-nuclear states. Although the idea has evoked interest in intellectual circles in both countries, it has not been explored in intergovernmental channels. Whatever its theoretical merits and demerits, a proposal of this nature has no promise unless the superpowers first make major strides toward muting the tensions between them. It is worth noting, however, that the record of cooperation on proliferation issues and the clear sense in Moscow and Washington that they stand in a similar posture toward potential proliferators identify this issue as one on which collaboration might be carried to its maximum lengths.

Along the spectrum from minimal arrangements to the hypothetical option of condominium lies a broad array of possibilities for orchestraint, including elements of more active engagement verging on entente. They include political and economic measures, as well as additional security arrangements affecting numerous states. Beyond the strategic arms proposals occupying center stage, conventional ideas include confidence-building measures and mutual force reduction in Europe, steps to relieve friction over human rights issues, expanded East–West trade, and concerted action to deal with a large number of regional trouble-spots and problems, including Afghanistan, Nicaragua, El Salvador, Angola–Namibia, the Iran–Iraq war, the Arab–Israeli conflict, continuing violence in Southeast Asia and South Africa, renegade states like Libya, and the division of Korea.

It is here that the real business of world politics will be transacted. The need is not so much for new options on the menu of superpower diplomacy as for fresh approaches to identified problems. Of special significance may be the fact that Moscow and Washington are edging into regional political discussions simultaneously with serious negotiations on nuclear arms issues. Across-the-board progress on regional disputes is not in the offing, but three regions stand out as ripe for superpower orchestraint: Central America, Afghanistan, and the Middle East.

## SPHERES OF COOPERATION

However offensive the phrase *sphere of influence*, Central America and Afghanistan invite analysis as contemporary instances of that classical property of world politics. That is why a number of experienced observers have suggested,[4] usually *sotto voce*, that there may be a basis for an arrangement involving (a) U.S. restraint in supporting the guerrillas in Afghanistan as part of a movement toward political settlement of the invasion/civil war there, perhaps under United Nations auspices; and (b) Soviet restraint in backing Cuban/Nicaraguan/Salvadoran guerrilla activities in Central America, coupled perhaps with Contadora-type agreements to promote democratic processes in the region in conjunction with disengagement of foreign military elements.

Such a bargain will be difficult to contrive and could not readily be acknowledged by either superpower, but it deserves priority attention. The United States cannot in conscience abandon freedom fighters in Afghanistan, but it is in no position to help them prevail; if the *mujahedin* are offered reasonable terms to seek national reconciliation in the context of Soviet military withdrawal, the United States cannot in conscience exploit the circumstances for geostrategic purposes by encouraging guerrilla recalcitrance. There are good reasons to believe that the Soviets have found their Afghanistan involvement longer and more burdensome than expected and, while they can continue to bear it, they could welcome a compromise that met their concern for border security without requiring permanent Soviet military operations in the country.

By the same token, the Soviets will not easily relinquish the opportunity to nettle the United States in its own hemisphere. Nor will they wish to appear hesitant in applying the doctrine of national liberation movements to Central America. But the Soviet Union cannot expect wider comity with the United States so long as it is thought to be a prime sponsor of troubles on America's doorstep. An intriguing and suggestive remark came from former Foreign Minister Andrei Gromyko when he told former Secretary of State Alexander Haig, in a moment of exasperation, that "Cuba is your problem." If the statement means anything, it surely reveals an awareness that Moscow's capacity to operate through intermediaries in the Western Hemisphere has definite limits. Bringing its leverage into play to lower the level of violence in Central America, whether spawned by Cuba or not, could buy the Soviet Union considerable credit in the high political accounts of superpower relations.

The circumstances of the Middle East are quite different, and far past the stage when either power could assume the prerogatives of a tacit sphere of influence. It is not clear what specific initiatives the two could take to help terminate the simmering bloodbath between Iran and Iraq, but the topic should be on the bilateral agenda. A more concrete opportunity may exist in the intermittent peace process that has gone to seed after the flowering of Camp David. The United States has found it difficult to coax that process forward; it has sternly resisted the notion that the Soviet Union, so often seen as a disruptive presence in the area, should take an active role.

Several reasons argue for a reassessment of that policy. Foremost among them is the fact that King Hussein has framed the latest Jordanian–Palestinian overtures with a view to Soviet involvement in an international conference, out of which direct Arab–Israeli negotiations would emerge. That framework reflects a credible judgment that, especially as Syria's principal patron, the Soviets already possess essential influence over key aspects of any political movement in the region; better to have them inside the tent than out, said the Bedouin sage, Lyndon Johnson.

From the American perspective there are additional reasons to rethink the matter. The exclusion policy dates from the years before Anwar Sadat transformed the situation by expelling Soviet military personnel from Egypt and making his historic journey to Jerusalem. The earlier assumption that Iraq was gravitating into Moscow's orbit no longer holds. There are tantalizing hints of Soviet willingness to resume diplomatic relations with Israel. There are, to be sure, hard arguments in *Realpolitik* terms for resisting Soviet participation, but the occasion could well provide a crucial test of Moscow's willingness and capacity to play a constructive role in working for a more expansive détente.

The Soviets are in the Middle East, but in a weakened condition. There may not be a better time to run the risk of experimenting with their presence in the peace process. That is all the more true when, if they prove unhelpful, other options will remain available and attractive. Inviting the Soviets into the process would throw light on how the new leaders in Moscow view their responsibilities to help manage international conflict. It would also meet their long-standing complaint that exclusion from the Middle East process denies them recognition as a great power with legitimate interests in the region. In or out of the formal procedures, Moscow can impede or facilitate them; it may be more inclined to facilitate them if it is an active party, and if the process is linked to the larger attempt to shape an affirmative superpower relationship.

These key regional conflicts illustrate cases in which the superpowers need to enrich the narrower conceptions of détente applied in the past, because frictions over such Third World issues have fed back into the central relationship in ways which cast doubt on its true direction. Collaboration in these realms, needless to say, cannot substitute for progress on bilateral strategic and political issues or on the Eurocentric problems which consume so much of their attention. But, apart from its intrinsic importance, such collaboration could make the central agenda less vulnerable to disruption.

## ARMS CONTROL OPPORTUNITIES

Of the central agenda on arms control opportunities, only the essentials can be mentioned here. President Reagan and General Secretary Gorbachev may well have the greatest opportunity in history to strike a basic bargain maintaining strategic stability while reducing nuclear weapons. Granted that pitfalls exist, there are numerous paths towards such stability through reductions, and honest negotiation can discover the ones most agreeable to the parties. Nibbling at the edges of the problem will not suffice. What is called for is a package deal, incorporating useful precedents from the SALT and Test Ban negotiations and making fair trade-offs between the concerns and advantages of both nations.

At the heart of the bargain, evidently, must be a mutually acceptable arrangement relating strategic defensive activities to the proposed offensive force reductions. Mr. Reagan has stressed that the immediate task is to end the erosion of the 1972 ABM Treaty, and that any research on the Strategic Defense Initiative (SDI) should take place within the terms of that agreement. He has also said that if the research is successful, the United States would share the resulting technology with the Soviet Union. Under those criteria it should be possible to clarify the boundary between permissible research and prohibited development, perhaps specifying certain activities which could only take place under joint supervision. As former National Security Adviser Robert McFarlane assured the British in 1985, the U.S. government recognizes that any eventual transition to greater reliance on defenses would require the cooperation of the Soviet Union. Whatever the ultimate fate of SDI and its Soviet counterpart, cooperation in defining the future defense regime will have to begin now if actual force reductions in offenses are to be achieved.

That task has grown more problematic as the administration has coupled its declaratory commitment to abide by the ABM treaty with dubious interpretations of its provisions. Clearly, the treaty cannot survive self-serving interpretations of convenience by either party. And equally clear is the certain failure of attempts to resurrect superpower negotiations on offensive force reductions if there is bad faith in managing the existing treaty regime on strategic defenses. Excessive zeal in catering to the president's interest in research on strategic defense by subverting the ABM treaty that he is sworn to respect may cast a cloud over his good faith and jeopardize his goal of achieving real reductions in offensive weapons at the very moment when he has elicited significant movement in the Soviet bargaining stance. Evidently, the two sides will have to clarify these interpretive issues.

Among the myriad details involved in the strategic arms negotiations, three questions are overriding. The first concerns the boundaries for strategic defense activities. Interestingly, private discussions with knowledgeable Soviets reveal considerably more forthcoming attitudes about strategic defense research than official positions convey. The large portion of the SDI devoted to surveillance, acquisition, tracking and kill assessment, multi-purpose technologies which are difficult to monitor, might well be acceptable to the Soviets provided there were adequate constraints on other critical technologies. Specifically, agreement not to test large-scale lasers and other weapon components in space might encourage Soviet acquiescence in a wide range of research on other elements of strategic defense. Similarly, in order to maintain confidence that neither side was seeking to break out of defensive restraints (in other words, to give effect to President Reagan's pledge that any eventual transition to greater reliance on strategic defense should be cooperative) the two sides might limit the size and potential of power sources approved for deployment in space, subject to mutual visitation rights and possibly to exceptions for joint systems. In principle, amendments to the ABM treaty could focus restraints on a few identifiable technologies, leaving considerable latitude for the kind of research Mr. Reagan wishes to authorize for the benefit of his successors. There should be no impediment on America's part to such a selective approach, because *regulating* SDI in no way amounts to *abandoning* SDI. Larger uncertainties surround the degree to which General Secretary Gorbachev would be willing to narrow his wholesale opposition to SDI.

The second critical question bears on the relationship between superpower and third-country nuclear forces. Although the complexities surrounding these latter forces are severe, they should never have been allowed to confound Soviet–American arms diplomacy. Gorbachev's gambit of offering separate discussions to the British and the French on European nuclear forces points up an untenable situation. The Soviets and Americans cannot negotiate about the nuclear forces of other countries, but neither can they disregard their existence in determining the scale and character of possible reductions in superpower deployments. Over the years of SALT, START, and INF, this issue has been finagled in various ways, obscured in side deals and tacit trade-offs, but has never been addressed forthrightly. It now demands a straightforward approach for the simple reason that without one, substantial reductions in the major powers' forces are unlikely.

While those powers cannot constrain the weapons of other states, they can make explicit a common standard for their own response to any expansion of those weapons that jeopardizes possible reductions in Soviet and American deployments. That standard might take the form of an agreement that, in reducing forces to a specified level of delivery vehicles and warheads, each superpower reserves the right to retain additional forces equivalent to any third-country deployments above a fixed percentage of that level. Such an arrangement would be equitable, but more importantly it would embody a political reality that must be advertised: neither superpower will continue reductions for long if other states increase their nuclear forces indefinitely. An agreement along these lines would create a powerful political stake for third countries in the process of superpower reductions. It would be a weighty responsibility for any of them to trigger suspension of that process by excessive buildups of their own. And a provision of this nature could pave the way for formal negotiations with Paris, London, and Beijing at a later stage. Both France and Britain have indicated that they would be willing to consider how best to contribute to arms reductions, once the superpowers have actually embarked upon a reductions program.

The third overriding question goes to the scope and content of offensive reductions. It is obvious that incorporating precedents, criteria and counting rules previously negotiated could do a great deal to expedite such a bargain. Gorbachev's confirmation that Moscow accepts the necessity to lower both launcher numbers and warhead totals steers discussion in the right direction. Making warhead reductions workable will require reasonable counting rules, which SALT II provides for ballistic missiles. That agreement also offers a basis for avoiding an endless wrangle over how to treat weapons carried by bombers; it equates bombers not equipped for cruise missiles with single warhead ICBMs. Given the different characteristics of those systems, that is a fair standard, and it could prove critical for balanced reductions. Just as Soviet missile throw-weight is likely to exceed that of the United States in a reduced force posture, American bomber advantages are likely to persist. For both sides, these residual capacities would provide useful hedges against a collapse of the agreement, in which case missiles could add warheads and bombers could add cruise missiles.

Because both countries have begun to add air-launched cruise missiles to some of their bombers, a central task will be to relate constraints on ALCM-carrying bombers to reductions in ballistic missile warheads. Again, SALT offers a suggestive counting rule of 20 weapons for ALCM bombers, compared to the maximum of 10 warheads permitted on heavy ICBMs. One possibility would be to set a delivery vehicle sub-ceiling to cover both heavy bombers carrying ALCMs and heavy ballistic missiles. Equating the two for purposes of the sub-ceiling would balance the larger number of slow-reaction cruise missiles on bombers which face active defenses against half that number of fast-reaction weapons on heavy ballistic missiles. Analysts can argue forever about the specifics of any formula, but political inventions of this kind will be necessary if the two sides are to phase down their very different strategic postures. Handling of bombers and heavy missiles in this integrated manner should make feasible reductions of central strategic forces to the 6000-weapon range.

Needless to say, no reductions will take place if either government feels that stability will be undermined. Ideally, the two sides would describe a long-term evolution away from relatively vulnerable MIRVed systems and toward more survivable single-warhead ballistic missiles. It is an open question whether development of counterforce-capable SLBMs will proceed so rapidly as to rob the parties of the potential benefits to stability envisaged by the Scowcroft Commission. Relaxing limits on the number of small, single-warhead ICBMs permitted under a reduced ceiling — perhaps by allowing a trade of one MIRVed ICBM for two single-warhead missiles — would be prudent. In any case, the decisive fact is that the dynamics of reductions will impose greater discipline and new incentives on both military establishments. In a smaller force, the premium will be on survivability. To a considerable extent one can rely on rational military planners to attend to that requirement as forces are compelled to shrink.

In short, the new fluidity in the strategic arms control process demands fresh and imaginative efforts to craft a viable reductions program. There are many ways to exploit this opportunity as well as to reconcile the differing inclinations the parties bring to the negotiation. To do so, however, will require a better sense of timing than either government has usually shown. The unfolding force growth and impending technological excursions lend urgency to the mission.

Success in striking a deal on the central strategic balance can open the door to moderation of political and military stresses in Europe as well. Intermediate nuclear forces will have to be treated in the strategic accords, but conventional and tactical forces will remain on the agenda in the Conference on Security and Cooperation in Europe (CSCE) and the Mutual and Balanced Force Reduction (MBFR) talks. Those negotiations have long been stymied because they are dependent variables in the overall equation. Resumption of productive diplomacy on strategic forces should improve the chances of forward movement in both CSCE and MBFR. The candidates are plentiful: more substantial confidence-building measures, phased pullbacks of tactical nuclear weapons and armored forces on both sides, incremental reductions in manpower, perhaps provisions to reduce the ambiguities and potential instabilities associated with dual-capable systems. The parties' habitual disagreement over the actual numbers of forces in the theater may now be susceptible to resolution by creative blending of recent Soviet and Western proposals. No program to cultivate a spreading orchestraint can prosper without concrete innovations in the European security arena.

## THE NEED FOR ACTION

This chapter does not pretend to set forth a comprehensive and systematic scheme for settling the cold war once and for all. What it aspires to do is advance a more hopeful perspective on previous efforts to move beyond that unhappy era, along with a more ambitious outline for the effort to forge a credible and durable relationship between the superpowers. As the two governments embark on that ineluctable challenge, wariness is in order; a sense of futility is not. Their predecessors wrought better than they have been given credit for; they have provided many building blocks with which to erect a sturdier structure. Their successors are unlikely to have a better opportunity than they themselves have now. Unless today's incumbents act decisively, they will bequeath a sad legacy: mounting military deployments, increasing economic distress, prolonged political tensions, and decreasing security for the nations they serve.

Lingering questions abound. Are the Soviet and American peoples mature enough to acknowledge that the failures of détente are shared failures, shortcomings for which both sides bear responsibility? Do leaders on both sides have a clear enough view of past mistakes and frustrations in the relationship to avoid them in the future? Do they perceive the more positive legacies of détente, on which they can begin to erect a sturdy strategic and political orchestraint? Or do the arrival of Gorbachev and the departure of Gromyko portend a turning away from emphasis on U.S.-Soviet relations, either in despair or opportunism? Can the "surrogate enemy"—the shared dread of nuclear catastrophe—motivate Soviet and American governments to subordinate their ongoing political competition to the discipline of orchestraint? Answers to these questions will only emerge from a lengthy period of active engagement between the superpowers.

When Ronald Reagan completes his term of office, he will have presided over nearly one fifth of the nuclear age. Mikhail Gorbachev, who will be younger in the year 2000 than Mr. Reagan is today, may hold power for a third of it or longer. How will they make use of their stewardship? On the answer to that question hinges not only their place in history, but the course of history itself.

## NOTES

1. Vernon Van Dyke applies Maslow's thesis to the behavior of nations in *Pride and Power* (Champaign/Urbana: University of Illinois Press, 1964).
2. Simon Serfaty, "Introduction: Neither Détente nor Containment," in Serfaty, ed., *U.S.-Soviet Relations*, Foreign Policy Institute School of Advanced International Studies, The Johns Hopkins University, August 1985, p. 2.
3. Raymond Garthoff, *Détente and Confrontation: American-Soviet Relations from Nixon to Reagan* (Washington: Brookings Institution, 1985).
4. See for example Zbigniew Brzezinski, "Afghanistan and Nicaragua," *The National Interest* 1 (Fall 1985): 48-51.

# 11 CONTAINMENT, NON-INTERVENTION, AND STRATEGIC DISENGAGEMENT

## Earl C. Ravenal

It has often been said that "containment has stood the test of time." Yet, "compared to what?" asks the hoary joke. Containment must be arrayed against its costs, the expectations held of it, and the projected costs and expectations of alternative doctrines of national strategy. Indeed, containment has been subjected to critiques from both sides: that its accomplishments have been meager, and a more ambitious strategy is in order; or that its costs and risks are excessive, well beyond the necessary and beneficial.

For almost four decades, since the beginning of the cold war in the late 1940s, America's national strategy has been devoted to the containment of the Soviet Union and Soviet-inspired communism. In that time, the paradigm of America's national strategy has consisted of two basic elements: deterrence, and forward defense or alliance—both devoted to containing communist power and influence. *Deterrence* is roughly equated with our strategic nuclear forces; we seek to maintain at least a balance of strategic nuclear arms with Russia and to provide a nuclear umbrella over our allies and various other countries. *Forward defense or alliance* involves our protection, mostly by means of general purpose forces, of allies and other countries that occupy strategic positions or have sympathetic social and political values.

The problem with the strategy of containment has not only been the continuing high costs associated with the requisite military preparations and the occasional egregious costs of heightened crises and regional wars; it has also been the risk, under certain circumstances, of being plunged into nuclear war. The costs can be attributed mostly to the generation of conventional forces, primarily for the defense of Europe; the risks can be attributed to reliance on the earlier use of nuclear weapons, also particularly in a confrontation arising from a conventional war in Europe. To some extent, cost can be transmuted into additional risk and risk can be transformed into mere cost — that is what is meant by "lowering" or "raising" the nuclear threshold. But the choice itself arises from the policy of containment.

Perhaps the high cost of our present national strategy could be tolerated, if it could be demonstrated that the cost was already more than strictly necessary to implement the strategy, and if the nation found itself in comfortable fiscal circumstances. Neither is the case. Powerful critics assert, with considerable empirical support in the quantification of global and regional power balances, that even the $314 billion that the Reagan administration requested for defense for FY 1986, let alone the $289 billion that Congress finally granted, is grossly insufficient to execute the present task of containing Soviet communism around the world. William Van Cleave proposed a 1986 defense budget $50 billion higher than Reagan's request.[1] And Leonard Sullivan, Jr.'s estimate for projecting a confident conventional defense against Soviet arms envisions defense authorizations reaching 10% of GNP — a budget of about $446 billion for 1987.[2]

So, if anything, we are spending too little, not too much, to implement our present policy of containment.[3] Another indication of this fact is the continuing shift of strategic concern to the Persian Gulf at the relative expense of Europe. This process, begun in the last two years of the Carter administration, can be measured in terms of the number of American land divisions, tactical air wings, and naval carrier battle groups primarily allocated to the Gulf (for 1987, $5\frac{2}{3}$ land divisions and an equivalent portion of tactical air and surface navy, out of a total of 21 land divisions, army and marine). Our explicit acquisition of this "new" area of strategic responsibility would not, still, be troublesome, were it not for the administration's additional assumption of multiple simultaneous deployments. In his FY 1986 posture statement, for example, Secretary of Defense Weinberger states:

> Our forward-defense strategy dictates that we be able to conduct concurrent deployments to widely separated areas of the globe. Our present goal is to achieve the capability to deploy forces to a remote theater such as Southwest Asia, while maintaining an acceptable capability to reinforce NATO and key areas of Northeast Asia.[4]

The intention to deploy forces simultaneously raises the issue of double counting. A close reading of the force allocation embodied in Secretary Weinberger's statement indicates that, to some extent, the Pentagon intends a double assignment of certain units — characteristically for the Persian Gulf and also for Europe or East Asia and the Western Pacific. This not only violates the first law of thermodynamics, but also raises the question of the strategic overextension of general purpose forces. In more general terms, it suggests an imbalance of commitments and resources.

This problem did not originate with the Reagan administration. It has characterized U.S. force planning since the two-and-a-half war doctrine of the Kennedy–McNamara administration and even the one-and-a-half war doctrine of the Nixon–Kissinger–Laird administration — and before either of those, the Eisenhower–Dulles–Radford–Wilson administration. But the Reagan administration has exacerbated the contradiction, with its implication of a wider strategic scope of simultaneous responses to Soviet aggressions, and with its more tangible implementation of the commitment to defend the Persian Gulf and Southwest Asia without significantly increasing the force structure or overall military manpower. Of course, there is no law against creating such gaps and contradictions, and they can often be maintained for some time, since these states of affairs are not always tested sharply or conclusively by events. But ultimately, events, or the foreshadowing of events by analysis, will challenge these relationships. And something will have to give.

The urgent question, then, is whether the United States can afford even its present scope of containment, let alone the more rigorous, demanding, and consistent version of the Reagan administration's strategy proposed by its still more hawkish critics. How can we pay for it and in what ways? What the United States faces, toward the end of the Reagan administration, is a crisis of solvency, in several pertinent senses of the word: not merely fiscal solvency, but also a gross misalignment between the country's strategic objectives in the world and its manifest willingness to pay for them.

It will not do for proponents of vigorous containment to impugn the patriotism of those who see our situation as arguing for significant retrenchment, or to dismiss the fiscal problem by reciting the abstract proposition that our economy could support even higher defense spending, for example, by sharply raising taxes. The fact that there are options does not make them more desirable than current policy, or more politically feasible. All of the fiscal options (taxes, inflation, more government borrowing) are not simply unpalatable, but destructive. Resources (and support) are not automatic; to be available to the state, they must be mobilized from society. Even if the government could balance its books by exacting more resources in the form of taxes (and possibly also conscription at low military wages) to support a large defense establishment and extensive foreign commitments, that would be just the end of one problem and the beginning of another.

Solvency means that the external and internal stances of this country comport with each other. An extensive, engaged foreign policy and a large, active military posture require big, intrusive, demanding government. If, as we were promised, the Reagan administration favors a more reserved, less extensive government, then we must have a more detached, disengaged foreign policy. The dilemma is especially cruel for this conservative president, who said in his first inaugural address that "government is the problem."

## THE PROBLEM OF ANALYSIS

Thus, the broad challenge to contemporary American foreign policy is how to perpetuate containment of the Soviet Union in an era of multiple constraints, both international and domestic. Some of these constraints are limits, and thus are more or less unalterable. Others are trade-offs — that is, the price we have to pay, in terms of the larger objectives of our state and society, to contain the Soviet Union. We must consider whether our society is really committed to pay that price, not just rhetorically, but objectively; that is, not just in the verbalizations of a crust of elites, but in the supportive actions of all of society, taken as a policymaking system. For the question of the perpetuation of containment will not be determined by its abstract desirability, or even by its "necessity," but rather by whether containment is viable strategically and consonant with domestic values. Among those values are economic solvency and the quality of society, including our accustomed freedoms and the unique political system that we undertake to defend in the first place.

The question of perpetuating containment is therefore profound and complex. Yet, in typical critiques of containment, the goal of containing the U.S.S.R. is assumed; it is taken as indispensable, not challengeable in itself. True, various constraints (e.g., budgetary, demographic, resource, popular support) are often enumerated. But such exercises generally move abruptly, negligently, and optimistically to a proposed series of mild correctives. Questions relating to the sufficiency of the proposed moves are begged, simply in the way the moves are described. Often, as a centerpiece of these proposals, certain "force-multipliers" or other gimmicks are suggested, such as "dual-missioning" of our forces — that is, treating the units the United States keeps in Europe and Northeast Asia as expeditionary forces, available for broader regional assignments.[5] Such superficial analyses and wishful prescriptions usually ignore the obvious dilemma: that global "flexibility" can be achieved only by robbing the primary areas of some measure of our protection.

Such proposals fail because of their underlying methodology, a way of thinking that characterizes much of the current debate on containment itself. Simply put, containment may be a nice idea, but foreign policy is not made of attractive ideas peddled with competitive virtuosity and zeal. Certainly a policy such as containment is not self-executing; there are the essential questions of what may be needed to implement the policy, whether those things will be forthcoming, and at what price. Only in the context of these questions can we understand the scope of our choices or even understand what it means to "choose." Most policy writing, whether official or critical, consists of lists of things that "must" be done. Rarely is it based on an assessment of costs, limits, and feasibility, or a comparison of alternatives. Rarely does it invoke numbers, or even imply quantities of things that must be exacted or expended. Gaps are bridged, if at all, by pure verbalisms, exhortations of "will," or the mere advocacy of shifts in our orientation.

But policy, particularly foreign policy, is not a set of items that must be obtained, preserved, or remedied in the world, without reference to situation or contingent cost. It is certainly not the official expression of objectives of state. Rather, policy is an entire system's probable responses to future contingent challenges over a range of issues and geographical areas. Many of the elements that form these responses will not be determined by national authorities. Some policy determinants consist of institutional, military, and resource dispositions that make it more likely that we will respond in a certain way. Other determinants include situations at the time of future decisions or actions, also to varying degrees beyond our control, though not totally beyond our prediction. That is why the description of a proposed foreign policy must begin by tracing the constraints of the international and domestic systems. These are the starting points in the partially predictive process that indicates what our foreign policy orientation "ought" to be.

The pages that follow attempt to apply this kind of real-world analysis to containment as the emblematic American foreign policy of the past four decades. An old expression inquires whether the game is worth the candle. Any critique of containment should ask: (a) What is the game? (b) What is the requisite candle? (c) Can we afford the candle? and (d) Is there another game in town?

## UNIVERSALITY AND THE MIRAGE
## OF SELECTIVE CONTAINMENT

We start with the name of the game—the concept of containment. At the outset, we encounter an essential dispute: Was containment originally intended to be universal in its application? More interestingly, is containment by its very nature, or rather by the nature of the threat it is designed to meet, universal?

A literal reading of George Kennan's original "text" indicates that containment was to be universal. Indeed, Kennan made containment's universality the centerpiece of his published analysis of Soviet conduct in 1947, in his celebrated image of the Soviet threat:

> Its political action is a fluid stream which moves constantly, wherever it is permitted to move, toward a given goal. Its main concern is to make sure that it has filled every nook and cranny available to it in the basin of world power.

Further, Kennan prescribed:

> a long-term, patient but firm and vigilant containment . . . [through] the adroit and vigilant application of counter-force at a series of constantly shifting geographical and political points, corresponding to the shifts and maneuvers of Soviet policy . . . a policy of firm containment, designed to confront the Russians with unalterable counter-force at every point where they show signs of encroaching upon the interests of a peaceful and stable world.[6]

Kennan now claims that he has been grossly misinterpreted; that he always intended to emphasize geographical selectivity (that is, Europe and its approaches from the east, the south, and the sea), and to confine our response primarily to economic means[7] — a retrospective exegesis, or prosthesis, for which there is some support in his unpublished and State Department work at the time.[8] Nevertheless, given Kennan's characterization of the Soviet threat, one wonders how a geographically and functionally limited American response could have been sufficient. That is particularly so if the purpose of containment was not to make a token defense, but to present Soviet leaders with such a prospect of frustration that the motives and dynamic of their society would be profoundly altered. Hydraulic metaphors, no less than their subject, should flow in all directions. If the threat is of such a character that there is a case for containing it at all, then containment must be universal. Selectively containing that kind of threat is like trying to hold water in a two-dimensional vessel.

Nevertheless, selectivity is the most prevalent kind of argument purporting to mitigate the need for extensive armament and deployments in the implementation of containment. It can take two forms: selectivity of *commitment*, that is, of the objectives of our policy and strategy; and selectivity of *means*, of the military forces and weapons which support it.

Selectivity of commitment is proposed as a way of bringing obligations and costs into line (and also as a way of minimizing the occasions for war). The argument for selectivity fixes on places and defensive objects that "matter," that make a difference according to some criterion. Virtually all proponents of selectivity would still contain our adversaries in some sense; but they are selective in that they strive for some principle of limitation and impute to their more extreme opponents the scheme of "universality."

Most proposals of selective intervention — as diverse as those of Kennan, Robert W. Tucker, Stanley Hoffmann, and Ernst B. Haas[9] — are subject to the same problems. In the last analysis, all lead back to, or are operationally indistinguishable from, the more comprehensive versions of containment. This is true in several respects. (a) They support virtually all the same objects of our defense; objects, as it turns out, that comprise the major portion of our present and projected defense expenditures.[10] (b) They would implicitly support, in addition to the supposedly necessary prime objects, a host of minor, intrinsically dispensable objects "for the sake of" the major objectives. (c) When and if these proposals are costed out, they may turn out to be even more expensive than the supposedly universal schemes they would supplant. This is because, in emphasizing certain situations as "vital," they tend to add these to all the others, which they are wary of discontinuing. (d) Finally, the logic of threat and response, coupled with the diagnosis of the nature or "source" of the threat, leads these supposedly limitationist arguments back to an espousal of any act or response that would constitute effective containment. Selectivity becomes universality, though the authors of these proposals sometimes disown or disfigure their intellectual offspring.

An able statement of selectivity is that of Robert W. Tucker. Tucker argues for "moderate containment," or "a limited policy of containment," and he would "concentrate" American strategic attention on the Persian Gulf.[11] His requirement for intensified defense of the Gulf seems at least halfway toward the ability to stand off a Soviet incursion, as well as to discourage an indigenous disruption or refusal of oil on assured and reasonable terms. Though he does not demonstrate how our military force would accomplish this result, it is clear that it would require a larger, more ready and sustainable rapid deployment force.

We already spend some $49 billion a year to prepare to defend the Persian Gulf (out of about $65 billion that can be considered to be attributable to regions other than Europe and East Asia). Tucker's scheme for a more comprehensive defense of the Gulf might add another $10 or $12 billion a year to the defensive cost of this region. And since Tucker would not give up the defense of Western Europe, which costs $133 billion a year, there is no category of arms that he would cut appreciably, except such minimal forces as we keep for intervention in Central America; and even there he asserts the propriety of American force if Soviet or Cuban support is discovered.

George Kennan, too, starts by seeking a principle that limits American political and military intervention and ends by asserting and implying a scope of instances that is tantamount to virtually universal involvement. In his book *The Cloud of Danger*, Kennan advocates "the reduction of external commitments to the indispensable minimum . . . the preservation of the political independence and military security of Europe, of Japan, and — with the single reservation that it should not involve the dispatch and commitment of American armed forces — of Israel."[12] True, Kennan would like to abandon "several obsolescent and nonessential positions: notably those at Panama, in the Philippines, and in Korea."[13] But he cannot deny the extent to which the primary commitments depend, physically and psychologically, on those "nonessential" positions.

In fact, one should not be unduly impressed by modifying and mollifying adjectives such as "limited," "selective," or "moderate"; for when one becomes concrete, the imperative of containment usually overrides the qualifications. The problem is generic to selective versions of containment. Containment, of its essence, must remain contingently open-ended. The circumstances of Soviet aggressive or expansive behavior are not subject to American definition and delimitation; implicit in the definition of "the Soviet threat" is that the Soviets exercise the initiative. Therefore, once committed to containment, how can we keep it limited?

Stanley Hoffmann also proposes a "selective policy." He criticizes the "new orthodoxy" and its "fundamentalist response": "projection of a bipolar grid" on the world, "neo-nationalism," "emphasis on military power," "too militant [a] view of Soviet expansionism," and a "world-wide crusade." But he would defend essentially the same places and objects as his more extreme opponents, and in much the same ways, especially in Europe, where the conventional force balance trends are "disturbing" and where we "need . . . middle-range nuclear weapons capable of hitting the Soviet Union."

Throughout Hoffmann's critique there is an avoidance of choice. In the Persian Gulf, for instance, "the U.S. would be in a tragic position if it had to choose between economic disaster and a military intervention that could be economically futile and would be politically catastrophic." (Yes, but which way would his argument fall if we had to choose?) Again, "the aim of foreign policy ought to be to make it possible for each of the two powers to play its own game, in such a way as not to violate the vital interests of the other." (A good rule. But should we adopt it unilaterally, asymmetrically, if "their" game *does* violate our vital interests?) In another place, Hoffmann proposes "to provide extended deterrence by means other than American military and nuclear might alone." (What is the function of "alone"? If we have the nuclear might, what else do we need? If we do not have it, what good are the other means?)[14]

The problems of selectivity are seen even more clearly in the essay of Ernst B. Haas. Haas' plan "scales down and redefines some American world order values, recognizing that we cannot, without risking our own ruin, continue the attempt to mold the world in our image." It also aims at a "delinking of issues." Haas even permits himself to be skeptical of the existence of "a 'Soviet threat,'" or, for that matter, a "free world." Confronted with the question, "where should we be ready to fight?" Haas recites the familiar litany: "Western Europe, Japan, South Korea, and the Pacific." To this he adds, "regimes so close to the United States as to afford the adversary an opportunity for offensive action . . . Canada and Mexico. . . . " To this already substantial list Haas appends two non-strategic criteria: "the military defense of all democratic countries against Soviet threats, provided these countries wish to be defended . . . [and] threats by allies of the Soviet Union against Third World countries with a democratic tradition." There is yet another, economic, objective: "key commodities that are essential for the economic welfare of the democratic countries."[15]

These proposed objects of American protection are not in themselves absurd. The point is that, in the name of "selectivity," they add up to a good part of the world — all we are now committed to defend, and perhaps more. My calculation is that the areas and objectives that Haas mentions are already costing the United States about $237 billion out of the $240 billion we plan to spend for general purpose forces in the 1987 defense budget. Verbal criteria, such as "selective engagement," do not save Americans much or absolve us from the risk of confrontation and escalation.

In the end, "selective" containment is not the only alternative to universal containment. Rather, it is just a middle position between universal intervention and consistent non-intervention (the uninvited guest at this contentious banquet). Limitationists think their middle positions must be more realistic, simply because the extreme positions are unacceptable or unmentionable. But because of its contradictions and its operational correspondence with more extensive containment, this middle position is instead almost fictional. It is an artifact of the debate, not a real policy of state. The extremes of universal containment and consistent disengagement may be unpalatable, but that is just the point. The choice of extreme positions approximates the present predicament of the United States. In the face of this real and poignant choice, the formula of "selective" intervention or "moderate" containment is more an incantation than a proposal.

## DEFINING THE CONTAINMENT PROBLEM AWAY

But selectivity in its various forms is not the only false approach invented to avoid the burdens and risks of containment. Several positions of the liberal center and liberal left either deny the need to contain or attempt to subsume the containment paradigm in a new and presumably more acceptable framework.

Some of these arguments deny the empirical premise—the "threat"—and attempt to explain away a succession of Soviet moves, both regional intrusions and arms buildups. There are three variants: (a) "we are still ahead"; (b) "their moves are not what you think they are"; and (c) "their moves are somehow our fault, reactions to our own provocations." All are the familiar stuff of the former revisionists of the cold war. They may have once been useful correctives, but over the past decade they have had to become more imaginative, even fanciful. For some reason, whether compensatory or aggressive, the Soviets *have* mounted a major political and military challenge to the West; at least they have done a collection of things that equate to such a challenge, and done so in the knowledge that they would be so interpreted. Rather than deny the problem in order to justify doing less, a realistic analysis would admit the seriousness of U.S. inaction in order to measure its consequences against those of confronting the problem directly.

Another escape (generally a liberal one) from the responsibility of dealing frontally with "the threat" is the positing of "deals," a new round of global negotiations with the Soviet Union. Though proponents of this course of action would be uncomfortable with the parallel, this would be tantamount to another Yalta in three respects. First, the concept is grandiose; a new deal would not be a series of *ad hoc* technical agreements, but a comprehensive renegotiation of the boundaries of "East" and "West" and the rules of conduct in and between those spheres. Second, "deals" do not represent one nation's adjustment to situations; they are not unilateral, consisting of measures entirely within our own competence to devise and execute. Indeed, they toy casually with the fate of other nations, whose abandonment or preservation are the agenda of the two superpowers. Third, above all, if there are to be deals at all instead of unilateral counter-threats, they must codify the farthest reaches of Soviet penetration and influence, and leave the rest, as in Lenin's dictum, "negotiable." Thus, deals simply define away the problem of our inability to act by making it part of the settlement.

Still another attempt to solve the problem of America's situation in the world is to displace it, to find a surrogate goal that is more congenial or putatively more amenable to solution than the unilateral pursuit of security. The classic solution is to posit "world order norms," conditions of the international system that should be sought instead of the narrower and presumably more contentious security interests of the United States. An elaborate expression of this thesis is Stanley Hoffmann's book, which embodies in its title the choice he sees as meaningful and critical: *Primacy or World Order.*[16]

But the kind of world order we would recognize as congenial or livable would include a vast component of American primacy. World order is not self-enforcing, and no one can hope for overarching impartial mechanisms or wish for the dominance of another great power. So in the critical cases it would even be hard to distinguish world order from effective American primacy. More important, it would be hard to distinguish the amount of American power needed for the more direct and comprehensible tasks of self-protection from the amount (presumably, Hoffmann would say, the lesser amount) sufficient to establish world order. Indeed, it might take a concentration and persistence of American power far in excess of the more modest requirements of our own security to enforce world order. That effort would often be misspent, and might also be frustrated. Our simple will to move the international system toward a more cooperative, "managed" basis would likely meet the residual suspicion of our major antagonists in the world, or the competition of ambitious, rising regional contestants, or the hostility of a myriad of other less powerful but dissatisfied nations who do not relish our intrusive distribution of the things of the world, however constructive we may think it is.

## THE QUESTION OF MEANS

If the objects of containment cannot be selectively limited, and the containment problem itself cannot be defined or subsumed out of existence, perhaps some relief from the burdens of extensive containment can be found in the means through which the policy would be executed. One approach is to assert that military means are interchangeable with "non-military means," and that the substitution is a matter of choice or preference. But this proposition is not much more than a placebo. Everyone hopes that in a crisis of conflicting interests, diplomacy, economic inducements, and sympathetic ties will help resolve the problem. But it is fair to ask, what if those non-military instruments do not work? Or what if they work only because military instruments lurk in the background—that is, if they depend for their efficacy, in the last analysis, on the threat of force? Simply to ignore this problem is to be thrown back on a non-policy: hoping that nothing happens.

The argument for "non-military means" amounts to a displacement, actually a transcendence, of the security problem. Again, one version is represented in the current writings of George F. Kennan. Kennan's attitude toward the current Soviet challenge and America's predicament is expressed poignantly in an article in *The Atlantic* called "Cease This Madness,"[17] which is an impassioned appeal directed to the leadership of both the United States and the Soviet Union. Laying about him even-handedly with imputations of blame—equating, for example, the Soviets' depriving their youth of liberty with our society's granting them too much liberty—he proceeds to impugn the "madness" that underlies the "dreadful militarization of the entire East–West relationship." He avers: "For the maintenance of armed forces on a scale that envisages the total destruction of an entire people there is no rational justification."

There is no question that Kennan is describing a real peril to humanity; but his remarks only underscore the tragic predicament of both nations, the perverse but still recognizable rationality of arms competition. What one would call, ruefully, strategic interdependence is not "madness" in the ordinary sense of the word. Kennan's frequent charge of "militarization" and his rather vague advice, ". . . thrust [these] destructive powers . . . from you," in the end simply reflect his long-standing impatience in the presence of military factors, an impatience born of the disdain of the diplomatist to do his homework in the military stuff of the strategic nuclear age. What remedy follows from this dual ascription of cause: madness and militarization? Simply, that "the decisionmakers of the two superpowers . . . should . . . take their military establishments in hand and insist that these become the servants, not the masters and determinants, of political action," as if the military created the foreign policies of either state.

A variant of the argument for "non-military means" is the well-worn thesis of the disutility of military force. This is another attempt to avoid the price, and even the calculus, of our national objectives. The argument plays upon an equivocation: first, that U.S. military power, in relation to that of others, is in decline; second, that military power *in general* is less usable, less translatable into political advantages.

It is probably true that pure application of military force is declining in its effect on situations, that it is increasingly cost-ineffective, and that its means are becoming more widely diffused among multiple centers of political and strategic initiative. But military force is still integral to the structure of international relations. Indeed, the debate that underlies assessments of the efficacy of military force is over the extent to which the *structure* of the international system is determined by strategic or non-strategic factors, resting, in turn, on the distribution and exploitation of military or non-military resources and advantages.[18] And, of course, military power can be decisive if asymmetrically possessed in a particular situation.

As for non-military means, one can cite a variety of instruments to influence other parties, through incentives as well as threats.[19] Everyone favors non-military instruments, where they are appropriate. But one needs force, or at least residual force, to defend a nation's security decisively and confidently. If the object is to minimize the use of military force, then the task is to devise a system and a foreign policy that do not occasion violent intervention. Non-military means might have to be taken into the calculus, but they do not excuse us from the calculation.

An associated confusion arises when we ask whether our political leaders could enhance American power in the world by mobilizing national
"will." It had become a fashion to deplore the supposed absence of "presidential leadership," at least until the Reagan restoration of 1981, in which
America was dealt the semblance of presidential leadership in spades.
Now various pundit-journalists, professorial strategists, and even many
national security bureaucrats talk almost obsessively about will. Foreign
challenges and problems are seen as tests of our resolve; Vietnam was a
"trauma" that impaired our capability to respond to threats; we are para-
lyzed by a "failure of nerve."

But this terminology itself is a tissue of anthropomorphisms and reifica-
tions. We are not talking about "will" in some primal personal sense; we
are talking about the operation of a complex political and social system,
not even an organism except in a mostly misleading metaphor. "Will"
represents a construct, that is, a complex resultant or relationship, which
includes as just one interactive component the ability of a president to
generate and sustain the support of the rest of the political system for
some specific purpose. What we are really describing, then, is the structure of a problem, and the structure of the system that deals with the
problem.

The politics of "will" stems from a profound misconception of the
nature and function of foreign policy, embodying a curious mixture of
necessity and choice. The necessary, proper, and exclusive referent of foreign policy is held to be *external*, having to do with the state of the outside world, not the impact of it on our own political or social or economic
system; and rather *abstract*, such as global and regional power balances
and assessments of relative credibility. "Interests" are held to reside objectively, and almost implicitly, in objects of our foreign policy or in situations themselves, when in fact they are more the result of our own
perceptions of relevance and immediacy, and of our tangible commitments, which forge the linkages between events elsewhere in the world
and our own indicated responses.[20] And yet, in apparent contradiction,
our responses are seen as a matter of choice, an exercise of will. Indeed,
policy itself is most often defined as a set of authoritative declarations of
intent when, operationally, policy is more a set of contingent predictions
about our own probable future responses—in short, what we will be *able*
to do as much as what we would *like* to do.

Thus, our interests, far from being unarguable external impositions on
us, evolve more from our predilections for global architecture, the
abstract sense we insist on making of the world, and the way we intellec-
tualize foreign objects and situations. And policy, far from being a matter
of pure choice or will, is more determined by constraints, both external
and internal. If there was a trauma occasioned by the Vietnam War, it

has to be analyzed in terms of what the war revealed about the constrained operation of our own system and about our constrained ability to coerce the conduct of others in the international system. What is not appreciated, even by those who consider themselves foreign policy "makers," is that you don't "make" foreign policy as you make boats or houses or gadgets or soup. The question is not even who makes policy, but *what* makes policy.

To determine the responses of our system, then, we cannot look to factors of will, predilection, or even intention. Rather, we are thrown back on the analysis of (a) the strategic orientation that is conditioned by our preparations and built into our institutions, and (b) our capabilities and constraints. Those factors constitute, respectively, the logic and the logistics of national action. They are what make certain responses both "necessary" and yet at times impossible.

Thus, a proper theory of national conduct would have to include:

1. The probable limits of Soviet expansion and other challenging activity, without our deterrence or counterintervention;
2. The ability of the United States to live with these situations;
3. What it could cost to counter Soviet or other actions at various stages, and the comparison of these costs with the costs of other things our system could do; and
4. The alternatives we have, and the effects that would occur in the international system if we were to exercise some large-scale alternative choices.

## AN ALTERNATIVE TO CONTAINMENT

The entailments and disabilities of containment suggest the consideration of a major, coherent alternative. Such a policy would be one of strategic disengagement and non-intervention. In such a program, both of the cardinal elements of the present U.S. strategic paradigm would change. Instead of deterrence and alliance, we would pursue war avoidance and self-reliance. Our security would depend more on our abstention from regional conflicts and, in the strategic nuclear dimension, on finite essential deterrence.

In a program of non-intervention, the United States would defend primarily against an umbra of direct threats to those values that are so basic that they are part of the definition of state and society: our political integrity and the safety of our citizens and their domestic property. Because those values are inalienable, their defense would *ipso facto* be credible. We would also defend against a penumbra of challenges that are indirectly threatening but are relevant because of their weight, momentum, direction, and ineluctability. We would be looking for a new set of criteria — decision rules, if you will — that condition and bound our responses to future events that could be considered challenges. This definition is intensive, rather than extensive, in nature.

Nor are these rhetorical terms. As I have discussed at greater length elsewhere,[21] our military program would be designed to defend the most restricted perimeter required to protect those core values, a much smaller perimeter than the one the United States is now committed to defend. We would defend against military threats directed against our homeland. That is not, in the first instance, an overtly geographical criterion, and deliberately not. We should not be fixated on drawing lines in the sand; rather, we should be concerned to characterize correctly the nature and import of other countries' actions, and appreciate the characteristics of foreign events that cause us to consider them "threats." Functional criteria may be less definitive than geographical ones, but they are more important.

The concomitant of this restricted definition of American interests and of the threats to them is that the United States would encourage other nations to become self-reliant, to hedge. In fact, many foresighted countries already discount American protection in a wide range of possible cases, despite our formal obligations to come to their assistance. This does not imply that all these countries face imminent threats; simply that some are impressed more by the reality of our circumstances than by our reassurances and have drawn the appropriate conclusions.

War avoidance invokes primarily, though not exclusively, the strategic nuclear component of this counterparadigm. We will always need a strategy that discourages direct nuclear attacks on our homeland or intolerable coercion of our national political choices by nuclear threats. But today, given the parity between the nuclear arsenals of the two superpowers, our safety depends on maintaining a condition that is called crisis stability, wherein both sides have a strong incentive to avoid striking first with their nuclear weapons.

A design for nuclear stability would look like this: Since an enemy's first strike must logically be a damage-limiting attack against our nuclear forces, we should eliminate systems as they become even theoretically vulnerable to a Soviet preemptive strike. Land-based systems are inevitably vulnerable, despite the efforts of a succession of administrations to put them in multiple or closely spaced shelters (as with the MX), or to acquire a redundant and dispersed force (as with the prospective Midgetman single-warhead missiles). Instead, we should move to a dyad of strategic nuclear forces: ballistic missile submarines and bombers armed with medium-range air-launched cruise missiles. Then, to discourage further a Soviet first strike, we should not target Soviet missiles (nor does it make any strategic or moral sense to aim at Soviet cities). Rather, we should develop a list of some 3,000 military targets such as naval and air bases, concentrations of conventional forces, military logistical complexes, and arms industries that are relatively far from large civilian population centers. Finally, since nuclear war is most likely to occur through *our* escalation in the midst of conventional war, probably in Europe, or possibly in the Middle East, we must confront our attitude toward the first use of nuclear weapons. I believe we should impose upon ourselves an unconditional doctrine of no first use.

The two elements of war avoidance and self-reliance constitute a new paradigm, a principled policy of non-intervention that should be a major alternative. We would no longer consider peace to be seamless and indivisible. There might well be continuing troubles in the world, including cases where a Soviet-sponsored faction perpetrates a forcible revision of the local military balance. If we were to intervene, we might win a few rounds, as in Grenada in November 1983. But the list of feasible interventions is far shorter than the list of desirable ones, and even shorter than the list of "necessary" ones.

But what of the expected, and frequent, charge that a non-interventionist foreign policy would lay the world open to Soviet expansion or revolutionary violence? In the last analysis, a true non-interventionist position does not depend on trust in Soviet intentions; it takes Soviet power seriously. It simply accepts the possibility of suffering some foreign losses in order to preserve the integrity of our own economy, society, and political system. Yet there are reasons, also, to doubt the unvarnished projection of a Soviet political–military windfall. These reasons depend on a more sophisticated calculus of the motives (the propensity to intervene) of a potential aggressor; on an unavoidably complex analysis of the course and future of the international system; and on a somewhat speculative projection of the status of Western Europe without America.

First, it is difficult to determine just how the Soviet Union would react to a non-interventionist American foreign policy. However, a potential aggressor will consider not simply the odds of victory or defeat; he must weigh whether his potential gains, minus the predicted costs of achieving them, exceed what he could achieve without attacking. That is a very different, and a much more discouraging, calculus.

Beyond that, a serious proposal of non-intervention must make some assumptions about the world — that is, the global political–military balance, specifically between the United States and the Soviet Union, and the situation in strategic regions of the world. The international system is not just an inert environment for the making of foreign policy, or so much malleable clay or putty for the designers of an active and manipulative foreign policy. The structure or design of the international system is also in important ways a determinant of foreign policy, a framework within which each nation must choose. Its characteristics are to some extent alterable by individual nations, more or less according to their power, and the United States will continue to have pre-eminent ability to set and modify those parameters through its own choices and actions. But to do so requires a further expense or effort and is arguably less efficient than a policy of operating within the parameters.

The evolving international system will offer increasing challenges and temptations, but it also will impose greater costs and risks for less ample and less secure gains, all within the social, economic, and political constraints of the domestic system, which are themselves becoming tighter and more troublesome. The world that we will confront as we move beyond the turn of the millennium will evolve further from the world that we have experienced during the past four decades, in six critical dimensions.

The first is the high probability of troubles, such as embargoes, expropriations, coups, revolutions, externally supported subversions, thrusts by impatient irredentist states, and calculated probes of defense perimeters; these will be neither resolved nor constructively equilibrated by some benign balance of power mechanism.

The second tendency is increasing interdependence. But this has a different implication from the one which proponents would recognize. Interdependence is a set of functional linkages of nations: resources, access routes, economic activities and organizations, populations, and the physical environment. These areas harbor problems that could be aggravated to the point where they became threats to the security of nations, demanding but not suggesting solutions.

The third element of the future international system is the probable absence of an ultimate adjustment mechanism, in the form of a supranational institution that can authoritatively police the system, dispensing justice and granting relief, especially in those extreme cases that threaten to unhinge the system.

The fourth factor is an interim conclusion of the first three: Stabilization, the long-range action of states to bring about conditions in the external system that enhance their security, will take the form of unilateral interventions rather than collaborative world order.

The fifth future condition—perhaps the most important one—is the unmanageable diffusion of power, beyond some ideal geometry of powerful but "responsible" states. Instead, this process is likely to proceed to a kaleidoscopic interaction of multiple political entities. By all measures of power—military (nuclear or conventional, actual or potential), economic (total wealth or commercial weight), or political (the thrust to autonomy and achievement)—there may be 15 or 20 salient states, not necessarily equal, and not necessarily armed with nuclear weapons, but potent to the point of enjoying the possibility of independent action. This diffusion of power will have several aspects. One is that limits will become evident in existing polities, and cracks will appear in existing military alliances. Another aspect of diffusion is the impracticality of military power, whether nuclear, conventional, or subconventional — quite a different matter from the absolute or relative disutility of military force.

The sixth condition that will complicate the enforcement of international order is the *incoherence of domestic support*, not just in our country but to a certain extent in all, and not just when political systems are free from external pressure, but precisely when they most need steady support. The lack of public support might not prevent intervention, but it might critically inhibit its prosecution. (This, in my view, is the enduring lesson of Vietnam.)

The net result of these tendencies is that general unalignment, as a pattern or type of international system, is likely to succeed the present multipolar balance of power, just as the balance of power succeeded the earlier regime of bipolar confrontation. This would be a world of circumscribed regional powers. Though absolute technological and military disparities might increase, there might be more equality of usable power among the present superpowers, great powers, and middle powers, including some accomplished or would-be "regional hegemones."

In the face of such a world, the policy choice for the United States is whether to attempt to control its environment, or simply to adjust. Although challenges and opportunities will arise, it will be increasingly unnecessary and undesirable for the United States to intervene in regional situations. It will be unnecessary because the very presence of either a regional hegemone or a perpetually conflicted situation will be an obstruction to the other superpower, or to any other external power. There would be less potential profit for any intervenor, making our own abstention less risky. It will be increasingly undesirable for the United States to intervene in regional situations because these situations will be messy and interminable. They will tend to be profitless, because intervention will be expensive, and results, even if achieved, will be transient.

Of course, for the United States the most important region is Europe. What would be the probable status of Europe without American protection? I would envisage a Europe that is independent politically and diplomatically and autonomous strategically, and that acts in greater military concert, though not political unity. Actually, Europe could go quite far toward defending itself without American help. It need not be "Finlandized," either in whole or in part. If the United States were to withdraw, the principal European countries would probably increase their defense spending gradually, perhaps to 5% or 6% of their gross national product. The countries of Western Europe, even if not formally united in a new

military alliance, have the economic, demographic, and military resources, and the advantage of natural and man-made barriers, to defeat
or crucially penalize a Soviet attack.[22]

The United States can make large cuts in its defense budget *if* and *only
if* such a policy of strategic disengagement and non-intervention is
adopted. We could defend our essential security and our central values
with a much smaller force structure than we have now. Such a force
structure would provide the following general purpose forces: 8 land divisions (6 army and 2 Marine Corps), 20 tactical airwing equivalents (11
air force, 4 Marine Corps, and 5 navy), and 6 carrier battle groups. With
the addition of a dyad of nuclear forces (submarines and cruise-missile-
armed bombers), this would mean manpower of 1,185,000 (370,000 army,
315,000 air force, 365,000 navy, and 135,000 Marine Corps). The total
defense budget at the end of a decade of adjustment would be about $158
billion in 1987 dollars. In contrast, the Reagan administration originally
requested, for 1987, 21 land divisions and 46 tactical airwing equivalents,
with 14 carrier battle groups; this force requires 2,181,000 men and a
budget authorization of $312 billion.

These differences will multiply greatly unless we change our course.
The way we are headed, the defense budget will be about $530 billion by
1996, and cumulative defense spending during that decade will be over
$4.1 trillion. Under a non-interventionist policy, the 1996 defense budget
would be 58% less, and the cumulative cost over a decade would be under $2.6 trillion.[23]

## CONCLUSION: THE SHAPE OF THE DEBATE

The case for non-intervention is not a pure prescription of a state of
affairs that is inherently and universally attractive. It is prescription min-
gled with prediction. Non-intervention is proposed as an adjustment to
the world as it is shaping up and to the constraints of our polity, society,
and economy. Our national orientation should not depend entirely on
whether some objective, such as containment, is worthy of our commitment. Worthy causes are not free. As in all things, there is a price to be
paid, and that price has been growing higher. The multidimensional costs
of containment (the specific acts and the general stance of perpetual pre-
paredness) should be weighed against the consequences of not containing
and not preparing to contain. Part of the prediction is that our country,
taken as a decision-making system, will not pay those costs.

The consistent pursuit of non-intervention by this nation will entail a
fundamental change in its foreign policy and national strategy. We would
have to test our foreign and military policies against the harder questions
about national security. In the first instance, this means distinguishing

sharply between the interests of our allies and dependents and the interests of our own country. We would also have to learn to differentiate even our own interests from our security. This is not to deny that our other interests (defined in terms of the objective goals of actual individuals and organizations) are real, and mostly legitimate. It is rather to challenge the automatic notion that we must prepare to defend our panoply of interests by the use or threat of force, overt or covert, wholesale or piecemeal, through proxies or by ourselves.[24] And it is to challenge the notion that "milieu goals" — the shape and character of the international system, "balance" in general or with a particular antagonist, and even the more abstract concept of order in the system — should be assimilated into the schedule of objects that we must pursue and, by implication, defend. Sometimes, in the typical inflated and debased political rhetoric of our time, these more abstract and generic milieu goals are disguised as more immediate, even vital, security interests. But "vital" should be reserved for those truly supreme interests that derive so strictly from our identity as a nation that they could not credibly be alienated, even by an official expression.[25]

When put up against these more stringent criteria, most interests are alienable, in the sense that we can choose not to defend them against all kinds of threats. We can draw back to a line that has two interacting and mutually reinforcing characteristics: credibility and feasibility — a line that we *must* hold, as part of the definition of our sovereignty, and that we *can* hold, as a defensive perimeter and a strategic force concept that can be maintained with advantage and within constraints over the long haul.

Such a national strategy would not, admittedly, maximize gross American "interests" in the world. But it would be designed to optimize the net interests of American society in the world, in terms of the value of these interests measured against the costs (and costs disguised as risks) of defending them. Ultimately, we may have to settle for less than we would like — even for less than we think we need.

## NOTES

1. "Defense Strategy: A Debate," in George E. Hudson and Joseph Kruzel, eds., *American Defense Annual, 1985–1986* (Lexington, MA: Lexington Books, 1985).
2. "The FY84 Defense Debate: Defeat by Default," *Armed Forces Journal International*, May 1983.
3. This is an entirely different argument from that of the critics of containment who ridicule its passive stance and its failure to bring about the originally advertised downfall or evolution of the Soviet government. The latter point of view is sometimes labeled "containment-plus." It is the program of, for

example, most of the authors gathered in the recent volume, Aaron Wildavsky, ed., *Beyond Containment: Alternative American Policies Toward the Soviet Union* (San Francisco, CA: ICS Press, 1983).

Wildavsky himself denigrates existing American policy as "minimal containment," "piecemeal resistance," and "defensive." He proposes to bring about nothing less than "political pluralization" within the Soviet Union, indeed as a necessary condition for avoiding the eventual Soviet move to "subjugate" the United States. Yet, as is typical of such advocates, Wildavsky purports to eschew "physical force," instead begging the essential question by postulating the sufficiency of mere "political warfare," a sort of Radio Free Europe writ large, a lot of noise at ramparts more substantial than the walls of Jericho. For instance, Wildavsky would "unmask" through "publicity" Soviet privilege and corruption, by "broadcasting . . . consumer information" to Soviet citizens. The most that can be said for this sophisticated troublemaking is that it is cheap — except that Wildavsky and other such militant hawks would add it to, not substitute it for, everything we are doing in the tangible defensive dimension.

4. *Annual Report*, FY 1986, p. 39.

5. There are several problems, for example, with the proposal made by John Endicott in "Forward Deployed Expeditionary Forces," in Terry L. Deibel and John Lewis Gaddis, eds., *Containment: Concept and Policy* (Washington, D.C.: NDU Press, 1986). First, the forces he would generate or liberate from their overall units and contingently deploy to other regional situations are not sustainable. They are rump units, or rather, detached arms and legs without their torso, which has been left behind. They are dependent on a few days of transportable supplies, then on pre-positioned logistics that will be vulnerable, because they will be known and high-value targets for a determined enemy.

Second, even the flexibly deployed forces are costly. Their pre-positioned supplies are, after all, redundant. The lines of communication to their assigned outposts must be protected by our anti-submarine systems and our carrier battle groups against determined attempts at interdiction. The locations to be reached are, by definition, the farthest off, and therefore require the greatest amounts of airlift and sealift. Moreover, the equipment to be lifted is not as light as proponents of these forces indicate. Airmobile units, with their helicopters, are notoriously bulky, and the high rates of fire that must be sustained entail heavy logistics, even if the units are classified as "light." There will be a need for a thick base structure along the way to the far-off theaters, and this, in turn, will entail subsidies and defensive obligations to local countries.

Third, above all, proponents of dual-missioning have to cope with the prospect of simultaneous conflicts, for example, in Europe and in Southwest Asia. Our adversaries will not be so obliging as to play to American convenience. Serious trouble in a peripheral area is bound to be accompanied by tension at the center. In any case, nervous allies will not cheerfully part with the cutting edge of American forces primarily detailed to their defense. That, among other things, is already the trouble with the Rapid Deployment Force under Central Command — at least with Secretary of Defense Weinberger's concept of such forces: they are to be double-hatted or even triple-hatted units. But we are not fooling anyone but ourselves; certainly not our allies, and even less our adversaries. (One is reminded of Kurt Vonnegut's description, in his novel, *Galapagos*, of the Ecuadorian navy: It consists of four submarines, which choose to remain submerged and incommunicado and have not been heard from for 15 years.)

The proponents of this dual-missioning scheme assure us that "political costs should be minimal," since "U.S. commitment to the defense of Western Europe and South Korea would be evident and continuing." But I would not be so sure of this proposition. Long before such units were actually shifted out of their primary region of deployment, in some crisis, the designation of these units as swing forces would have illustrated the inconstancy of our commitment. In any case, if such forces were more needed in the outlying theaters, we would have, or should have, permanently deployed them there in the first place. (Indeed, in the case of Asia, the scheme of force flexibility rests on the ability of South Korea and Japan to handle their own conventional defense.) Why, then, shift American forces merely temporarily? (And, ironically, the worst time to move them would be in a crisis.) Why not withdraw them in any case, and entirely?

6. "X" [George F. Kennan], "The Sources of Soviet Conduct," *Foreign Affairs* 25 (July 1947): 566–582.
7. See "'X' Plus 25: Interview with George Kennan," *Foreign Policy* (Summer 1972): 14ff., referring to Kennan, *Memoirs: 1925–1950* (Boston: Atlantic Little, Brown, 1967), *passim*.
8. See, for example, John Lewis Gaddis, *Strategies of Containment* (New York: Oxford University Press, 1982).
9. George F. Kennan, *The Cloud of Danger* (Boston: Little, Brown/Atlantic Monthly Press, 1977); Robert W. Tucker, "The Purposes of American Power," *Foreign Affairs* (Winter 1980–1981): 241–274; Stanley Hoffmann, "The New Orthodoxy," *The New York Review of Books*, April 16, 1981, and "Foreign Policy: What's to Be Done?" *The New York Review of Books*, April 30, 1981; Ernst B. Haas, "On Hedging Our Bets: Selective Engagement with the Soviet Union," in Aaron Wildavsky (ed.), *Beyond Containment: Alternative American Policies Toward the Soviet Union* (San Francisco: ICS Press, 1983).
10. The three main theaters, which virtually all proponents of supposed selectivity of American commitment, intervention, and deployment would retain (Europe/NATO, the Middle East including the Eastern Mediterranean and the Persian Gulf/Southwest Asia, and East Asia/Western Pacific) take $224 billion of the $240 billion for general purpose forces, out of the $312 billion initially requested defense budget authority for FY 1987. Thus, the peripheral regions, some part of which most proponents of selectivity might dispense with, take only about 5% of the defense budget. There may be good and even sufficient reasons for not intervening in such peripheral areas, but they are not budgetary. In this respect, at least, selective containment is hardly less demanding than supposed global containment.
11. Tucker, "The Purpose of American Power," p. 256.
12. *The Cloud of Danger*, p. 229. No doubt Kennan would now also include the Persian Gulf/Southwest Asia. Evidence for this surmise is in Kennan's article on the Op-Ed page of the *New York Times* in the immediate aftermath of the Soviet invasion of Afghanistan in late December 1979, in which, after calling for "mature statesmanship," he hastened to reassure: "These words are not meant to express opposition to a prompt and effective strengthening of our military capabilities relevant to the Middle East . . . [As for the] big stick . . . who could object?" "George F. Kennan, On Washington's Reaction to

the Afghan Crisis: 'Was This Really Mature Statesmanship?'" *The New York Times*, February 1, 1980.

13. *The Cloud of Danger*, p. 230.

14. Hoffmann, "The New Orthodoxy" and "Foreign Policy."

15. Haas, "On Hedging Our Bets."

16. Stanley Hoffmann, *Primacy or World Order: American Foreign Policy Since the Cold War* (New York: McGraw Hill, 1978).

17. George F. Kennan, "Cease This Madness," *The Atlantic*, January, 1981.

18. This is a debate conducted by, among others, Seyom Brown, "The Changing Essence of Power," *Foreign Affairs*, January 1973, and *New Forces in World Politics* (Washington, D.C.: Brookings, 1974); and by Robert W. Tucker, "A New International Order?" *Commentary*, February 1975, and *The Inequality of Nations* (New York: Basic Books, 1977).

19. A striking inventory of such non-forcible (or at least non-violent) means is presented in Richard W. Fogg, "Creative, Peaceful Approaches for Dealing with Conflict," *Journal of Conflict Resolution*, June 1985.

20. A further word about "threats": No pile of facts (for example, about the military capabilities or the intentions of the Soviet Union), no matter how high or deep, leads by itself to any conclusion, particularly a policy conclusion. What is essential in disposing a nation's response to some challenge or state of affairs is the "*major* premise," which is always an "if-then" proposition; in other words, a general policy statement. Indeed, a nation's "policy" can be considered a summation of the important major premises relating to possible events or occurrences across geographical areas or in functional areas of national activity. Thus, it is well to take seriously the facts of, say, the Soviet state and leadership. But such sobriety in itself neither disposes the factual determination nor dictates the policy conclusion. Odd as it may seem, there is no necessary connection between taking threats seriously and doing something about them.

21. See Earl C. Ravenal, *Defining Defense: The 1985 Military Budget* (Washington, D.C.: Cato Institute, 1984).

22. See the more ample treatment of this point in Earl C. Ravenal, *NATO: The Tides of Discontent* (Berkeley, Cal.: University of California, Institute of International Studies, 1985).

23. These figures, based on official Pentagon estimates for the first five years, assume, for the five-year period 1992–1996, 4% inflation plus 2% real annual increases. My alternative assumes, for the entire period 1987–1996, 4% inflation only, with my prescribed cuts taken over a 10-year period.

24. As in the case of the Persian Gulf, some national interests cost more to defend than they are worth. See the analysis in Earl C. Ravenal, "Defending Persian Gulf Oil," *Intervention*, Fall 1984, and "The Strategic Cost of Oil," testimony before the Subcommittee on the Panama Canal and the Outer Continental Shelf, Committee on Merchant Marine and Fisheries, U.S. House of Representatives, 27 June 1984.

25. For the purposes of this discussion, it is a postulate that we ought not adopt a defense policy that prejudices our sovereignty. But it is not inconceivable that, in a situation that forced a choice between incurring or committing unspeakable destruction and relinquishing some of the prerogatives of national sovereignty, we ought to give up the prerogatives. Such a case would be a choice between the sovereignty (what we are as a collectivity) and the "we" (what we are as individuals, either our physical existence or our moral identity).

# 12 TOWARD A LESS LIMITED CONTAINMENT

## Dimitri K. Simes

Since World War II, U.S. policy toward the Soviet Union has been dominated by containment. Containment has been practiced with different degrees of intellectual and rhetorical clarity, with differing mixtures of foreign policy tools, and with varying degrees of vigor. Yet, regardless of the personal preferences and ambitions of American presidents, there has been neither an escape from containment nor a way to go much beyond it.

President Jimmy Carter brought to office a hearty disdain for containment. Yet during his presidency he managed to expand containment rhetorically, if not quite in reality, to the Persian Gulf. Conversely, President Ronald Reagan initially talked about putting Soviet communism "on the ash heap of history." His advisers included individuals who argued that U.S. policy should be aimed at transforming or at least considerably modifying the Soviet system. But on the eve of the 1985 Geneva summit with Mikhail Gorbachev, in an interview with the BBC, Mr. Reagan took the position that there is not "any reason why we can't coexist in the world, [and] where there are legitimate areas of competition, compete. But do it in a manner that recognizes that neither one of us should be a threat to the other."

The evolution of the attitudes of Mr. Carter and Mr. Reagan is another reminder that containment is more than a policy option. The very structure of the world environment, the increasing dependence of Soviet foreign policy upon military exploitation of global trouble spots, and the character of the U.S. political process turn containment into more than a necessity — it has become a fact of life.

## THE ROOTS OF CONTAINMENT

The complexity of the international system notwithstanding, in terms of power the world is still bipolar. Quite apart from Moscow's intentions, the emergence of global Soviet power presents a major structural problem for the United States. The mere projection of Soviet force into new regions inevitably imposes constraints on American conduct. The appearance of a new and formidable actor changes the power equilibrium to the U.S. disadvantage. It encourages American foes, it concerns American allies, and it forces U.S. policymakers to take into account the possibility of Soviet counteraction. Accordingly, even a relatively benign or temporary expansion of Soviet presence cannot but limit U.S. freedom of geopolitical maneuver.

That does not mean, of course, that any spread of Soviet influence anywhere and in any case should automatically cause alarm in Washington. What it does mean is that such a spread is inherently against U.S. interests and cannot be perceived with indifference.

Of course, Soviet advances are not universally accomplished through benign means. While in a number of instances, most notably in Indonesia, Egypt and Somalia, Soviet presence has proven to be short-lived, in many others it has demonstrated considerable staying power. Moreover, even a temporary Soviet role in turbulent areas may result in a real threat to important U.S. interests. There would have been no Somalian invasion of the Ogaden desert without a roughly $2 billion Soviet investment in Mogadishu's military machine. And the outcome of the conflict would, in all likelihood, have been quite different if the U.S.S.R. had not switched sides and supported Ethiopia.

In the Middle East, Soviet military assistance and superpower patronage enabled Egypt and Syria to attack Israel in October 1973. Soviet support of the Arabs did not preclude President Anwar Sadat's breaking from Moscow. Nevertheless, it triggered a situation in which U.S. forces had to be put on alert. American relations with the Arab world experienced a painful if temporary setback. More ominously, there was a dramatic rise in oil prices which did damage, not just to the Western economy, but also to the very social fabric of industrial democracies and the cohesion of NATO.

Perceptions are an integral part of international reality. And when the Soviets and their proxies successfully act as arbiters of Third World disputes (even when these disputes and the regions in which they take place are not of great strategic significance to the United States), America's credibility as a superpower inevitably suffers in the process. Furthermore, the definition of what is of strategic significance cannot be divorced from the role played by a competing superpower. An area not terribly crucial to the United States in itself can quickly acquire importance if, as in the example of Angola, it offers facilities for the Soviet navy and air force, hosts (for whatever reason) 35,000 Cuban expeditionary troops, or becomes the recipient of major quantities of sophisticated Soviet weapons.

It is doubtful that any diplomatic arrangement could persuade the Soviets to downplay military and security assistance as their principal policy tools in the Third World. Moscow is well aware that the Soviet model of development has lost much of its appeal, that Soviet technology and consumer goods are of inferior quality, and that Soviet ideology, and more broadly, Soviet culture are of extremely limited attraction.

Thus, when the Soviet leadership is asked by the United States to limit the rivalry in the Third World to a strictly peaceful competition, the perception in the Kremlin is that they are being asked to compete with both hands tied behind their back. There was a time in the late 1950s and early 1960s when, under Nikita Khrushchev, Moscow held romantic illusions about the great common revolutionary goals shared by the U.S.S.R. and newly independent nations. Those illusions are gone. By now the Politburo is perfectly aware that it is regional turmoil that provides opportunities to expand and maintain Soviet influence, and that military force, coercion, and security assistance offer the best chances for success.

Surely, Mikhail S. Gorbachev and his associates have to balance the quest for global influence against other Soviet priorities. These include avoiding an all-out confrontation with the United States and deriving benefits of economic cooperation with the West. But the quest, even if pursued in a careful and calibrated fashion, exists. And it allows the United States little choice but containment.

Containment is also a domestic political imperative in the United States. The U.S. political process, despite its periodic masochism, has little tolerance for Soviet geopolitical advances. Americans envision their worldwide mission to be the promotion of democracy and free enterprise. When any country moves into the United States' sphere of influence — especially when such a move is at least partially the outcome of the Soviet Union's own actions rather than the free will of the people in question — that move inevitably triggers a strong public outcry in the United States. As President Carter discovered, downplaying Soviet geopolitical advances can carry a heavy political price. Although it was the Soviet invasion of Afghanistan that made Mr. Carter a convert to containment, he certainly was under strong pressure for some time to respond to Soviet Third World exploits in a more vigorous manner.

## THE OBJECTS OF CONTAINMENT

Containment, then, is an integral part of any effective and sustainable policy toward the Soviet Union. It is not, however, adequate as a policy in itself. On the one hand, there is always the question of which broader political objectives containment should enhance and support. On the other, the appropriate tools to carry out these objectives must be determined.

Today, realistically, a qualified containment of Soviet power in areas truly vital to U.S. security may be taken for granted. Containment is not automatic, of course. But if an adequate American effort is made, and a national consensus in favor of such an effort exists, both Western Europe and the Far East are beyond Soviet reach. The conventional superiority of the Soviet Union in Europe is not sufficient to assure the Kremlin of a successful blitzkrieg, particularly since Soviet military planners cannot be quite certain whether East European armies would be more of an asset or a liability in the event of a protracted conflict in the European theater. The relatively smooth and painless deployment of U.S. missiles in Europe, despite a major Soviet propaganda drive, served to demonstrate NATO's will and cohesion. And a near collapse of Eurocommunism has contributed to the domestic stability of European democracies. These considerations are in addition to whatever uncertainty the remnants of extended deterrence can still generate in the Soviet mind.

The political and military situation in the Far East is no more conducive to Soviet military adventures than in Europe. Japan's rearmament under the Nakasone government, coupled with the political stabilization and modernization of China, severely limits opportunities for Soviet probing. The relatively orderly expansion of democracy and economic growth in South Korea is another contributing factor. All in all, despite major improvements in the Pacific fleet and other categories of Soviet forces, containment in the Far East appears to be as solid as ever. The peaceful transition of power in the Philippines has eliminated, at least for the time being, an opportunity for Soviet meddling.

In the Persian Gulf the situation is more murky. Unlike in Europe and the Far East, there is no neat dividing line between the two systems of alliances. A number of pro-Western regimes feel vulnerable to Islamic fundamentalism and left wing radicalism. The image of the United States as a principal sponsor of Israel contributes to anti-American sentiment and makes governments friendly to Washington subject to intensely emotional, even violent criticism. And the United States' apparent inability to be a reliable source of arms for its moderate Arab partners can only weaken its position.

Yet the ability of the United States to project power in the Gulf is superior to that of the U.S.S.R. and will continue so as long as Iran maintains its distance from Moscow. Also, this region is not quite on the periphery of the Soviet Union, and the Soviets tend to act with greater care at longer distances from their borders. Moreover, the Soviet leadership has already demonstrated its tacit respect of U.S. interests in this region by taking the position (both publicly and privately) during the hostage crisis in Tehran that the United States has legitimate security and economic concerns in the Gulf. Of course, the Politburo would not accept an attempt by the United States to bring the Persian Gulf into the American orbit through a unilateral use of force. And the Soviets have claimed that they must be included in any arrangement to guarantee security of the Gulf. To illustrate its seriousness, Moscow has continued providing assistance to Iran, extended its naval facility in South Yemen, established diplomatic relations with Oman, and made approaches to Saudi Arabia.

However, the Soviet Union does not seem to have given much priority to creating mischief in the Gulf. Because of lack of an opportunity, innate caution, or a reluctance to invest scarce resources, the Soviet Union has maintained a rather low-key posture in the region. The oil glut made the United States less exposed to turbulence in the Gulf, while probably signaling to the Soviet Union that chances to create major mischief were limited for the time being. Without predicting the future direction of Mr. Gorbachev's foreign policy, it is fair to observe that his leadership to date does not seem overly enthusiastic about making additional high-risk Third World commitments. Assertive retrenchment, rather than a search for new involvements, appears to be the name of the game for Moscow in the Middle East.

In summation, unless there is a drastic change of circumstances in the region, or of priorities in the Kremlin, the United States should be in a position to sustain containment in the Persian Gulf.

The real dilemma for the United States is whether to go beyond a containment policy limited to Western Europe, the Far East and the Persian Gulf. Common sense suggests that global containment of communism, or even more narrowly, of the Soviet Union, cannot be foolproof. An attempt to put a straitjacket on the Soviet empire could produce an embarrassing gap between perceived U.S. interests and the power to protect them. An indiscriminate commitment to stopping the Soviets in the Third World could involve the United States in more Vietnams, shattering the American domestic consensus in favor of a tough-minded policy toward the U.S.S.R. in the process. And spreading U.S. resources too thinly may result in failing to constrain Moscow where it really matters.

But if global containment of the Soviet Union cannot reliably work everywhere, does it follow that the only alternative is selective containment in areas of vital interest to the United States? A containment strictly limited to the defense of a few particularly important regions is about as unrealistic a notion as the idea of a foolproof global containment. If the Soviet Union is allowed to acquire geopolitical momentum and if U.S. credibility as a superpower could be damaged in the process, how long would it take before the American ability to implement even more modest containment schemes would be questioned by friends and foes alike?

And containment, after all, is very much in the eye of the beholder. It reflects not only the balance of forces, but also the balance of perceptions.

Second, an appreciation that the United States has neither the resources nor the will to take a stand at every point of Soviet penetration does not mean that the only other option in areas of less than vital interest is passivity. If the Soviets are making advances in areas where the United States does not have vital interests or where local circumstances do not favor a major American involvement, an appropriate U.S. response may still be limited action.

The purpose of such action would be not necessarily to win, but rather to upgrade the costs for the Soviet Union. Global powers cannot be effective if they agree to become involved only when a complete victory is probable. Something short of total victory may also constitute a considerable success. Surely a stalemate on the ground, as costly as it may be in human terms, is preferable from a geopolitical standpoint to the imposition of a Soviet-supported regime. If the objective is not so much to achieve a rollback of the Soviet empire as to exercise containment on uncertain Third World turf, bringing Moscow's advance to a halt would be a meaningful accomplishment. American aid to the Duarte government in El Salvador has as yet failed to defeat the communist guerrillas, but it has been instrumental in depriving them of victory.

Even if a stalemate is beyond reach, U.S. involvement on the side of pro-Western elements can be beneficial in some instances. Consider the case of Nicaragua. As long as the Sandinistas are busy fighting the contras they will have few resources and little energy left for their notorious "revolution without borders." Also, at a time when Mikhail Gorbachev's Politburo is preoccupied with the modernization of the Soviet economy and the technological arms race with the United States, it may be less inclined to up the ante in relatively unimportant Third World areas if major political and economic investments are involved.

Accordingly, in establishing criteria for an indirect American intervention, three conditions should be noted. First, the cost to the United States should be less than the cost to the Soviet rival dealing with a U.S.-aided movement. Second, American clients should have an authentic base of support to which U.S. assistance can be sustained over time (but not necessarily indefinitely). And finally, while the United States cannot and should not be deterred by toothless criticism from Third World nations or even from its allies, it has to avoid interventions so controversial that they could alter the geopolitical equation in the Soviets' favor. If these criteria are observed (and they should not be applied too restrictively), the chances are good that a vigorous, but indirect, U.S. involvement in the Third World would contribute to the containment of the Soviet Union.

Moreover, it is a safe prediction that, if the United States routinely makes low-key commitments to those opposing its rival in a variety of trouble spots, American clients somewhere are bound to win. That is how the U.S.S.R. has supported numerous so-called national liberation movements for decades. The Kremlin was rarely certain that any one of them in particular would come to power. It was enough to know that some were likely to deliver on the Soviet investment. Also, the Soviets were comforted by the thought that they had to invest less in these movements than the West had to spend, both financially and in terms of political capital, to cope with them. Keeping a rival busy that cheaply is not a bad geopolitical strategy.

Consequently, there is no necessary contradiction between pursuing global containment and avoiding indiscriminate commitments. Vital interests require vigorous defense, including if necessary the use of military force. Peripheral interests justify marginal investments. But the sum total of marginal U.S. investments can considerably restrain the Soviet geopolitical drive.

In Nicaragua a token but sustained contribution to the contras—even if insufficient to dislodge the Sandinistas—would put the Soviets and the Cubans on the defensive while forcing the Kremlin to allocate additional funds just to keep its clients in power. In Angola, U.S. support for UNITA, particularly supplying it with Stinger surface-to-air missiles and anti-tank weapons, is already forcing Moscow and Havana to make additional costly commitments to the MPLA without much prospect of defeating Jonas Savimbi's forces. In Kampuchea, the largely symbolic American aid to non-communist factions fighting the Vietnamese complicates the situation for Hanoi and Moscow. And U.S. assistance to the rebels in Afghanistan turns that country into a bleeding geopolitical wound and a source of constant embarrassment for the U.S.S.R.

In none of these cases are vital U.S. interests at stake. And keeping the U.S. role reasonably covert—to the extent possible in the context of American democracy—helps to keep the U.S. commitment carefully measured in order to avoid undesirable escalation. Washington has an opportunity to pursue a dynamic containment of Soviet power without an excessive commitment of American resources and prestige.

Should the ultimate purpose of containment be limited to this objective? Those who believe in "containment without confrontation" would caution against more ambitious designs. They would argue that success of containment is partly dependent upon Soviet cooperation. If the Soviets view containment as a part of a broader strategy to deny them superpower status (to say nothing of encouraging instability inside their empire) they may respond with unpredictable violence.

Nevertheless, it is fairly obvious that instability inside the Soviet orbit inevitably strains Moscow's assertiveness. The Soviet preoccupation with just protecting itself and its own makes containment easier to implement. Reasonable people may disagree over what the United States can realistically do to put the Soviet Union on the defensive in its own sphere of influence, and they may debate the consequences of destabilization for East–West relations. But is is hard to see how limiting the Soviets' freedom to maneuver in dealing with the East Europeans and other clients could be contrary to American interests, including those which fall under the requirements of containment.

Obviously, unlike the Third World, Eastern Europe is an area where the Soviet Union has vital interests and a long history of engagement. The United States has to act with extreme care and sensitivity toward local concerns to avoid unwittingly pushing East European governments further into Soviet hands or provoking Soviet interventions. Still, by pursuing a more vigorous and purposeful policy of differentiation, by building independent relationships with East European regimes, by helping these regimes become integrated into the world economy, by signaling to them that the United States (while disapproving their internal practices) does not challenge their political legitimacy, the United States has an opportunity to make headway inside the Soviet orbit. Of course, this is easier said than done. The Soviets can be relied upon to oppose stronger ties between the West and their satellites. And a commendable and politically inevitable U.S. sympathy with opposition movements, such as Solidarity in Poland, runs the risk of delivering a message to governments in the region that their survival depends upon a close alliance with Moscow. Nevertheless, it is fair to say that for a long time U.S. policy toward Eastern Europe has been largely *ad hoc*. It has suffered from incoherence rooted in a lack of a conceptual framework and an inability to make difficult and politically unpopular choices. The room for improvement is enormous.

Simultaneously, the United States is pushed both by the development of military technology and the growing mobility of Soviet forces in Europe to rethink American conventional posture and doctrine. Static defense becomes increasingly obsolete. An introduction of precision-guided munitions coupled with a new emphasis on maneuverability can provide NATO with some limited offensive options behind enemy lines. Such options are needed just to maintain credible deterrence as the U.S. nuclear umbrella increasingly loses credibility. But the very same options, even if they are developed for strictly defensive reasons, have a potential, whether NATO intends it or not, of raising questions in the Kremlin regarding Western performance if the Soviets attempt another intervention in countries contiguous to NATO. That may reduce chances for Soviet invasions if a Hungarian revolt or a Prague spring were repeated.

There should be no illusion: nothing the West can realistically do would prevent the Soviet Union from crushing any opposing anti-Russian forces aspiring to power in Eastern Europe. But extending a token of Western deterrence behind the great divide can make a difference when the Soviets are confronted with a more ambiguous situation. After all, in 1968 there was a communist government in Prague proclaiming its intent to maintain basic ties to Moscow. And communists in the Imre Nagy government in Budapest in 1956 also tried to give similar assurances. A perception in the Kremlin that reliance on force could trigger a Western counterintervention, however limited in scope, might encourage the Soviet leadership to give the search for political solutions a greater chance.

Needless to say, dominant West European thinking is strongly against any step threatening a military confrontation with the East. Severe budgetary constraints also preclude the possibility of giving NATO a credible offensive punch. Yet the historical direction of NATO defenses favors maneuver and deterrence based less on attrition and more on retaliation. If the Reagan administration made European conventional modernization its genuine political and military priority, and if this modernization was presented to the allies as an alternative to the nuclear arms race and a prescription for drastic cuts in strategic weapons (which it is), the traditional wisdom that the West has no military options whatsoever behind the Iron Curtain could gradually become a thing of the past.

An effective containment does not have to be (and indeed, simply cannot be) merely defensive. It has to be incorporated as an indispensable element of a more general policy of disciplining the Soviet power, disciplining it to the greatest possible degree not only outside, but also inside the Soviet sphere of influence.

## THE TOOLS OF CONTAINMENT

The tools of containment may be somewhat artificially divided into three categories: coercion, abdication, and cooperation. In the 1980s, the Western arsenal of coercion, in addition to the traditional tools of extended deterrence and maintenance of the system of alliances, was complemented by a number of resistance movements in areas under Soviet influence. There is a growing sentiment that these movements represent, not only an inherently moral cause, but also a promising foreign policy instrument. At the same time, a counter argument is gaining strength that supporting these movements is an ethical and political blunder. The rebels are often not quite knights on white horses — witness the contras in Nicaragua. Moreover, some argue that few are likely to prevail and that aid to them would only result in greater Soviet military involvement — witness Afghanistan. Also, some of these movements are supported by outcast governments and are guilty by association — witness UNITA in Angola.

Such arguments cannot be easily dismissed. But they only point up the impossibility of engaging the Soviet Union in a vigorous geopolitical competition without incurring some moral and political costs. Each situation, of course, should be assessed individually. But the lens through which these situations are viewed must be colored by a recognition that stopping, and where possible, reversing Soviet advances is a dominant political and moral imperative for the United States.

Using the tools of abdication requires U.S. determination not to help the Soviet Union manage its empire with Western assistance. Again, the practical choices are not easy. What about the starving in Ethiopia? What about the Polish people, who would suffer if their government defaults? Using innocent civilians as pawns in the geopolitical rivalry is inherently contrary to the American ethos. Yet, in disregarding the option of abdication the United States fails to exploit one of the most important Soviet vulnerabilities, namely the economic and social failure of the Russian-style model of communism. Those who choose to be allied with the Soviet Union should be prepared to expect the associated internal costs.

The Soviet Union is reluctant to pay the full price of maintaining its global empire. Accordingly, Moscow is not opposed to Third World nations seeking economic assistance from the West. In a way, the Kremlin benefits from a curious division of labor when the East accepts responsibility for maintaining Third World Marxist–Leninists in power while the West keeps their economies afloat. There is a school of thought in the United States that argues in favor of such an arrangement. It suggests that, in the long run, economic relations with industrial democracies will make Third World radical regimes less dependent upon the Soviet Union.

The trouble is that, for governments like those in Nicaragua, Ethiopia, and Angola, a relationship with Moscow is more than an alliance of convenience. Lacking domestic legitimacy, they desperately need the kind of security assistance that only the Soviet bloc is willing to provide. There is also a matter of ideological urge. The Soviet communist model has a very limited international appeal. But fundamental beliefs of Marxist–Leninist authoritarianism still attract supporters among Third World revolutionaries. They are pragmatic enough to become willing and even demanding recipients of Western economic assistance. But like their Soviet mentors, they feel little gratitude and no political closeness to their capitalist benefactors. The Mengistu government in Ethiopia, for instance, responded to U.S. famine aid with strongly worded attacks on the United States for having allegedly failed to offer adequate and timely help.

Most African nations suffer from gross economic mismanagement. Yet up until now, they could both receive Western aid and conduct policies detrimental to Western interests. The United States is in no position to force all Western allies to deny assistance to left-wing radical regimes. But

America can, without causing too much controversy inside NATO, deprive its Third World opponents of any American contribution. Unfortunately, that would result in additional human suffering. But, on the other hand, it would force Moscow's Third World friends to make some important choices. Some might opt to distance themselves from the U.S.S.R. and to control their anti-American impulses. Others might become basket cases, vividly demonstrating the futility of exclusive association with the Kremlin. Some might even be overthrown. Meanwhile, the Soviet Union, confronted with additional costs of the empire, might adopt a more conservative approach to exploiting Third World hotbeds of instability.

The outcome would be a more prosperous and safer future for peoples who otherwise could become targets of Soviet expansionism. That would not only be inherently geopolitically advantageous to the United States but also profoundly moral. In his speech at the 27th Communist Party Congress, Mikhail Gorbachev signaled reluctance to make a greater investment in Third World causes. Surely it is not the responsibility of America to pick up the bill for Moscow's troubled clients, at least not as long as they maintain a posture of defiance toward the United States.

Finally, there are the tools of cooperation. A useful, if somewhat artificial, distinction can be made between those intended to contribute to a climate of relative interdependence, which supplements the basic rivalry with useful shock absorbers, and those essentially designed to promote U.S. geopolitical interests. In the first category is direct trade with the Soviet Union; in the second are economic arrangements with and aid to East European and other countries (e.g., Mozambique) which are striving for a modicum of foreign policy autonomy from Moscow. The latter are not terribly controversial. There are good reasons to offer a reward to governments prepared to distance themselves from the Kremlin. The former raise some tough questions. Mutually beneficial, unsubsidized, nonstrategic trade is unobjectionable in its own right. The real issue is how much leverage the West can buy with it as long as the U.S.S.R. is denied what it wants most: high technology and major, long-term, subsidized investment. To accommodate the Soviet desire means running the risk of contributing to Soviet military power and to the attractiveness of the Soviet model. But the failure to accommodate Soviet requests significantly reduces one potential for political leverage.

Historically, economic cooperation has failed to have a major impact on Soviet political ambitions. It has created some valuable bonds between the two sides, but the bonds have been useful only at the margins of managing the rivalry in a more rational and controllable fashion. The lesson of the past 40 years is that containment cannot be based on anything but a forceful unilateral effort. Today, conditions for such an effort are uniquely favorable. But, as in the past, the absence of this effort — the refusal to make critical (even if unpleasant) choices — can cost dearly.

## DEALING WITH ASSERTIVE RETRENCHMENT

Contrary to what some Reagan administration officials seem to believe, the Soviet Union is not on the run. Nor is there evidence to support the claim made by a number of their liberal critics that Gorbachev's preoccupation with domestic economy automatically discourages a global diplomacy of force. Under the new general secretary's ambitious leadership the Soviet Union, without changing any of its fundamental objectives, acts with a greater vigor and sophistication. The Kremlin may be reluctant to make further expansive commitments. But Gorbachev hardly projects an image of a statesman willing to preside over the dismantling of the Soviet empire. The Soviet Third World policy may be described as an assertive retrenchment. Where the Soviets are already involved, they are willing to go a long way to avoid a humiliating retreat. Such a retreat is viewed by the Soviet elite not just as a geopolitical setback but also as a challenge to the very legitimacy of their system, to the credibility of Manifest Destiny, Soviet style. And the very structure of international politics, rich with turmoil and anti-Western sentiment, virtually assures that the Kremlin will encounter opportunities too tempting to resist.

No *modus vivendi* is possible between two such ambitious and messianic nations as the United States and the Soviet Union. Soviet and American global political and economic interests rarely overlap. And contrasting political systems and values further exacerbate the inevitable conflict. Yet, there is little danger that the conflict will deteriorate into a direct military confrontation. The central strategic balance is sufficiently stable, and nuclear overkill is sufficient to assure great caution on both sides. Moscow and Washington alike recognize each other's vital interests and avoid challenges with a high potential for disastrous escalation.

It is on murky Third World turf that the United States can best pursue a robust policy without the risk of war with the Soviet Union. Optimists may hope that this policy will eventually make the world (or at least some new parts of it) safe for democracy. But at a minimum, a dynamic pursuit of containment in the Third World can deprive the Soviet Union of geopolitical momentum. It was the image of this momentum that finally killed détente in the 1970s. Accordingly, a more vigorous opposition to Soviet advances on that ground might paradoxically generate a better political climate for superpower cooperation in the late 1980s and beyond.

# 13  THE RISE AND FALL
## OF CONTAINMENT*

*Norman Podhoretz*

Two perspectives on containment are essential to understanding its history and its applicability to our current circumstances. First, containment should be seen as a national reaction to the lesson of Munich. Second, as such, it was successful in enlisting bipartisan support during the first years of its existence. There was deep, abiding, national support for a policy that seemed to be at once morally ennobling, politically viable, and conducive to the most vital of American and Western values. It was because the lesson of Munich — that is, the lesson that appeasement leads to war and that tardy resistance to totalitarian aggression is the road to war or defeat or both — had been absorbed by virtually all elements in our political culture that this new anti-Munich policy was not only conceived but also received with such enthusiasm.

Fundamentally, containment was based on two simple propositions — simple, but by no means uncontroversial, in 1947 and still today. The first of these propositions was that there was a "clear and present danger," a Soviet threat, to the free institutions of the West. The second proposition, equally simple and perhaps less controversial then than it is today, was that only American power could successfully cope with or "contain" that threat.

The resistance to these two propositions came both from the left and from the right. On the left, it was denied that there was a threat. The Soviet threat was seen as the figment of a paranoid anticommunist American imagination. It was denied that the Soviet Union had aggressive or expansionist intent and it was asserted that any Soviet actions which seemed aggressive or expansionist were really defensive responses to American provocation. This challenge to containment's view of Soviet behavior

---

*This chapter is an edited version of informal remarks given by the author at "Containment and the Future," a symposium held at the National Defense University, Washington, D.C., November 7, 1985.

found political expression through the leadership of Henry Wallace and the Progressive Party in their 1948 presidential campaign against Harry Truman. I was an undergraduate at Columbia University during that campaign, and a supporter of Wallace. I was still too young to vote, but I remember attending a Wallace rally on the Columbia campus, chaired by the late Mark Van Doren, then the single greatest literary star on the Columbia faculty. Norman Mailer appeared to make a pitch for Wallace's candidacy, and a folk singer named Pete Seeger (some things never change) was there to entertain us.

We were told that Henry Wallace would get 10 million votes. In the end, in fact, he got under a million. Because Wallace failed so badly and was so humiliated at the polls, the position that he represented was discredited as a serious point of view in the mainstream of American politics. That took care of the left-wing attack on the fundamental premises of containment. The phenomenon that has come to be rather loosely known as McCarthyism then conducted what might be called a mopping-up operation.

There was also a right-wing attack on containment. We need only remind ourselves that the young Richard Nixon spoke of Secretary of State Acheson's "Cowardly College of Communist Containment," and actually accused Dean Acheson of being soft on communism. Many people today think of Richard Nixon — with some justification — as having grown a bit soft on communism himself. Younger people are also amazed to hear that John F. Kennedy successfully attacked Nixon for being soft on Cuba in the 1960 presidential campaign, and that it was Kennedy who was the hard-line candidate in that contest. (Some things *do* change: look at the Democratic Party today.) But the young Nixon spoke for the wing of the Republican Party which believed that the trouble with containment was not that it misconstrued the nature of the Soviet threat, but that it misconstrued the nature of the strategy needed to meet that threat. In other words, they attacked containment for being timid and defensive. What the right wing was calling for in those days was a policy that used to be known as rollback or liberation.

Rhetorically, rollback or liberation maintained a lively existence until the election of Dwight Eisenhower. Richard Nixon was Eisenhower's vice president, and John Foster Dulles, the great exponent of rollback and liberation, was his secretary of state. It would have been reasonable to suppose that they were about to embark on a policy of rollback or liberation. In fact, the Eisenhower administration did no such thing. As its response to the Hungarian revolution of 1956 vividly demonstrated, it had no intention of practicing anything remotely resembling a policy of rollback of Soviet power.

Eisenhower's failure to follow right-wing Republican tactics meant that the policy of containment as developed by the young George Kennan became a bipartisan policy, representing a broad national consensus. The nation was willing to support the idea that American political, economic, and, if necessary, military power should be used in order to hold the Soviet Union behind the lines that had been set at the end of World War II. As an indication of our seriousness, we had sent troops into Korea, the invasion of which was seen as a direct challenge to the policy of containment. We spent blood (about 33,000 American lives) and treasure, and there was very little dissent from the decision to go into Korea in the name of containing Soviet or communist expansionism. (Indeed, no distinction was being made, at that point, between the two.)

## DETENTE AND THE LESSONS OF VIETNAM

As we all know, this happy American consensus on containment was destined to be destroyed by the Vietnam war. Some of us believe that American intervention in Vietnam was mandated by the same intellectual imperatives that had mandated the intervention in Korea. Our intervention in Vietnam may, as I myself have argued, have been an act of imprudence. But in principle, John F. Kennedy's decision to go into Vietnam was entirely consistent with the policy of containment, both as defined in the abstract and as embodied in concrete action by the Truman and Eisenhower administrations.

Defeat in Vietnam, of course, destroyed the consensus that had crystallized around containment. If containment was the policy developed in response to the lesson of Munich, it was destroyed in its turn by the lesson of Vietnam. For an entire generation, and indeed for virtually the entire political culture, Vietnam replaced Munich as the grand symbol of "Never Again." Just as the world had pledged almost unanimously that there would be "No More Munichs," so the guiding principle in the United States now became "No More Vietnams."

What exactly was the lesson of Vietnam? When we marked the 10th anniversary of the fall of Saigon, the debate over that question reemerged, still unresolved. But in the 1970s, the lesson of Vietnam was widely taken by our political culture to be not that going into Vietnam might have been an imprudent, reckless, or unwise application of a fundamentally sound strategy, but rather that the strategy, namely containment, had been wrong from the beginning. In fact, the lesson went even further than that. The lesson was putatively that the entire basis of American policy in relation to communism and the Soviet Union since 1947, since the enunciation of the Truman Doctrine and the publication of the "X" article in *Foreign Affairs*, had been fundamentally flawed. Vietnam, it was thought, had torn the mask off that policy and exposed it as based on illusion at best and on evil intent at worst. The alleged illusion concerned the Soviet threat which, so it was said, had been wildly exaggerated. We had gone into Vietnam in response to a threat that did not exist.

Vietnam was also very widely thought to teach the lesson that American power, whose purposes had seemed to be good, benevolent, and even noble, was in fact morally deficient. American power had been deployed in support of immoral and indeed criminal ends. And not only was it morally flawed, it was also operationally flawed. The supposedly greatest power on earth couldn't even win a war against a Third World guerrilla army. So what was our power worth?

Here, in the starkest possible terms, was the traumatic disintegration of the national consensus we had enjoyed since 1947 on the main issue in our foreign policy. In response, a Republican administration led by the same Richard Nixon who had spoken of the Acheson "Cowardly College of Communist Containment" developed an alternative policy which was built on the principle of strategic retreat. I think it is fair to say that détente represented, at least in the minds of Richard Nixon and Henry Kissinger, an effort to salvage as much of containment as possible under conditions that made the continued pursuit of such a policy impossible.

This is the heart of what came to be called the Nixon Doctrine. What did the Nixon Doctrine, coming almost exactly 20 years after the Truman Doctrine, say? The Nixon Doctrine said that the United States would no longer use its own military power to contain Soviet expansionism. The Soviet threat was still recognized and acknowledged by Nixon and Kissinger. In that sense, détente did not represent a departure from or an abandonment of containment's vision of the Soviet Union: the Soviet threat was there, it was real, and it was serious. But it could no longer be dealt with directly through the use of American military power, either deterrent power or the actual deployment of American forces. Substitutes for American power had to be found, and what the Nixon Doctrine proposed was the appointment of surrogate powers to do the job in various regions of the world. We could help them with military aid, economic aid, and political support, but we would leave the fighting to them. Who were they? Iran under the shah in the Persian Gulf and in the Middle East generally and, more significantly as it would turn out, China in the Far East.

In the opening to China, which I see as part of this new policy of strategic retreat, the Nixon Doctrine was in effect identifying the enemy to be contained not as *communism*, but rather as the Soviet Union, defined as a traditionally expansionist nation-state. There was a change in understanding here: a threat that was previously seen as ideological and military was now assimilated into the traditional terms of great-power conflict and diplomacy. Was the Soviet Union comparable to Wilhelmine Germany, or was it comparable to Nazi Germany? Were we trying to avert World War I, or were we trying to avert World War II? The debate over which analogy really applies seems to some people an academic and even frivolous argument. To me, it goes to the heart of the matter.

In the years between 1947 and 1968, we implicitly looked upon the Soviet Union as comparable to Nazi Germany; the threat emanating from the Soviet Union was viewed as comparable to the threat that had come from Nazi Germany. When I say *we* I don't just mean the Foreign Service or the politicians, but also the intellectual community, which was in those days very heavily influenced by such works as Hannah Arendt's *The Origins of Totalitarianism*, a book whose entire point was to portray the Soviet Union as a mutation of the same species as Nazi Germany. Its thesis was that totalitarianism was a new phenomenon in history. Nazi Germany was one expression of it, the Soviet Union another; they were exactly comparable, morally and politically.

Containment in its first phase, I believe, implicitly accepted the parallel to Nazi Germany. The difference under détente was not to deny that the Soviet Union was a threat, but to deny that the Soviet Union was *that kind* of threat. Some academic defenders of détente (Stanley Hoffmann of Harvard, for example) explicitly invoked the analogy of Wilhelmine Germany. Helmut Sonnenfeldt, when he was counselor at the State Department under Henry Kissinger, used the same image. In this view, the Soviet Union was an expansionist power, but not a revolutionary actor on the world scene trying to create a new international order in which it would enjoy hegemony. It was, rather, an ambitious outsider seeking an equal place for itself in the imperial sun, like Wilhelmine Germany. That is what the new understanding of the Soviet Union alleged that the Soviet Union was — at least among those who were willing to grant that the U.S.S.R. represented any kind of threat at all.

But however one looked at the Soviet Union, there was general agreement that American power was no longer capable by itself, or even with help from U.S. allies, of coping with that threat. We were weakened and demoralized, and neither Congress nor the media nor the relevant political constituencies were willing to back the kind of forceful policies or the level of defense spending that would be required to continue classical containment. Therefore, a retreat was necessary, along with the creation of substitute power in the form of surrogates, which is what the policy of the Nixon and Ford administrations provided. During the first three years of the Carter administration, there was an even further slide down this particular slippery slope, as high officials of that administration — the president himself and his secretary of state — began saying that there was no Soviet threat at all.

At that point, one of the two fundamental pillars on which classical containment had rested was challenged for the first time. Not only high officials of the Carter administration, but also a vast majority of academic specialists in the universities and the foreign policy institutes, were now telling us that the Soviet Union had become a status-quo power. Secretary of State Cyrus Vance said in a speech that President Carter and Leonid Brezhnev shared the same values and aspirations. The president himself congratulated the nation on having overcome what he called its "inordinate fear of communism," a remark which led some to ask what an ordinate fear of communism might be.

Not content with denying that there was a Soviet threat, and not content with this radical assault on one of the two fundamental premises of containment, the Carter administration went even further into a fantasy that should have shaken the military. The administration said that military power had become or was becoming obsolete in our time as compared with other forms of power, suggesting that the use of military power, whether for deterrent purposes or actually for shooting purposes, was in almost any situation no longer to be regarded as necessary. That dictum completed a thorough and radical departure from containment.

## REAGAN AND THE LESSONS OF THE
## POST-VIETNAM ERA

History sometimes has a way of impinging upon the false or deluded consciousness of those who attempt to shape it, and so it did in the Carter administration. First came an event that did not directly impinge on the Carter *Weltanschauung* itself, but which had consequences for it— namely, the fall of the shah of Iran and the rise of the ayatollah. In failing to do what was necessary to prop up the shah when he was under assault, we as a nation simply abandoned the Nixon Doctrine. If one of the main surrogates for American power could not depend on American support when he was in trouble, as a result of a challenge from anti-American forces, then the whole doctrine was nonsense. It simply exposed itself as a brilliant scheme on paper and empty in action. No matter how many speeches anyone made to the contrary, it was clear that surrogates were not an adequate substitute for our own power.

But if the fall of the shah discredited the Nixon Doctrine, it was the invasion of Afghanistan that discredited the Carter view of the Soviet Union. However, the president himself, unlike many people, was willing to admit that he had been wrong. He said that in a single week he had learned more about the Soviet Union than he had known in his whole life before. Evidently, Mr. Carter had really believed that the Soviet Union was not a threat, that military power really was obsolete, and that Mr. Brezhnev really did subscribe to the same values as we did. But the Soviet

Union rudely contradicted him by sending more than 75,000 troops into Afghanistan, the first use by the Soviet Union of its own troops outside Warsaw Pact territory since the early postwar period. Although Mr. Carter realized that he was mistaken about the Soviet Union, one has to wonder how much the political education of Jimmy Carter had cost the country in the previous three years.

At the same time, his eyes, and the eyes of a lot of other people, were opened to another illusion, namely, that the Soviet Union was only interested in parity with us in nuclear weaponry. People who had resisted the warnings of groups like the Committee on the Present Danger about the Soviet military buildup suddenly, in the post-Afghanistan climate, began to entertain the possibility that they might have been wrong, that Paul Nitze and Eugene Rostow and a few others might indeed have been right in their Churchillian warnings that the Soviets were trying to achieve not parity but strategic superiority.

In his fourth year as president, remarkably, even Jimmy Carter emerged as a born-again hawk. Carter had been a very enthusiastic supporter of the Vietnam war in his younger days, and his conversion to a dovish position came late. But after the Afghanistan invasion, he proposed a big increase in the defense budget. He withdrew SALT II from the Senate. He instituted a grain embargo against the Soviet Union. He even enunciated a new presidential doctrine. Ten years after the Nixon Doctrine, we were given the Carter Doctrine, in which the president said that the United States would use any measure up to and including military force to prevent an outside power (everybody understood whom he meant) from taking control of the oil fields of the Persian Gulf region. Many presidents have been haunted by the ghosts of past strategies and past policies; Jimmy Carter was clearly haunted by the ghost of Harry Truman, the ghost of containment past. (Of course, Carter never had an opportunity to show us what he might have done if he had been reelected. Judging from the way he has talked since he left office, he would have lapsed again into born-again appeasement — if one wanted to be polite, one might call it détente.)

At any rate, by 1979 it seemed as though we were back again to 1947, and in some ways as a nation we were. The polls from 1979–1980 show an extraordinary degree of support for serious increases in defense spending: over 70% which, on an issue like defense, is unprecedentedly high. Alarm over the Soviet threat also moved sharply upward around the same time. In addition, there emerged what was called a new patriotism or a new nationalism, which had a good deal to do with frustration and rage over the hostage crisis in Iran. There was a feeling that it was because we had allowed ourselves to become weak that we were being attacked and humiliated in such a way. In a sense, the state of public opinion was not dissimilar to the state of public opinion in 1947–1948, with Iran and Afghanistan now serving as the galvanizing events, just as the coup in Czechoslovakia and the threat to Greece and Turkey had done then.

Ronald Reagan clearly was swept into the White House on the tide of this new public feeling both about the Soviet threat and about the need for a reassertion of American power. It was felt that not just a military buildup was necessary, but that a concerted effort to reverse a perceived decline in American power in general was needed; an effort to rediscover and to recapture the lost sources of American greatness. Reagan seemed the best leader for such an effort. The subliminal and sometimes even explicit message of Jimmy Carter's candidacy was that the decline of American power was inexorable, inevitable. There was nothing we could do about it. A mature people, which is what he exhorted us to be, would make its peace with this decline. Reagan said no: the decline of American power was a result of bad policy, and he knew how to reverse it. What the American people said in electing Reagan in 1980 was that they were not quite ready to be "mature" and to accept decline as inexorable. They wanted another shot at national greatness.

However, "ghosts" also haunted Reagan. In his first years in office, the ghosts of the young Richard Nixon, of Douglas MacArthur, and of John Foster Dulles (before he became secretary of state) floated through the White House. The ghostly doctrine of rollback or liberation haunted Reagan's rhetoric when he spoke of the Soviet Union as an "evil empire" and when he said that communism would be consigned to the ash heap of history. This kind of talk instilled a good deal of hope in some people and aroused hysteria in a lot of other people.

But the ghost of rollback haunted only Ronald Reagan's rhetoric. It did not go so far as to haunt his actual policy. His actual policy was haunted by a different ghost: the ghost of détente, the ghost of an older Richard Nixon. It was, to be sure, détente as Mr. Nixon then began defining it in speeches and articles — détente of the hard-headed variety, not, as he saw it, of the soft-headed variety that Carter had adopted. Once, when criticizing something I had written about détente, Helmut Sonnenfeldt said, "You don't understand; détente to us meant an iron fist in a velvet glove." If that were the case, what Nixon, Sonnenfeldt, and others were saying was that Jimmy Carter had removed the iron fist, leaving only a velvet glove good for nothing but stroking. In that context, we might say that the Reagan administration, at least in its rhetoric, was trying to put the iron fist back into the glove, though in its actual policies it did a bit of stroking itself.

I think one could make a very solid and well-documented case for the thesis behind this playful metaphor. Even the tough policies of the Reagan administration, whether rhetorical or real, are entirely consistent with the theory of détente as spelled out by the post-presidential Richard Nixon, and in some of the writings of Henry Kissinger, because their conception of détente did indeed involve a component of power. Détente had to be policed, and the only policeman available was the United States. So if the Soviet Union stepped out of line, we had to be prepared to do something, such as call an alert, send a ship, or send a tank. But as Nixon and Kissinger saw it, because Watergate destroyed executive authority and because Congress would not supply the means with which, say, to help Savimbi in Angola, this necessary component of the strategy was eliminated, frustrating Kissinger's design and leaving Carter with a policy that was, for all practical purposes, equivalent to appeasement.

In bringing the Nixonian tradition back into its own policies, the Reagan administration also aimed at reestablishing a system of incentives and penalties that would serve to restrain Soviet behavior and, in turn, make it possible for Reagan to arrive at an accommodation similar to the one that had been outlined in the Basic Principles of Détente agreed to by Nixon and Brezhnev in Moscow in 1972 (which, however, the Soviets immediately began to violate).

## THE LESSONS OF MR. X

All these ghosts are still haunting our efforts to define a sense of ourselves and a sense of our responsibilities in relation to the Soviet threat. The truth of the matter is that we have not returned to the spirit of 1947. We have not returned to the clarity of 1947, and we have not returned to the state of national will that we were able to mobilize in 1947. Since 1979, we as a nation have been floundering in search of a policy or a strategy that will help us come to grips with who we are, what our responsibilities as a nation are, and what it is we are trying to accomplish.

But why should we be floundering in this way? Let me suggest that the problem is fundamentally not political, but what I would call in the broad sense, cultural.

I am an unreconstructed and unrepentant admirer of the "X" article and the George Kennan of 1947, and I am just as severe a critic of the George Kennan of today. D. H. Lawrence once gave this advice to literary critics: "Never trust the teller," he said, "trust the tale." The tale in this case is "The Sources of Soviet Conduct," Mr. Kennan's famous *Foreign Affairs* article. I believe that this article, which develops the two fundamental principles of containment and the principles around which a national consensus mobilized so enthusiastically, remains valid even today. I would go so far as to say that it is more valid today than it was in 1947. We are floundering because we have permitted ourselves to forget what Mr. X taught us in 1947, namely, that what he called "Russian expansive tendencies . . . cannot be charmed or talked out of existence." They can only be restrained — and these are Mr. Kennan's words — "by the adroit and vigilant application of counter-force at a series of constantly shifting geographical and political points corresponding to the shifts and maneuvers of Soviet policy." We have forgotten the wisdom and realism behind that view of the Soviet Union, and I believe that Mr. Kennan himself has forgotten it. We are floundering because we have also forgotten the purposes to which we once dedicated American power. These, too, were outlined in the "X" article, which defined the objective of the policy of containment as being to promote "tendencies which must eventually find their outlet in either the breakup or the gradual mellowing of Soviet power."

How are we to bring ourselves to remember these principles? We can begin by recognizing that Mr. X was right in everything but his timing. The Kennan of 1947 thought it would take only 10 or 15 years for containment to bring about the breakup or mellowing of Soviet power, not an eternity of confrontation. Ironically, of course, 15 years brought us to the intervention in Vietnam and the beginning of the breakup of *American* power.

But even though Kennan's timing was off, his prediction was right. What he said, turning the Marxist tables on the Soviet Union, was that the idea of internal contradictions (by which the capitalist world was supposedly doomed) was much more applicable to the Soviet Union. Internal contradictions would make it impossible for the Soviet Union to exist in the same form indefinitely, provided that its "expansive tendencies," which Kennan saw as a kind of safety valve or escape from those internal contradictions, were contained. If the Soviets were held behind the post-World War II line, the pressures would build up, and a mellowing or breakup would gradually result.

We have to recognize that mellowing is an impossibility for the Soviet Union; to expect it to mellow is to expect an entire political class to commit suicide. This is a class which owes its legitimacy to its commitment to the Leninist mission in the world at large and cannot forsake that commitment without calling its own legitimacy into question. Whether its members subjectively believe in communism or not does not matter. Some people say there are no communists left in the Soviet Union; perhaps that is true. Perhaps the members of the so-called *nomenklatura* do not believe in communism, but communism believes in them. There is no way that they can maintain themselves in power if they repudiate the Leninist commitment. And here I would ask, from its own point of view, does the *nomenklatura* have any good reason to do so?

To look forward to a mellowing of Soviet power, then, is to harbor an illusion. On the other hand, to look forward to the breakup of the Soviet empire is to look forward not only to a reality, but to what I would argue is a virtual inevitability. There are some people who think that of all the empires in history — the Assyrian, the Babylonian, the Greek, the Roman, the British — only the Soviet empire is eternal. But the Soviet empire is no more eternal than any other empire known to history. It will break up someday. The question is when and under what circumstances?

Once, we understood what our role in that process ought to be. We understood it in the post-1947 period under the tutelage of men like George Kennan. I think we need to recapture the courage to follow a strategy that would promote tendencies which are now much more richly developed than they were in 1947 and that might lead to a breakup of the Soviet empire. These tendencies include demographic problems, economic problems, and so on. Concretely, what form would such a strategy take? I think it would not be all that different from the strategy that was outlined by the "X" piece itself, updated to meet certain new realities.

First, we would have to be determined to prevent Soviet military power from outstripping our own. I rank this as the very minimum, as a first priority, and as the necessary foundation for all the other steps we might take. We would have to maintain a healthy military balance. I would like to see us actually achieve superiority, but at the very least, we need to keep the Soviets from achieving superiority. The second thing we should be doing is helping the various anti-Soviet insurgencies that are now operating on the periphery of the empire, such as those in Afghanistan, in Angola, and in Nicaragua. The third would be to practice economic denial in dealing with the heartland of the empire, so as to exacerbate the economic crisis within.

The fourth, which I rank last not because I think it has the lowest priority (in fact, it may have the highest priority) is to recapture our sense of what this struggle is all about. I believe it is a struggle with the primary remaining mutation of the totalitarian curse which has been the twentieth century's distinctive contribution to the history of despotism and tyranny. Our willingness to assume the responsibility to defeat the other principal example of this accursed contemporary species of tyranny (namely, Nazi Germany) was matched by an equally courageous and morally noble determination in 1947 to set ourselves against the triumph of the Soviet Union, even though, for tactical, prudential reasons, we had made an alliance with the Soviets when the Nazi threat was the more urgent "present danger." We have to teach ourselves once again that we are not in this struggle to establish some kind of classical nineteenth-century balance of power or to serve dubious theories of *Realpolitik*. We are involved, rather, in a clash of civilizations, and it is a clash that will not, as Mr. X said, be charmed or talked out of existence. This means we have to learn once again to talk about what communism is, and in what sense it represents a mortal curse and a threat.

Will anyone support such a policy? Are there any politicians willing to sponsor it? Very likely, there are not. Nevertheless, I find myself going back repeatedly to the concluding words of the "X" article, which, again, I think are no less applicable to our situation as a people today than they were in 1947. Indeed, they are more applicable, given the kinds of spiritual and cultural changes, as well as political, economic, and military changes that have occurred. Kennan spoke with the eloquence that he so inimitably commands no matter what position he argues. He said that "the thoughtful observer of Russian–American relations" would find no "cause for complaint in the Soviet threat." And then he concluded with these words:

> The thoughtful observer . . . will rather experience a certain gratitude for a Providence which, by providing the American people with this implacable challenge, has made their entire security as a nation dependent on their pulling themselves together and accepting the responsibilities of moral and political leadership that history plainly intended them to bear.

I can think of no better contemporary exhortation to the people of the United States (and indeed of the Western world generally) than those magnificent words.

# 14 CONTAINMENT IN A NEW ERA

*Donald S. Zagoria*

Despite the doubts of many, the West has been extremely successful in containing Soviet power during the past 40 years. Moreover, there is no reason why we should not continue to be successful in the years ahead, when we will be faced with a continuing Soviet challenge though under quite different circumstances. But if we are to be successful in containing Soviet power, we will have to avoid the counsels of both extremes in the United States: those who allege that containment is too passive, who oversimplify and exaggerate the Soviet challenge, and who regard every negotiation and every agreement with Moscow as a sign of weakness; and those who fear that containment is too dangerous in a nuclear age, who minimize the Soviet challenge, who long for an end to the competition, and who rationalize every Soviet advance.

People who know the Soviets best have no doubt that they are a formidable adversary, determined to alter in their favor what they call the "correlation of forces." The Chinese call the Soviets "hegemonists" with a "southern strategy" designed to outflank Europe. The North Koreans, when they were freer to speak their minds, called the Russians "dominationists." Seweryn Bialer talks of the "unrelenting drive of the Soviet leaders to sustain and advance Soviet power in the global arena," and he and many others speak of the insatiable Soviet appetite for "total security."[1] Zbigniew Brzezinski calls Soviet global strategy a "unique organic imperialism" born out of territorial insecurity.[2] Hans Morgenthau would call them "imperialist" because they are dissatisfied with the existing distribution of power in the world.[3] We would be wise not to ignore these assessments.

The Soviets are not only an expansionist power, but they are also highly secretive, relentless, and ruthless. With a younger, more stable leadership, and with global military reach, they could be even more formidable in the years ahead.

To be sure, as Kennan has noted, Americans face a variety of challenges, ranging from environmental problems to the national deficit, in addition to that of the Soviet Union. But no American president has been able to escape from the Soviet challenge, even though several have tried.

There is no question that the containment of Soviet expansion will remain the proper strategy for the United States in dealing with the Soviet Union, and that it will be a necessary strategy far into the future. Such a containment strategy is not incompatible with arms control or limited détente or even cooperation on some issues of common concern. But the Soviet Union is and will remain our most important challenger. In many ways it is a stronger and far more effective challenger than it was 20 or 30 years ago.

The nature of the containment problem has changed because the world has changed. The real question we should be asking is how to adapt the containment strategy to the new global environment of the 1980s and beyond. Containment was successful from 1945 to 1985 because it confronted the challenge of restoring the balance of power shattered by World War II. If containment is to be successful in the future, it will have to confront the new problems of growing Soviet military power and power projection, regional conflicts, Third World instability, and chronic Soviet opportunism designed to alter important regional balances in their favor.

## CONTAINMENT IN THE PAST:
## REASONS FOR SUCCESS

By the 1960s, the three pillars of containment were already in place. First, there was a continuing U.S. diplomatic and military presence on the Eurasian continent and a NATO alliance of free nations committed to checking Soviet expansion. Second, there was a strong and resurgent Europe. Third, there was an independent China. I would add a fourth element: an economically strong and dynamic Japan allied to the United States. By the 1970s, there was added to these factors the success of many of the NICs (newly industrializing countries), particularly in Asia, so that by the end of the 1970s the Asia–Pacific region had become our principal trading partner and, along with Europe, an important second zone of U.S. strategic influence. All of this ensured containment's success. The Soviet Union was unable to dominate any of the major power centers in North America, Europe, or Asia, and the balance of power shattered by World War II was restored on terms highly favorable to the West.

There were also additional factors which accounted for the success of containment. Crude and counterproductive Soviet behavior has been one of the West's best allies. To a considerable extent, the Soviet Union has contained itself. From the Korean War to the Berlin blockade to the shooting down of an unarmed Korean airliner, and from Poland to Afghanistan, crude Soviet actions have helped to galvanize the West and drive many countries closer to the United States. As a result of the war unleashed by North Korea with Soviet acquiescence, the U.S. defense budget tripled or quadrupled. Similarly, the Soviet invasion of Afghanistan led to six or seven years of steady increases in U.S. defense spending. Soviet military pressure on the Chinese border and on the territories disputed with Japan has been partly responsible for driving both China and Japan closer to the United States. And the Soviet-supported Vietnamese invasion of Cambodia has unified the noncommunist countries of Southeast Asia (ASEAN) behind Thailand and prevented the further expansion of Soviet influence in that important region.

Another important factor has been the declining appeal of the Soviet model for a centrally planned economy. Both inside and outside the communist world, the limits of the Stalinist model of economic development are highly visible. Everywhere in the communist world, economic reform is on the agenda. In China, that reform has already gone quite far, and China's "open door" policy has potential consequences that no one can yet fully foresee. China's reform has even had an important impact on North Korea and Vietnam, and it is bound to have an influence throughout the Third World.

Another factor accounting for the success of containment has been the Soviet Union's difficulty with turning influence into control, especially in regions far removed from it geographically. Despite arms supplies, friendship treaties, and the Cuban–Yemeni–North Korean–East European "international brigade," the Soviet Union is still a long way from controlling any of its key Third World clients such as Syria, India, and Iraq. And it still lacks much influence in other important Third World states like Egypt, Saudi Arabia, Iran, Indonesia, and Nigeria.

The Soviet Union is engaged in an experiment, trying to turn influence into control in the smaller Marxist–Leninist states (such as Angola, Afghanistan, Nicaragua, and Ethiopia) through the formation of "vanguard communist parties" which it hopes will subordinate themselves to Moscow. But the prospects for this happening outside of nearby Afghanistan are not very bright. Indeed, as Jerry Hough points out, recent Soviet writing includes quite a number of pessimistic arguments that most of the alleged Marxist states in the Third World are unstable and unable to build "socialism" because of their backward conditions; in addition, they represent a huge drain on Soviet resources.

The best strategy for Third World countries to adopt, moreover, is not one of "leaning to one side" in the superpower rivalry. Rather, it is one of balancing between the superpowers in order to obtain the favors of both. China is now playing this game more effectively than ever before, and

India looks like it may move in this direction under its new prime minister, Rajiv Gandhi.

Finally, containment was successful because China became not only independent but actively opposed to Soviet expansion, particularly in Asia, where it continues to support the resistance in both Afghanistan and Cambodia. As China becomes stronger under the impetus of its four modernizations, it will be in a position to resist Soviet expansion in Asia even more effectively.

## CONTAINMENT IN THE FUTURE: THE CHALLENGES

When we turn from the past success of containment to the problems we face in containing Soviet expansion in the future, the picture is more complex. The most disturbing new elements in the picture are: first, the enormous growth of the Soviet military, particularly its power projection capabilities; second, regional conflicts, such as the Arab–Israeli conflict, and the chronic instability in the Third World which the Soviets ceaselessly seek to exploit; third, growing divisions within the Western alliance about how to deal with the Soviets; and finally, the breakdown of the U.S. domestic foreign policy consensus which characterized the critical part of the early postwar period.

There is little to add about the growth of Soviet military power to what is or should be widely known. The Soviets have built an impressive array of military capabilities for every conceivable contingency. Moscow considers its achievement of nuclear parity with the United States as its single most important accomplishment of the postwar period, one that has sobered the "imperialist world" and made it reluctant to intervene in various local conflicts. The Soviets are determined to attain not only nuclear parity on the global scale, but what they call parity in the European and Asian theaters as well. A Soviet general recently told an American academic that the Soviet Union was determined to have "parity" in Asia, a region where it is well behind in the overall "correlation of forces," indicating that the Soviets are very much aware of the importance of military power in determining regional balances.

It is in this context that we must view the Soviet deployment of SS-20s in Europe and Asia, the recent modernization of Soviet air and naval capabilities in the Pacific, the permanent Soviet naval deployments in the Indian Ocean and the South China Sea, and the indications that the Soviets have begun to build large aircraft carriers. The global balance of power is now determined to a considerable extent by regional balances. We will have to pay more attention to this phenomenon, because the Soviets will ceaselessly try to use military and other forms of power to alter these balances in their favor.

It is in the Third World that the Soviet challenge is likely to be most serious during the coming years. The main Soviet challenge to the West now and in the foreseeable future is not that Moscow is likely to launch a direct attack on the United States or its allies, but rather that it is determined to exploit global turbulence in order to weaken the United States and to expand its own interests. The Soviet Union, in other words, is a scavenger of global instability.

Moscow seeks global status neither by head-on nuclear war, which is too dangerous, nor by peaceful socioeconomic competition, for which it is unfit. As Brzezinski says, the only way open to the U.S.S.R. is "that of attrition and gradual disruption of stable international arrangements so that the United States suffers directly and indirectly. The most effective way of pursuing such a strategy of disruption is to achieve and maintain sufficient military power to deter U.S. reactions and to intimidate U.S. friends in those strategically vital areas which possess the greatest potential for a dynamic shift in the global balance."[4] These areas are, of course, the Middle East, the Persian Gulf, and Southwest Asia. Moreover, the Soviets are bound to have increasing opportunities in the Third World in the years ahead. The pressures of growing population, massive social, economic, and political inequality, and growing literacy are likely to contribute to radicalism, fundamentalism, and other anti-Western ideologies.

I am particularly concerned with what Gregory Massell calls the suicide of the pro-Western oligarchs. In Vietnam under Thieu, Iran under the shah, and Nicaragua under Somoza, the collapse of pro-Western authoritarian governments has had grave consequences for the West. In the Philippines, we were fortunate that the collapse of Marcos' regime led to a democratic, and not an authoritarian revolution. But Marcos' misrule helped produce a strong, radical left that is bound to play an important role in Filipino politics in the future. This left wants to eject the U.S. from its important naval and air bases in the Philippines. Were this to happen, it would profoundly change the strategic situation in the Pacific. Similarly, the radicalization of Egypt or Indonesia could dramatically alter the situation in other key regions. Yet anti-Americanism is growing in the Middle East. And even in such a staunch ally as South Korea, a substantial number of students are receptive to Marxist and neo-Marxist theories of "dependency."

The situation on our doorstep is also alarming. The Mexican population is doubling every 18 years or so, and it is a real question whether this phenomenon, combined with the debt problem and other pressures, will not eventually lead to an explosion. Were the United States to be confronted with a hostile Mexico and a hostile Central America, our own strategic situation would change markedly.

Even if we are relatively fortunate, and anti-Western movements in the Third World do not grow, the Soviets are likely to have increasing opportunities for political advance even among the more moderate states. Because they are losing faith in the United States as a friend and protector, and because they are losing hope that the Reagan administration has the will or the skill to play honest broker between the Arabs and Israel, many moderate Arab states are already edging away from the United States and making overtures to the radical Arab camp, to Europe, and to the Soviet Union. Many of these moderate Arab states see current U.S. policy as one of general neglect of their interests. In the Persian Gulf, Oman and the United Arab Emirates have already established diplomatic ties with Moscow, and Jordan has said it will have to consider buying arms from the Russians if it cannot get them from the United States.[5]

## A FUTURE STRATEGY FOR CONTAINMENT

In sum, the Third World is the "weak link" of the West, and any future strategy for containment will have to come to terms with this fact. Such a strategy will require a mix of many elements. There ought to be an increasing transfer of economic resources to the Third World. There also needs to be increasing pressure for economic and political reform there. We must have a better early warning system for signs of growing unpopularity of pro-Western governments. And when the warning sounds, we must take early action, not wait for crises to occur. If the radicals win, the United States should try to come to terms with them when this is possible. When it is not, we should support the opposition. Of course, the use of our power needs to be discriminating, and there are limits on our ability to influence such situations. But often that influence can be far from negligible.

Finally, we need a strategy to promote regional integration. The problem of containment in Asia is essentially one of fostering regional stability through integration. We should nourish ASEAN and seek to foster regional organizations and institutions elsewhere. To paraphrase Peter Jay, good regionalism is good containment.[6] Where there is effective regionalism there will be fewer opportunities for predatory outside powers like the Soviet Union to exploit regional conflicts.

A third problem for containment in the future is the growing difference within the Western alliance over how to cope with the Soviet Union. It is virtually impossible these days to hear a European, even a conservative European, talk about the Soviet Union in the same way as a conservative American. Within Europe, important elements in the Social Democratic Party of Germany and the Labor Party of England are calling for withdrawal from NATO. All of this is bound to stimulate Soviet appetites, and the Russians are likely to step up their efforts to split the Western alliance. It was, as the Soviets say, "no accident" that the new Soviet leader, Mikhail Gorbachev, met with French President Mitterand on the eve of his meeting with President Reagan and sought to get Mitterand to sign a joint condemnation of the U.S. Strategic Defense Initiative.

Finally, there is the problem of the lack of a foreign policy consensus at home for dealing with the Soviet Union. An important reason why we have been successful with containment up to now is that, for most of the early postwar period, we had a bipartisan foreign policy. If we are to be successful in the future, we will have to develop some procedures for institutionalizing bipartisanship. Some sensible suggestions have been made for how to accomplish this goal. Why, for example, could it not become standard practice for incoming presidents to appoint secretaries of state and defense who are broadly acceptable to both major parties? It might also be advisable to have a permanent bipartisan commission on the Soviet Union attached to the National Security Council. Such a commission could be charged with fashioning a bipartisan policy towards Moscow. The model for such a group would be the Scowcroft Commission, which was able to articulate a strategic weapons policy that was broadly acceptable. It will also be important for each president to develop a close working relationship with the leaders of the opposition party in the Congress.

## THE OUTLOOK FOR CONTAINMENT

Despite the rather serious problems we face in the future, I remain cautiously optimistic that we will be successful. Part of the reason for this confidence is that the United States has now reversed its military decline of the 1970s. The other reason for my confidence has to do with the flawed nature of Soviet power. Taken together, I think these factors signify that the late 1980s and the 1990s are not likely to be a promising decade for the Soviet Union in its drive to become an effective challenger to the United States.

First, the trends in the strategic competition are becoming increasingly unfavorable for Moscow. A series of U.S. strategic modernization programs — the MX, perhaps the Midgetman, the new, more accurate Trident missiles, the revived B-1 bomber, the advanced technology (Stealth) bomber, the Pershing II, as well as ground-, sea-, and air-launched cruise missiles — will soon enhance the American nuclear arsenal. Moreover, as Arnold Horelick has pointed out, "superior U.S. technology in such areas as sensors, computers, computer programming, signal processing and exotic kill mechanisms being harnessed in connection with President Reagan's Strategic Defense Initiative is bound to increase Soviet anxiety about the possible shape of the strategic balance in the years ahead."[7]

Second, the Soviet Union faces severe economic and social stagnation at home. Some Soviet specialists describe it as a systemic crisis, but it is important to understand its true nature. It is not a crisis of survival. The Soviet economy is not going to fall apart; there is not going to be a new Russian revolution. But there is a crisis of efficiency; and some Soviet intellectuals have been warning that, if present trends are not soon reversed, the "Polish disease"—disaffection within the working class—could spread to the Soviet Union.

The new Soviet leader, Mikhail Gorbachev, has suggested that the Soviet Union, unless it improves its technology and economic productivity, may not be able to maintain its present strategic position in competition with the West, a point Dimitri Simes makes as well. In a brutally frank report delivered on December 10, 1984, three months before he became General Secretary of the Soviet Communist Party, Gorbachev attributed the "slowdown of growth in the late 1970s and early 1980s" to the "stagnant retention" of "outmoded production relations." He warned that the ills of the system were of "truly tremendous scale" and that it would be a "titanic task" in terms of innovation and complexity to deal with them. What was at stake, he concluded, was nothing less than the need to make sure that the Soviet Union could "enter the new millennium worthily, as a great and flourishing power." And, in an unusually candid admission, he conceded that because of Soviet economic failures, the West was winning not only the economic and technological race, but the ideological competition as well. On June 11, 1985, Gorbachev added to this dire warning. He said that "urgent measures" were required to improve the economy because he could not cut social programs or reduce defense expenditures in the face of the "imperialist threat." He may yet be forced to do one or the other.

Declining trends in the strategic competition and severe economic difficulties at home are not Gorbachev's only problems. The Soviet Union is still bogged down in Afghanistan, and it faces a continuing crisis in Poland. Elsewhere in Eastern Europe, its economically hard-pressed satellites want greater independence and increased trade with the West. Some of them want to experiment with Chinese- and Hungarian-type economic reforms. A harshly worded *Pravda* article on June 21, 1985, reacted to these developments by warning Eastern Europe of the dangers of "revisionism" and even of "Russophobia."

Trends outside the empire are no more reassuring. In the Far East, the Soviet Union is increasingly "odd man out." In Europe, despite clumsy Soviet efforts to prevent the deployment of the Pershing IIs and cruise missiles, the deployments have proceeded on schedule. In the Persian Gulf, Iran has halted its natural gas deliveries to the Soviet Union and continues to broadcast revolutionary Islamic propaganda to Moscow's Muslim republics. Meanwhile, Iraq has been establishing closer economic ties to the West. In the Third World more broadly, Moscow faces armed insurgencies in almost all of its desperately poor client states. Finally, the American economy continues its recovery and President Reagan has launched the most sustained U.S. military buildup since World War II.

None of this means that Gorbachev is going to opt out of the international competition with the United States. But the problems he faces are formidable and deep-rooted; they cannot be solved quickly. It could take a decade or more just to begin a turnaround in the ailing Soviet economy.

Do these developments mean that Gorbachev will want a long period of calm in relations with the United States while he concentrates on his internal and imperial problems? We should find out if this is in fact the case, and we need to test Soviet intentions to do so. Of course, we should have no illusions about a return to détente. The rivalry between the superpowers will continue. But while we continue our necessary efforts to contain Soviet power, there may be an opportunity for arms control and for some easing of tensions, as called for by Alton Frye. Under the present circumstances, this is the best we can hope for. But it is not insignificant, and we must let neither visions of the ideal nor fears of the unreal inhibit whatever progress an imperfect world may allow.

## NOTES

1. Seweryn Bialer, "Andropov's Burden: Socialist Stagnation and Communist Encirclement," Address to the 25th Annual Conference, International Institute of Strategic Studies, 8 September 1983, Ottawa, Canada.
2. Zbigniew Brzezinski, "The Soviet Union: World Power of a New Type," *Ibid*.
3. Chapter 5, "Imperialism," in *Politics Among Nations*, 5th Revised Edition (New York: Alfred A. Knopf, 1978), pp. 48–76.
4. "The Soviet Union: World Power of a New Type," International Institute of Strategic Studies address.
5. Gerald F. Seib, "Moderate Arabs Are Losing Faith in U.S. as Friend, Protector After 1985 Reverses," *The Wall Street Journal*, December 24, 1985, Sec. 2, p. 13.
6. Peter Jay, "Regionalism as Geopolitics," *Foreign Affairs: America and the World 1979* 58 (No. 3, 1980): 485.
7. "The Return of Arms Control," *Foreign Affairs: America and the World 1984* 63 (No. 3, 1985): 527.

# INDEX

# ABOUT THE EDITORS
# AND CONTRIBUTORS

## THE EDITORS

**Terry L. Deibel** is a foreign affairs analyst, writer, and teacher whose career has combined academic pursuits and government service. He is now Professor of National Security Policy and Associate Dean of Faculty at the National War College in Washington, D.C., where he has taught since 1978. Previously he was Assistant Professor of International Affairs in the School of Foreign Service, Georgetown University, and he has also served with the International Programs Division of the Office of Management and Budget and in the Department of State's Bureau of Politico–Military Affairs. Professor Deibel has been an International Affairs Fellow of the Council on Foreign Relations, a senior staff member of the Center for Strategic and International Studies, and a Resident Associate at the Carnegie Endowment for International Peace.

**John Lewis Gaddis** is internationally recognized as a leading American historian of U.S. foreign policy during the cold war. He has taught since 1969 at Ohio University in Athens, Ohio, where he is now Distinguished Professor of History. Professor Gaddis has been Bicentennial Professor of American Studies at the University of Helsinki and Visiting Professor of Strategy at the United States Naval War College, and he is a recent recipient of the Guggenheim fellowship. Winner of the Bancroft Prize for History for *The United States and the Origins of the Cold War*, he is also the author of *Strategies of Containment* and is currently at work on a biography of George Kennan.

## THE CONTRIBUTORS

**James H. Billington**, a Soviet specialist with particular interest in the history, culture, and ideas of the U.S.S.R., has since 1973 been Director of the Woodrow Wilson International Center for Scholars of the Smithsonian Institution. He is a member of the editorial advisory board of *Foreign Affairs* and is a past chairman of the Board of Foreign Scholarships (which administers the Fulbright program).

249

**Alton Frye** is Washington Director and a Senior Fellow of the Council on Foreign Relations. A former Congressional Fellow, staff member of the RAND Corporation, and legislative and administrative assistant to Senator Edward W. Brooke, Dr. Frye specializes in legislative–executive relations, strategic studies, and arms control.

**Ole R. Holsti** is George V. Allen Professor of Political Science at Duke University, where he was chairman of the Department of Political Science from 1978 to 1983. A past president of the International Studies Association and associate editor of the *International Studies Quarterly* and the *American Journal of Political Science*, Professor Holsti specializes in belief systems and public opinion, conflict, international crises, and decisionmaking.

**Jerry F. Hough** is J. B. Duke Professor of Political Science at Duke University and a staff member of the Brookings Institution in Washington, D.C. A Soviet specialist, his areas of concentration include the Soviet leadership, political system, local party organs, urban politics, and foreign policy process, especially with regard to Europe and the competition with the United States in the Third World.

**George F. Kennan**, a former career diplomat in the U.S. Foreign Service, was first chairman of the State Department's Policy Planning Staff from 1947 to 1950 and served as Ambassador to the Soviet Union in 1952 and to Yugoslavia in 1961–1963. The author of 17 books and numerous articles on the Soviet Union and U.S.–Soviet relations, Ambassador Kennan is currently Professor Emeritus at the Institute for Advanced Study in Princeton, New Jersey.

**Norman Podhoretz** is the Editor-in-Chief of *Commentary* magazine, a member of the Council on Foreign Relations, and a member of the boards of the Committee on the Present Danger and the Committee for the Free World. His interests include literary matters, Jewish affairs, and American foreign policy in the postwar period, particularly the Vietnam War.

**George H. Quester** is Chairman of the Department of Government and Politics at the University of Maryland. A specialist in military strategy and arms control, American foreign policy, and international politics, he has taught at Cornell University and the National War College and is a member of the Council on Foreign Relations and the International Institute for Strategic Studies.

**Earl C. Ravenal,** a former official in the Office of the Secretary of Defense, is Distinguished Professor of International Affairs at the School of Foreign Service, Georgetown University, and Senior Fellow at the Cato Institute in Washington, D.C. He is the author of more than 140 articles and papers on foreign policy and national security, and has authored 9 books including *Never Again: Learning From America's Foreign Policy Failures*, and *NATO: The Tides of Discontent*.

**Dmitri K. Simes** is Senior Associate in Soviet Foreign Policy at the Carnegie Endowment for International Peace, Professorial Lecturer at the Johns Hopkins School of Advanced International Studies, and Adjunct Professor at Columbia University. A columnist for the *Christian Science Monitor* and member of the Council on Foreign Relations, he was also Research Associate at the Institute of World Economy and International Relations of the U.S.S.R. Academy of Sciences in the 1960s and early 1970s.

**Angela E. Stent** is Director of the Russian Area Studies Program and an Associate Professor at Georgetown University. Her specialties include East–West relations and trade, technology transfer, West European–Soviet relations, East and West Germany, and women in higher education. She speaks Russian, French, German and Italian.

**Richard H. Ullman** is Professor of International Affairs in the Woodrow Wilson School of Public and International Affairs, Princeton University. A specialist in U.S. foreign and defense policy as well as international relations theory, he has served on the staff of the National Security Council, the State Department's Policy Planning Staff, and the Office of the Secretary of Defense, as well as on the editorial board of the *New York Times*, as editor of *Foreign Policy*, and as Director of Studies and Director of the 1980 Project of the Council on Foreign Relations.

**Donald S. Zagoria** is a Professor of Government at Hunter College and the Graduate Center of the City University of New York, as well as a fellow at the Harriman Institute for Advanced Study of the Soviet Union at Columbia University. A specialist on Soviet foreign policy, Sino–Soviet relations, and the international relations of East Asia, Dr. Zagoria has maintained a life-long scholarly interest in the schisms of the communist world.